Modern and Contemporary Poetry and Poetics

Edited by Rachel Blau DuPlessis
Professor Emerita of English at Temple University, USA

Modern and Contemporary Poetry and Poetics promotes and pursues topics in the burgeoning field of 20th and 21st century poetics. Critical and scholarly work on poetry and poetics of interest to the series includes social location in its relationships to subjectivity, to the construction of authorship, to oeuvres, and to careers; poetic reception and dissemination (groups, movements, formations, institutions); the intersection of poetry and theory; questions about language, poetic authority, and the goals of writing; claims in poetics, impacts of social life, and the dynamics of the poetic career as these are staged and debated by poets and inside poems. Topics that are bibliographic, pedagogic, that concern the social field of poetry, and reflect on the history of poetry studies are valued as well. This series focuses both on individual poets and texts and on larger movements, poetic institutions, and questions about poetic authority, social identifications, and aesthetics.

Language and the Renewal of Society in Walt Whitman, Laura (Riding) Jackson, and Charles Olson
The American Cratylus
Carla Billitteri

Modernism and Poetic Inspiration
The Shadow Mouth
Jed Rasula

The Social Life of Poetry
Appalachia, Race, and Radical Modernism
Chris Green

Procedural Form in Postmodern American Poetry
Berrigan, Antin, Silliman, and Hejinian
David W. Huntsperger

Modernist Writings and Religio-scientific Discourse
H.D., Loy, and Toomer
Lara Vetter

Male Subjectivity and Poetic Form in "New American" Poetry
Andrew Mossin

The Poetry of Susan Howe
History, Theology, Authority
Will Montgomery

Ronald Johnson's Modernist Collage Poetry
Ross Hair

Pastoral, Pragmatism, and Twentieth-Century American Poetry
Ann Marie Mikkelsen

(Re:)Working the Ground
Essays on the Late Writings of Robert Duncan
edited by James Maynard

Women's Poetry and Popular Culture
Marsha Bryant

Poetry After the Invention of América
Don't Light the Flower
Andrés Ajens, translated by Michelle Gil-Montero, introduction by Erin Moure and Forrest Gander

New York School Collaborations
The Color of Vowels
edited by Mark Silverberg

The Poetics of the American Suburbs
Jo Gill

The Afro-Modernist Epic and Literary History
Tolson, Hughes, Baraka
Kathy Lou Schultz

Delmore Schwartz
A Critical Reassessment
Alex Runchman

The Poetics of Waste
Queer Excess in Stein, Ashbery, Schuyler, and Goldsmith
Christopher Schmidt

US Poetry in the Age of Empire, 1979–2012
Piotr K. Gwiazda

Global Anglophone Poetry
Literary Form and Social Critique in Walcott, Muldoon, de Kok, and Nagra
Omaar Hena

Modernist Legacies
Trends and Faultlines in British Poetry Today
Edited by Abigail Lang and David Nowell Smith

Writing Australian Unsettlement
Modes of Poetic Invention 1796–1945
Michael Farrell

Writing Australian Unsettlement

Available online or contact the author: limecha@hotmail.com

ode ode

BREAK ME OUCH

a raiders guide

Out of the Box: Contemporary Australian Gay and Lesbian Poets (co-edited with Jill Jones)

thempark

thou sand

open sesame

enjambment sisters present

same! same! same! same!

the thorn with the boy in its side

Long Dull Poem

Cocky's Joy

roughly proofed

Writing Australian Unsettlement

Modes of Poetic Invention 1796–1945

Michael Farrell

palgrave
macmillan

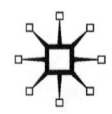

WRITING AUSTRALIAN UNSETTLEMENT
Copyright © Michael Farrell, 2015.

All rights reserved.

Some chapters have been published in earlier versions as below:

"A Poetics of the Plough: Ned Kelly's The Jerilderie Letter" published Southerly, Volume 72, Number 2, 2012. (Ch. 2)

"An Unsettled Community: Harpur's Carnival, Harris' Assonance, Mackellar's Code" published *Republics of Letters*. Robert Dixon and Peter Kirkpatrick eds., Sydney: Sydney University Press, 2012. (Chs. 4 / 5)

"Unsettling the Field: Christopher Brennan and Biodiversity" published *JASAL*, Volume 12, Number 1, 2012. (Ch. 6)

"The Colonial Baroque in Australia: On drover boab texts; Wiradjuri clubs; Charlie Flannigan's drawings." (Ch. 8) *Criticism*, forthcoming.

First published in 2015 by
PALGRAVE MACMILLAN®
in the United States—a division of St. Martin's Press LLC,
175 Fifth Avenue, New York, NY 10010.

Where this book is distributed in the UK, Europe and the rest of the world, this is by Palgrave Macmillan, a division of Macmillan Publishers Limited, registered in England, company number 785998, of Houndmills, Basingstoke, Hampshire RG21 6XS.

Palgrave Macmillan is the global academic imprint of the above companies and has companies and representatives throughout the world.

Palgrave® and Macmillan® are registered trademarks in the United States, the United Kingdom, Europe and other countries.

ISBN: 978–1–137–48571–7

Library of Congress Cataloging-in-Publication Data

Farrell, Michael, 1965–
    Writing Australian unsettlement : Modes of Poetic Invention, 1796–1945 / Michael Farrell.
       pages cm.—(Modern and contemporary poetry and poetics)
       Includes bibliographical references and index.
       Summary: "This book rewrites the history of Australian literature, through reading the unorthodox poetics of colonial life writing, from letters to tree carvings. Farrell examines page, punctuation and grammar to present a new version of Australian literature, including texts by poets, bushrangers, Indigenous stockmen, a Chinese miner and migrant women"—Provided by publisher.
       ISBN 978–1–137–48571–7 (hardback : alk. paper)
       1. Australian literature—19th century—History and criticism.
2. Australian literature—20th century—History and criticism.
3. Colonists—Australia—History. 4. Australian literature—Minority authors—Criticism and interpretation. I. Title.

PR9609.5.F37 2015
820.9'994—dc23
                                              2015012249

A catalogue record of the book is available from the British Library.

Design by Newgen Knowledge Works (P) Ltd., Chennai, India.

First edition: September 2015

10 9 8 7 6 5 4 3 2 1

For Martin

Contents

Acknowledgments		xi
Introduction		1
Chapter 1	The Hunted Writer: Ned Kelly's *The Jerilderie Letter* and Bennelong's "Letter to Mr Philips, Lord Sydney's Steward"	13
Chapter 2	An Australian Poetics of the Plough: *The Jerilderie Letter*	39
Chapter 3	Unnecessary Inventions: Jong Ah Sing's *The Case*	63
Chapter 4	Open Secrets: Dorothea Mackellar's Coded Diaries and Norman Harris's "Letter to Jim Bassett"	85
Chapter 5	Boredom: Charles Harpur's "Note to the Song of 'Good Night'" and Mary Fullerton's "Bromide"	107
Chapter 6	Unsettling the Field: *Ngarla Songs* and Christopher Brennan's *Musicopoematographoscope*	129
Chapter 7	Writing to Order: Gladys Gilligan's "The Settlement"	153
Chapter 8	Homelessness: Ann Williams's and Sarah Davenport's Travelling Diaries; Drover Bush Texts; Wiradjuri Club Drawings; Charlie Flannigan's Baroque Drawings 1893	175
Conclusion		195
Bibliography		199
Index		215

Acknowledgments

For humor and faith thanks go to my PhD supervisor Dr Justin Clemens. For support and grammatical advice, my associate PhD supervisor Professor Ken Gelder. For intellectual and personal support, Ann Vickery and Eddie Paterson. For encouragement and feedback, Kate Fagan and Martin Harrison. For chapter feedback, Fiona Hile, Beryl Langer, Stuart Cooke, Antonia Pont, Jessica Wilkinson, Matt Hall, Ella O'Keefe. For reading tips, Gareth Jenkins and James Field. For collegial support, Duncan Hose, Corey Wakeling, Tim Wright, Astrid Lorange, Sarinah Masukor, Sam Langer, Oscar Schwartz.

I would also like to thank the Australian Centre at the University of Melbourne for supporting me during some of the revision of this book.

Introduction

Like all histories, this book is a writing of the present as well as the past. It is about reading as much as writing: how we read the texts of the past after a century of radical changes in writing, and of the expansion of Anglophone poetics that dealt with those changes and proposed further. These developments were largely read, rather than written, in Australia, yet in the later twentieth century there were major reimaginings of Australia's cultural history that were "poetics by other means" (to adapt Marjorie Perloff), such as the writings of Paul Carter and Stephen Muecke. Poetry critics aware of this work include Martin Harrison (2004), who writes of the problem of our poetics' history:

> Classifying systems, largely derived from English and American critics and historians, are applied to Australian writing, as if genetic accounts and histories of evolution similar to those of British and American writing can be mapped equidistantly across the structures of connection, response and contact which form the local histories of a local art. Borrowed terms like "pastoral," "urban," and "landscape" for instance, may work very differently or simply may not work at all when applied to Australian poetry. (78–79)

This is not the book that Harrison suggests is necessary; yet I hope that it is in the spirit of what is articulated here. Rather than a system, I propose something that is more intuitive: the antisystem of "unsettlement." This unsettlement is not, however, "applied" to poetry either, for the most part, but to forms of what has become known as life writing, although some approach poetry much more closely than could have been perceived at the time of writing. They are also "networked" to poetry in myriad ways, not least through their poetics, but also biographically and circumstantially. I borrow this term from Philip Mead's *Networked Language* (2008), which is the major departure point for this book: while his work arrives at unsettlement, with the contemporary moment, mine retrieves it from Australia's networked history.

This book is also in the spirit of the following from historian Rodney Harrison (2008):

> Archaeology in Australia, as in other settler-colonial contexts, has a key role to play in "constituting that which has fallen outside the realms of discourse," making present that which has become absent from the history of the recent past.
>
> The idea of trace, or foundational "things," is integral to writing such histories. Imperial histories seek to erase the trace—this erasure is a fundamental tool of concepts such as *terra nullius* which seek to overwrite Aboriginal people's foundational influence on Australian society. Shared histories work directly against such a stance... (102)

Terra nullius is known in Australia as the formula that justifies the British takeover of the country, due to the land being "empty": of "civilization," which must (in the eighteenth century) be represented by buildings and agriculture. This doctrine was legally discredited, belatedly, in 1992 with the Mabo decision (named after its lead complainant Eddie Mabo). John Kinsella quotes from the court decision: "the common law of Australia recognizes a form of native title," adding that until this decision, and the subsequent passing by the Federal Government of the Native Title Act the following year, "Australia had been officially seen as a blank, *terra nullius*, a land open to claim" (Spatial 7–8). This was a major legal event, yet its effects are still being countered: as Harrison indicates, the term *terra nullius* is still active in erasing, not only Aboriginal history, but the history of that erasure. If we admit that erasure, however, we cannot pretend to know what has been erased. This book, then, following Eve Kosofsky Sedgwick, is an explicitly reparative one that seeks the pleasures of poetics in Indigenous and settler (and not just white settler) texts, and rejects "the monopolistic program of paranoid knowing" (22). It is a "shared history" that seeks equivalences and appreciates difference.

As references to pleasure indicate, this book is also an example of how I read, or a proposal of how—or what—others might. Many of the texts in this book have been written about by contemporary scholars, but for the most part not by those whose main interest is poetics, nor in what Australia's heritage of poetics might be. Nevertheless, some of their valuable work can be incorporated into such a project: one that I have framed as one of "unsettlement": one that is out of sympathy with the history of British settlement, both in its land and cultural colonization manifestations, that turns from what Peter Quartermain describes as "the attraction of firm punctuation...the attraction of the clear voice, which is in turn the attraction of the authentic and the sure: certainty is transcendent" (Sound 227). Punctuation is a key aspect to my readings of the case studies that follow, that and the page itself: supplementing what Jed Rasula calls the Foucauldian "adherence to language as primary resistance," and aiming to be literary in Garrett Stewart's sense of the term (as quoted by Rasula): "The reigning ideology in any period may be one of containment, but the material base itself is always insurgent...This insurgency is what, in and of itself, we call literary" (Understanding 253). The following, then, is a product of my reading experience and offers a new experience of reading (a history of) Australian writing, but does not seek to contain, settle, or dogmatize that experience. Rather, borrowing from Judith Halden-Sullivan's *Reading the Difficulties*, where she writes, "Experiencing contemporary American innovative poetry requires a revised sense of what reading can be," I mean to expand the notion of what reading Australian colonial writing can be. Halden-Sullivan quotes Gadamer:

> Experience stands in an ineluctable opposition to knowledge and to the kind of instruction that follows from general theoretical or technical knowledge. The truth of experience always implies an orientation towards new experience...The consummation of his experience, the perfection that we call "being experienced," does not consist in the fact that someone already knows everything and knows better than anyone else. Rather, the experienced person proves to be, on the contrary, someone who is radically undogmatic. (144)

This is not a conceptual critical project in terms of framing texts as poetry: but it is in poetry criticism that the work on the poetics of the page has been done. The critical work on prose as poetry has also had its effect, making any page of prose available for such a reading. There is a correspondence in what follows with the work of Kenneth Goldsmith, however, in that he writes of not wanting to add to "available text," but rather to "learn to negotiate the vast quantity that exists" (Uncreative 1). He is adding at that moment, as I am here: yet I want to defer adding to the writing on Australian contemporary poetics by first reviewing the poetics of some, to my mind, exciting precedents in Australian colonial writing, from the earliest (1796) case study, Bennelong, on. Ultimately, although writing and reading cannot be separated, I want to emphasize the agency of these writers, rather than that of readers, writers who wrote, generally, in much more difficult circumstances than most Australian writers today.

Despite the connotations of the term "settlement" as "deceptively benign and domesticated" (Coombes 2), the settlement of English literature in Australia functions as a state of exclusion—including racial exclusion—as much as the political settlement that it supports. Yet if "literature is an endless project that...denies...crystallization" (Picchione 196), then literary settlement, too, is an endless project. Rather than describe and critique this ongoing settlement of English literature—whether (to consider poetry alone) in the adapted ballad forms of colonial poets, the epic narratives that morph into explorer poems, or the local versions of Romantic and modernist lyric, not to mention more recent developments such as the influence of a range of international poetics, particularly North American, but including translations from Latin America, Europe, and Asia, I propose the possibility of an ongoing writing of unsettlement, through reading a series of exemplary unsettled texts from what might be called the long colonial era. These texts, though they may have appeared "deficient" (Iser 73) in terms of literature at the time of their writing, in retrospect seem to supply the deficiency of Australian literature in providing what can be read as an experimental poetics, preempting the modern, conventionally described as beginning with Kenneth Slessor in the 1930s, or a little later, with the fictional poet Ern Malley in 1943.

When the earliest of these unsettled texts were written, Australia was a new country with new social conditions: its topography, fauna, and flora were new to English depiction, requiring an extent of new coinage. New literacies also emerged: those of convicts; new British settlers with little education; settlers and sojourners (from China, for example) learning to write English for the first time; and, significantly, the beginnings of writing in English by Indigenous people. New forms and new uses of forms were inevitable.

In a speech made in 1853 by Daniel Deniehy (writer, politician, and supporter of the poet, Charles Harpur: the speech is quoted in Harpur's biography), Deniehy makes the claim that "in this country, Art has done nothing but Nature everything. IT IS OURS, THEN, ALONE TO INAUGURATE THE FUTURE" (Normington-Rawling 129). Deniehy conflates "Art" with settlement, in this *terra nullius*–inflected claim, denying any Indigenous presence or role. His statements correspond to a description of settlement in Michael Ackland's *That Shining Band: A Study of the Colonial Verse Tradition* (1994):

> Ensuing settlement involved taking physical and imaginative possession of the distant realm, and within this process poetry played an important role. Essentially its mission was to justify the ways of colonization, by fostering a sense of emotional and spiritual belonging in what was otherwise a place of exile, and by providing intellectually sanctioned title to the new domain. To this end...literary conventions were transported, and poetic

tableaux composed which vindicated dispossessing the original inhabitants. In particular, traditional, ideology-infused topoi and the implantation of advanced culture afforded compelling grounds for appropriating the antipodean landscape, while verse assumed implicitly a special status as the self-professed interpreter of, and guide to, the place of the newly founded colonies in a subsuming master-plan. The task of expounding the will of deity and of dealing prophetically with questions of national destiny would remain a permanent legacy, and, to some extent, a fatal model. (Shining 20)

In this scenario Australia's poetry and poets naturally come out of an existing British tradition, and a desire to serve the Commonwealth. Carter points to this implication too, quoting Keats: "The language of Poetry...naturally falls in with the language of Power" (Lie 7). Yet in asserting a "fatal model," Ackland refers to the effect on settler poets themselves: poet-suicides like Barcroft Boake and Adam Lindsay Gordon, rather than the effects on Aboriginal people, languages, land, and culture, an effect summed up by historian George Morgan: "The exclusion of all disturbing traces of Aboriginality was central to the process of settlement" (14).

In *Reading Australian Poetry* (1986), Andrew Taylor frames Australia's literary beginnings as that of an infant culture gradually outgrowing its (English) parent, through "submission...imitation...rebellion...self-discovery...independence." He compares this development to Harold Bloom's notion of the "strong poet" that "wrestle[s]" with their precursor (9). Taylor does not consider the possibility of a writing practice oblivious to the "parent" culture: prose or visual poetry that might come out of a differently literate, mature poetics; or of one written outside traditional modes. Although recognizing that his model is "nothing more than a trope" (9), Taylor asserts that "Within these limits we have Australian poetry. Beyond them we have something else" (10). Despite these strictures, Taylor nevertheless recognizes literary studies' problematic tendency toward conservatism:

> [O]ne of the paradoxes of literary studies [is] that while we claim that one of literature's greatest qualities is its ability to unsettle and disturb, the urge to relate, integrate, and even unify—the urge to privilege the familiar and the familial, that which works on us in ways which we can understand because it does not subvert what our understanding is grounded in—still activates most studies of literature. (16)

The limits of poetry described by Taylor indicate rather the limits of settlement poetry. Another version of this limit, proposed by Nicholas Jose in his introduction to the *Macquarie PEN Anthology of Australian Literature* (2009), is that of the "primary framework" of "English literature" (1). Jose implies that a qualified framework like "*Australian* literature" is, then, a secondary framework. Yet, as we will see, some of the anthology's inclusions challenge this paradigm.

In a relatively small literary culture, any overview tends to have a significant impact: therefore studies such as those by Taylor, Martin Harrison, and Paul Kane (1996) all appear to be major. It is, however, Mead's already mentioned *Networked Language*, which theorizes unsettlement, in order to argue for the future of postsettlement Australian poetry, from which I take my cue. Using a figure that bears some resemblance to the network, I have also adapted Deleuze and Guattari's "assemblage." It is a highly flexible term, in its ability to refer to differently scaled structures; it also allows for implications of agency to be ever present (the English term of assemblage being a translation from the French *agencement*). I use it in recognition of the assemblage nature of all texts and writing scenes: their multiplicity, difference and materiality, and their potential to be disassembled and reassembled: and because of the possibilities thereby invoked, of the assemblage and disassemblage of settlement. As Deleuze and Claire Parnet's translators emphasize, the term "has both an active and a passive sense" (Tomlinson and Habberjam xiii). This could also be said of the term "settlement." I refer to textual assemblages as having "agency," deriving my use of the term from Giddens:

> Agency refers not to the intentions people have in doing things but to their capability of doing things in the first place. Agency concerns events of which an individual is the perpetrator in the sense that the individual could at any phase in a given sequence of conduct have acted differently. (9)

I argue that such agency is the case, in the unsettled texts that follow: that they are not aspirational attempts to write something more literary, yet do enact creative, poetic choices. The texts could always have been written differently (even if the writers themselves claim they could not have acted differently). My readings consider how each respective text is assembled, as well as disassembled and reassembled by their editors. In order to read in such a way that de-privileges the semantic and grammatical—the privileging of which constitutes literary settlement as such—I examine the circumstances of each case study's assemblage, and the material facts of each text as assemblage. Finally, the term "assemblage" also suggests a more visual approach to reading, in turn suggesting the space of the text.

One conventional kind of textual assemblage is that of the edited anthology. Anthologies frame and produce, for example, literature. They define limits and canons by including and excluding, and arguing with each other. An ongoing assembly line of anthologies aspires to represent Australia's national literature, and national literary histories function similarly. In what follows I refer to a number of anthologies, in particular the *Macquarie PEN Anthology of Australian Literature* and the *Macquarie PEN Anthology of Aboriginal Literature* (2008). The former includes a substantial component of the latter and is a significant attempt to present a national literature that includes Indigenous writing; it is very much a "shared" project, in terms of Indigenous and non-Indigenous writing. It includes, for example, extracts from Ned Kelly's *The Jerilderie Letter*, a text that is not conventionally considered literary, nor even grammatical. Although such efforts of inclusivity are admirable, what has come to be considered literature in this instance is that which has historical importance. This is not to say that the texts do not have "imaginative" or otherwise literary qualities. They are, however, received into the anthology context without any attempt to frame (or rather reframe) them in terms of genre or poetics. The inclusion of these texts may unsettle Australian literature: or it may settle the texts themselves.

The word "unsettlement" is being used with increasing frequency in a range of Australian literary critical contexts. Usually, its use is one that exploits its affective, punning quality, as in this quote from Ross Gibson's *Seven Versions of an Australian Badland* (2002): "As one old frontier veteran explained to the 1861 Parliamentary Inquiry into the Native Police, 'You go into the scrub, the blacks are all around you, and you can see nothing of them.' Here was country for European *un*settlement" (98). My use of the term refers to the text's relation to settlement as such, and its material negation or resistance. Unsettlement takes place regardless of sentiment or intention, and, conversely, is not guaranteed by antisettlement sentiment (such as might be found in the poems of Henry Lawson, for example). It is effected through writing practice; through writing in terms of other literacies; through reinventing writing and genre; and through material location.

Uses of the term "settled" or "settling" can themselves appear to be unsettled. Delys Bird's essay "The 'Settling' of English," which serves as the second chapter of *The Oxford Literary History of Australia* (1998), suggests its negative term through the ways in which "settle," is employed. Bird's is an account of the "self-definition" of "English in the Australian colonies" up "to 1850" (21). While Bird consciously aligns the settlement of the English language with that of English-speaking people, she also, through the use of quote marks around "Settling" in her title, distances Australian literature from complicity with English settlement. Bird acknowledges her discomfort with this relationship in a footnote:

> In this chapter I am necessarily writing from a Eurocentric perspective since my concern is with the ways English literary traditions were transformed and "Australianised" in the experience of colonisation. I must, then, use terms like "settlement" and "settler" rather than the now multiple alternatives to describe colonisation and the imperial activities of English, and will refer only briefly to representations of Aboriginality and Aborigines in my discussion, since the previous chapter [Adam Shoemaker's "White on Black / Black on Black"] is devoted to these issues. (365)

Such separation of Aboriginal and Settler literature is typical, and enforces the sense that these postsettlement literary histories are distinct and don't speak to each other, despite both being, for the most part, in English. While anthologies such as the *Macquarie PEN* do appear to offer a shared history, they can also be read metonymically as coming from separate cultures, when little is done critically to counter this assumption. Mead's chapter on contemporary Indigenous poet Lionel Fogarty and Greek Australian poet ΠO is a rare and unsettling comparative instance, and one that I have also adopted in several of these chapters.

Bird uses "settlement" as if that is her only option, as if she is without agency. The punctuation of the quote marks, and the use of the footnote are her unsettling concessions. She concludes her essay past the prescribed boundary of 1850, looking to the future of the bookshops and novels that "begin the consolidation of the conflicted history of the settling-in of English" (43). This phrasing seems deliberately ambiguous and contradictory. "Consolidation" is not resolution: can a "conflicted history" be consolidated? More pertinently, her use of the figure of the "settling-in" of literature, with its suggestion of an already established culture or home, differs from the pioneer term of settling "on" the land. Bird implies the literal "consolidation" of shopfronts, and of solid fat books into libraries and learning institutions. But that it is "conflicted" also suggests there is discomfort associated with the "settling in."

By contrast, the use of unsettling can appear to be, ultimately, a settling one. An essay by John McLaren on mid-twentieth century poets titled "Unsettling the Southland: Myths of Possibility and Origin" is framed as an "engage[ment]" with "the costs and rewards of settlement." McLaren suggests that for certain poets, Australia is "one of the places where humans might work out their own destiny with their environment and the culture they brought to it." Although McLaren criticizes the "pastoral dream" and the "neglecting [of] the reality of the land and its first dwellers," there are no Indigenous poets mentioned (204). McLaren and other literary critics use the term of "unsettling" in ways that evoke a disruption of settlement, but do little with the term beyond the suggestive. (For an exception see Woodcock 263–273).

In the many readings of the political act, historical fact, and literary trope that is "settlement," it seems that, far from being a critical term, it is an uncritical term. Reference to literary settlement commonly demonstrates a passive acceptance of settlement or appears to serve a hallowing of the writers invoked, without in any substantial way pointing to the real possibilities of unsettlement in terms of new writing or reading practices.

Mead charts Australian poetry from its modern founders (Slessor, Judith Wright, and James McAuley), through to the postmodern (Malley, John Tranter), and concludes with the contemporary (Fogarty and ΠO). He writes that "Poetry is networked language in the sense that it is designed to generate meanings through structure and connection" (4). His final chapter is titled "Unsettling Language": "unsettling" understood as both adjective and verb: language that unsettles the reader and is unsettled itself. Mead takes this notion further, however, and makes an explicit case for unsettling language in the context of a settlement that he argues is "breaking up." By focusing on language rather than poetry as such, Mead challenges the notion of language's instrumentality and transparency. He refers to the history of Australian literature's role in these terms:

> From the beginning "Australian literature," viewed as a consciously undertaken program of cultural *settlement*, to use a loaded word, privileged all the historical, formal and linguistic categories necessary for its self creation and development. Inevitably, this founding of tradition included anxious, assertive and sometimes violently maintained narratives of history, selves and language. Preoccupied with its own belatedness, our national literature has been reluctant to realise its own neocolonialist assumptions and the ways in which the thematics of white belonging— "nation, landscape, the literature of the soil"—belong to the "toxic legacy of colonialism." Now, as the pressures of neo-liberal economics and globalization are reshaping contemporary culture, the literary paradigm that played a central role in underpinning that Australian settlement is breaking up. One effect of this break-up is to allow us to recognise more clearly the kind of poetries that best support that previous model of a national Australian literature, and those that don't. If "Australian literature," then, is to transform itself... [become] more inclusive and less "national"... it

has to come to terms with the *un*settling difference of Indigenous narratives of place and history and the plural knowledges of the multicultural present. (400; quotes from an essay by A. L. McCann, "The Literature of Extinction")

Here Mead describes an image of unsettlement, of disassemblage. The historical assembling of the nation both as concept and as ongoing enforcement had included the institution of a range of policies, such as the immigration policy known as "White Australia," as well as tariff protection. These policies came to be known retrospectively as the "Australian Settlement" (Woodward 3–4). Mead further urges the "abandon[ment of] the chauvinist discourse of a single Australian identity and an obsessive monoculturalism and monolingualism in favor of the plurality of local and minority languages and cultures, often creolised ones." He calls for the "reconceptualisation of a national literary history," and affirms Pierre Joris' theory of "nomad poetics" in suggesting a "giving up of the always potentially dangerous fiction that language and literature can provide *any* settled home for self-definition and national identity" (401). Mead locates a problem and points to a solution, indicating that this process is a historical as well as a contemporary one: a process that began alongside settlement. Indigenous and other unsettling modes have always been part of Australian writing, and in the readings that follow I take up Mead's challenge in order to "listen" to "difficult...poetic language[s]" (454) including the visual and spatial.

This study, then, despite its (post)colonial frame, takes part in the conversation of contemporary poetics and contributes specifically Australian possibilities. I am attempting something rather different from the usual studies of colonial literature, by rereading a number of texts from the colonial period according to a counter-device, or counter-lens, of "unsettlement." The texts that I read here are not only extraordinarily varied and fascinating documents, but have functioned (and continue to function in and for local literary and political histories) as "outside the limits" of "Australian poetry." In other words, these texts define the limits of Australian poetry. Foucault writes that "effective history...will uproot its traditional foundations and relentlessly disrupt its pretended continuities" (154). Foucault's statement efficiently summarizes the aspiration motivating this book. The point of the study is not, however, to raise up experiments or alternative modes of writing at the expense of the colonial canon. This canon itself only exists in the form of anthology inclusions and historical citations. The major colonial figures and texts are not widely taught in secondary or tertiary contexts. They are not even necessarily read as self-education by Australian poets. Previous generations were bored by the limited view of the bush; current generations are largely unaware of any view. The point, then, is to enliven and enrich Australian poetics by creating more interest in the colonial era; to provide points of comparison that go beyond the city versus bush paradigm; to include Indigenous writing in Australia's poetics history from the beginning; to unsettle automatic genre divisions made between Indigenous and non-Indigenous writing (and male and female); to insist on a more complete vision of the work of writers within the canon (Harpur, Brennan, Mackellar, Fullerton); to contribute to a history of Australian visual poetics; and to suggest new approaches (via punctuation, the page etc.) to reading apparently established (settled) texts.

With the exception of Mary Fullerton's unpublished "Bromide," which I found in Fullerton's archive at the State Library of Victoria in Melbourne, all the case studies owe, to some extent, their public profile to an editor, historian or critic.

The earliest publication, Harpur's "Note," is from Adrian Mitchell's selection from 1973 (written 1850); the most recent are the reproductions of drover texts (specific original dates unknown: late nineteenth and early twentieth century) in Darrell Lewis's article, included in Alan Mayne's history *Beyond the Black Stump* (2008). It is this interest by historians and anthologists that makes this study pertinent in terms of contemporary poetics. First, because those texts noticed by historians are largely ignored by poet-critics (despite, in the case of Kelly, for example, a determined literary framing by the *Letter*'s editor; the lack of fora for such noticing is another issue); second, because those texts that are included in literary anthologies are accepted on the basis of their historical interest, while any distinction with regard to their poetics is ignored; and, third, those texts that have been published by literary editors, despite their aberrance in the oeuvres of their authors, have a tendency to be excluded when later selections of those writers works are published (both Harpur and Brennan).

Chapter 1, "The Hunted Writer," focuses on the notorious bushranger Kelly's *The Jerilderie Letter*, as well as Indigenous traveller Bennelong's "Letter to Mr Philips, Lord Sydney's Steward," through the ambiguously key settlement activity of hunting. Chapter 2, "An Australian Poetics of the Plough," refers to an emblematic settlement activity, that of ploughing, but also to the object of the plough, through which Kelly's text can be read in a range of ways. Chapter 3, "Unnecessary Inventions," examines an extraordinary text by a Chinese goldminer that implicitly questions nation-building: Jong Ah Sing's *The Case*. In chapter 4, "Open Secrets," I oppose different elements of Australian political literary history, as expressed in the mode of secrecy of Noongar activist Norman Harris's "Letter to Jim Bassett" and Dorothea Mackellar's coded diaries: *I Love A Sunburnt Country*. In chapter 5,

"Boredom," I assess this dominant colonial mood through the carnivalesque, parodic aspects of Harpur's "Note to the Song of 'Good Night'" and Fullerton's quotation game, "Bromide." In chapter 6, "Unsettling the Field," I return to the fields of the plough and the hunt, reading the Indigenous collection of songs by stockmen that is *Ngarla Songs*, alongside the meta-symbolist work of Brennan's *Musicopoematographoscope*, through a range of contemporary theories of poetics, including ecopoetics and Charles Olson's "field." In chapter 7, "Writing to Order," I read Gladys Gilligan's enforced (by the Chief Protector of Aborigines, A. O. Neville) composition exercise "The Settlement," as another meta-colonial text that suggests the religious nature of settlement, before concluding with chapter 8, "Homelessness," in which I read a sweep of texts: new settlers Ann Williams's and Sarah Davenport's diaries; drover texts on trees and water tanks; Wiradjuri clubs; and Charlie Flannigan's baroque drawings. The readings of these texts point toward new, unsettled understandings of Australian poetics and its possibilities, and just perhaps, to new ways of reading the poetics of other, networked, histories.

CHAPTER 1

The Hunted Writer

Ned Kelly's *The Jerilderie Letter* and Bennelong's "Letter to Mr Philips, Lord Sydney's Steward"

The Jerilderie Letter. Written 1878: published in extract Webby 1989; published in full ed. McDermott 2001; extract Jose 2009. (Versions also published in newspapers and biographies at different times during the twentieth century, including its first publication in *The Herald*, 1930.)
"Letter to Mr Philips, Lord Sydney's Steward." Written 1796: published in van Toorn 2006; Heiss and Minter, 2008; Jose 2009.

This chapter shows the unsettling possibility of reading two historically significant texts, *The Jerilderie Letter* by Ned Kelly (1855–1880), and the "Letter to Mr Philips, Lord Sydney's Steward" by Bennelong (1764?–1813), through the practice of hunting. While Romantic poets wrote of such "imperial" activities, rather than participated in them (Carter, Lie 7), these two colonial writers were participants, as both protagonists and victims. It is this unsettling fact that informs the following readings.

Kelly, the son of an Irish convict, is not just "the most famous criminal in Australian history" (i), as the *Letter*'s Text Publishing blurb has it, but—within Australia at least—the country's most recognizable historical figure. A drawing of his iron helmet is enough to signify him. He is the subject of numerous poems, songs, and plays. There have been several movies based on his story: he has been played by both Mick Jagger and Heath Ledger. His image is used to sell pork in Castlemaine (Switzer n.pag.). The familiarity

Australians have with his image and story makes it natural to refer to him by his first name, as few other historical figures. He is known to have written only one letter in his own hand: the "Babington Letter," a short note written to a Sergeant Babington while Ned was still a teenager (Jones 49–51). Besides *The Jerilderie Letter*, dictated to gang member Joe Byrne, and its earlier version the "Cameron letter," Jones records that Kelly dictated three letters to the governor while in prison (279, 280, 284) and mentions a letter written to Kelly's sister, Kate (258). It is in this letter, however, that we get (Kelly's version of) the full story of him and his gang.

Bennelong, a member of the Eora people that fished in the vicinity of what would become Sydney Harbour, is also well known: there is an electorate named after him in New South Wales, as well as the place now known as Bennelong Point, the location of Sydney Opera House. His historical importance is a result of his being kidnapped by the first governor of New South Wales, Governor Arthur Philip. He became, then, the first example of an Aboriginal man who formed an ongoing relationship—though initially a forced one—with the white invaders and took on something of an ambassadorial role. He was the first Aboriginal, along with a man called Yemmerrawanne, to go to England and learn to speak English, of which the letter that survives is the evidence.

The concept of the hunted writer evokes images of paranoia, masochism, and oversensitivity. As metaphor, it suggests the seeking of the biographical subject, or in a fictional text, the biographical trace or plot clue. I am not seeking the writer behind these two remarkable texts, but rather considering the literal manifestation of Kelly and Bennelong being both the hunter and the hunted, and how this plays out in their writing. From here on I will refer to the texts as simply Kelly's *Letter* and Bennelong's "Letter," adopting the conventional distinction between a published book-length text and a shorter anthologized text. I theorize a settlement poetics of the hunt through the unsettling notion of the writer as hunter, but also as "game": this is the case with regard to police murderer Kelly, who, following his season of hunting, was in turn hunted by police, trackers, and others; and also with regard to Bennelong, who was arbitrarily hunted by Governor Philip's men as an Aboriginal specimen, and also later speared like a fish by his own tribe, and whose "Letter" further implicates its author in the practice of hunting.

The activity of the "hunt" is an ambivalent one, making possible the survival of the hunter, but resulting in the possible death or injury of the hunted. Hunting was a central part of Aboriginal life before settlement. Once settlers arrived, not only was hunting as Aboriginal practice under threat, Aboriginal people were themselves hunted by the whites: sometimes in reprisal for the "hunting" of cattle (Waterhouse 48–49). Michael Ackland describes this impact:

> Aboriginal wholeness and serenity had been interrupted by settlement... the intruders brought destruction to the old Aboriginal ways of life, broke up the hunting grounds, destroyed native morals, profaned the increase sites, fouled the water-holes and scattered the sacred churingas [objects]. (Shining 240)

Or to quote the title of a poem by Indigenous poet Oodgeroo Noonuccal (1920–1993) "No more boomerang" (Walker 32). That the meaning of hunting for Europeans is distinct from that of Indigenous Australians is illustrated by Michel Serres: "The horse calls man, who saddles the horse, who invents, shall we say, hunting, and who doesn't let the stallion go free after the kill...hunting is not primitive...Before hunting, hunting dogs have to be raised" (64). For Serres, European hunters are human "parasites," using dogs and horses for what they cannot do themselves, whereas the Aboriginal hunter tracks the land with his own knowledge (81). European-style hunting is, then, an "assemblage": needing not just a dog but a horse, not just a weapon but ammunition. Hunting as a general theme can be found in traditional Indigenous song, paraphrased by Stephen Muecke as "spearing kangaroos in this place / in this place forever spearing" (Honeysuckle 38); and in Charles Harpur's poem "The Kangaroo Hunt" (1860) (452–510). Adam Lindsay Gordon's well-known "The Sick Stockrider" (1870; made into a film in 1913) mentions hunting bushranger "'Starlight' and his gang"; the narrator and his friend Ned "emptied their six-shooters at them": to no result (Elliott 110). These examples present hunting as Indigenous practice precontact and as a practice of white settlement. Kelly and Bennelong unsettle these practices, as they embody examples of hunters who wrote: and who resisted, in very different ways, being "game."

The whites, like the Aboriginals, hunted for food and for skins, but also to get rid of animals (like kangaroos and wallabies, and later rabbits) who ate crops and grass, and others who were considered predators (dingoes, and later foxes). It became a common practice of settlement life (Waterhouse 70–72, 121–124). For the most part, it was a practical activity: though Richard Waterhouse writes that in the 1820s and 1830s hunts "were organised by squatters who rode to the chase formally dressed in green or scarlet coats. In those days there were no foxes, so native dog or dingo hunting was proclaimed as 'Fox hunting of the Antipodes'" (122). This activity was not typical, however. Lower class bush workers were as likely to learn bush skills from Aboriginals, including tracking (Ward, Australian 81).

Kelly's biographer, Ian Jones, suggests that Kelly himself may have learned hunting skills from Aboriginals (17).

The idea of hunted writers is one that unsettles our image of writing as much as that of hunting. The very naming of Kelly and Bennelong as writers unsettles the image of the civilized writer at a desk in a room. Yet the image of these two men as "quarry"—a term used aptly enough by Bennelong's biographer Isadore Brodsky—is also an unsettling one (21).

Ned Kelly was hung at the age of 25, following his capture, trial, and death sentence for the murder of police at Stringybark Creek, in the Wombat Ranges of northeast Victoria. The *Letter*, written while he was on the run, is Kelly's defense, detailing the extenuating circumstances and savagely denouncing the behavior of the police toward his family and himself. Kelly writes explicitly as an Irish nationalist in opposition to the English settlers. Though the *Letter* was intended for newspaper publication, and aspired to gain the sympathies of the general public, it was not published in Kelly's lifetime.

In rejecting the Australian nationalism of what he argues has become an outmoded literary model, Philip Mead opposes the "unsettled, wounded" text to the "vernacular" and "aggressive" (406): Kelly's *Letter* displays all these qualities. It was written by a figure since iconized and incorporated into British Australian nationalistic culture, yet is an exemplary unsettled, even homeless, text: written in the bush while wanted by the colonial police. It rejects the compromised and compromising life of settlement, of harassment by police and squatters. It definitively rejects the authority of the English and of the law.

Kelly's iconicity means that increased attention to his only extended piece of writing is probably inevitable. The *Letter* was fated to be read much later than its writer hoped, and was not generally available until 2001, when it was edited by Alex McDermott and published in book form. It has since been reprinted several times. Its contemporary popularity is due partly to the success of Peter Carey's novel *The True History of the Kelly Gang*, influenced by Kelly's *Letter* (McDermott xxix). The recent inclusion of an extract of the *Letter* in the *Macquarie PEN Anthology of Australian Literature* is but one example that what Mead calls the "reconceptualisation of a national literary history" (401) has begun. Yet its inclusion is and is not an unsettling event. The *Letter*'s inclusion is not framed in terms of its literary merit or its poetics; therefore, it can be read as merely a significant or interesting historical document, interesting perhaps as much for its lack of literary merit (its semiliterate grammar, for example) as its violent attitude and colorful descriptions of police. Other letters of what might previously have been thought of as nonliterary provenance are also included in the anthology.

As contributing editor David McCooey writes, "The question of what constitutes literature...has become more complex in recent decades" (42). Ivor Indyk, who reviewed the anthology in *The Australian*, questioned the inclusion of Kelly's "murderous...maniacal text": yet he also makes a comparison between the *Letter* and the Aboriginal "petition" letters, also included. Indyk further refers to the exclusion of contemporary poet ΠO, stating:

> Paradoxically, his omission highlights a strength of the anthology, which is its emphasis on voice...Since so many of our writers, and not just the earliest ones, are self-made, so the sense of belonging to a writerly tradition, let alone a national literary tradition, may also be indistinct. What comes to the fore in this situation, as the dominant feature, is voice. (n. pag.)

This emphasis on voice paradoxically erases orality as a settlement phenomenon and distracts us from the practice of textual literacy. Moreover, the two were often in relation, as is the case in the production of the texts of Kelly and Bennelong. A scholar of early Aboriginal writing, Penny van Toorn, writes that:

> there is no such singular thing as "literacy itself," no single set of reading and writing practices that are inherently and invariably correct, but instead a multitude of ways to practice literacy. Literacy can therefore only be validly examined in context, at particular sites, rather than in abstract general terms. (9)

Van Toorn's position implicitly resists that of the "prevailing mode" and the "primary framework": in a specific context, no particular mode necessarily prevails; no framework is necessarily primary. Elizabeth Webby, who included an extract of Kelly's *Letter* in her 1989 anthology *Colonial Voices: Letters, Diaries, Journalism and Other Accounts of Nineteenth-Century Australia*, writes:

> Perhaps the most curious of all is Ned Kelly's "Jerilderie" letter, a work of protest and self-justification intended for publication but never published. Maybe this is just as well. For any copy-editor would surely have cleaned up the erratic spelling to be found in the manuscript version reprinted here. (xxi)

The *Letter*'s "erratic spelling" is just one element of its textual poetics, a contradiction to the significance of "voice," a quality also privileged by Carey, whose front cover blurb of the *Letter* reads: "Kelly left his voice for us in his Jerilderie Letter. These 120-year-old pages are like Ned's DNA." The notional construct of Kelly's voice in the *Letter* is contradicted by Jones, who claims that the voices of Ned and Joe "blend" and that "Ned speaks as Joe believes he should speak—as Joe would speak if he were such a formidable man" (165). The view that the *Letter* is a mixed proposition is supported by McDermott, who suggests that it "prefigures the ambition of modernist literature to make the written and spoken words indivisible" (xxix).

Rather than denying the colonial practice (including the sense of rehearsal) of literacy, by cloaking it with the apparently democratic (everyone has one) concept of "voice," I am concerned with how poetics intersects with textual criticism—with the actual, material making of these texts. Primarily, however, I am concerned with the results. As James Thorpe writes in his *Principles of Textual Criticism*:

> The process of preparing the work for dissemination to a public...puts the work in the hands of persons who are professionals in the execution of the process. Similarly the effort to recover a work of the past puts it in the hands of professionals known as textual critics, or editors...The work of art is always tending toward a collaborative status. (McGann, Critique 42–43)

Thorpe's observation undoes the special status of collaboration, including that of Kelly's *Letter* as dictated to Byrne (the most educated member of Kelly's gang), and of Bennelong's with an anonymous scribe. My emphasis is not on the writer as such or the ultimate or ideal text, but the "unsettled" moment. Whereas the concept of "voice" alludes to the body, but is a metaphorical construction, colonial texts are physically written by someone's hand—and edited by further hands. The handwritten has its own poetic value; "voice" is symptomatic of the preference for "storytelling" and "song." In reading Kelly's *Letter*, however, I note the significance of oral culture. It is this culture that justifies the citation of "voice." The contemporary construction of voice is rather a paradoxical denial of the oral, denying as it does the oral's collaged and inconsistent nature. It is "Print culture," as Walter Ong writes, that "gave birth to the romantic notions of 'originality' and 'creativity,' and which set apart an individual work" (130). A further paradox then: that the concept of voice is produced by the printed word.

I don't want to overstate the effects of Kelly (or Byrne, his amanuensis's) illiteracy—or differently practiced literacy—as many of the *Letter*'s effects are metrical and assonantal; yet a poetics of illiteracy functions to positive ends in the *Letter*. (I note that Webby implies an affirmation of Kelly's (mis)spelling, as if it added distinction.) As Baudelaire wrote, "As for illiteracy, which forms (according to some blockheads) a part of moral ugliness—is it not superfluous to explain to you how this may be a whole naive poem of memories and delights?" (66). As long as the *Letter*'s voice is privileged over its written poetics, it can be still be read as "outside" while "inside" anthologies of Australian literature. If writing is unsettled from the mainstream in favor of voice, this has implications for the continuing invisibility of the other texts that I discuss. It is the marks on the page I am most concerned with.

The *Letter* was written while Kelly and his gang were wanted by the police. Kelly's aim in writing it was to literally call off the dogs, and to give his version of events. But as Jones asserts, the *Letter* is concerned with more than just local authority: in it "Ned's anger reached out past the squatters and police to the government itself—even to the British crown and the grey armies of men who sat at government desks and deliberated over baize-covered tables 12,000 miles away" (166). It was an ambitious, activist anger: "a warrior's fiery polemic" (McDermott xxix). As Sianne Ngai notes in her book *Ugly Feelings*, "thinkers from Aristotle to Audre Lord have highlighted anger's centrality to the pursuit of social justice" (35). It is the ugliness of this feeling that adds to the compelling quality of the *Letter*, but has perhaps also kept it from aesthetic consideration. Adapting the terms of another affect theorist, we might think of Kelly as a colonial "killjoy" (Ahmed 38–39). Nevertheless, Kelly's political ambitions—or mania—are evident in his recycling of the final section of the *Letter* for his and Byrne's manifesto, "Declaration of the Republic of North-eastern Victoria" (Jones 275–276). He had ideas, then, beyond destruction.

Perhaps Kelly "lost his head"—metaphorically—in shooting the police, but he kept it pretty cool afterward. His head, however, had a price on it from then on, and he was fated to lose it eventually: his body was buried without it (Jones 289). Two heads represent Kelly's headlessness: the empty head of the helmet that Sergeant Steele "held…aloft like a hunter's trophy" after shooting Ned (Jones 235), and the sculptured head of the death mask. These images appear on the front and back covers of the first edition of the published *Letter*. Kelly's actual skull has apparently been lost (Martin "Dead" 306). While these images may emphasize Kelly's cerebral nature, and the headiness of the *Letter*'s narrative, they also represent the *Letter* as letter. As Esther Milne writes in *Letters, Postcards, Emails*, "letters are often assumed to be cut off from their author's body" (84).

Critical interest in Carey's novels has brought renewed interest in the specific body of Kelly. In an article titled, "Dead White Male Heroes," which focuses on Kelly's "exten[ded]," "represent[ed]" and "metonymic" body, and which was published in a critical tribute to Carey, critic Susan K. Martin considers that:

> the anxiety about his [Kelly's] sexuality and the assertions of his heterosexuality [by Carey and also Robert Drewe; but questioned, for example, by Jones 62] are evident in the cultural investment in his physical body. Kelly is an excessively (re-)embodied and fabricated figure, memorialized and represented primarily through material objects: his body, or physical extensions of it, have become not just metonymic of him, but have taken his place. This is particularly true of the famous home made armour.... [Martin quotes Carey:] "the creature appeared from behind police lines. It was nothing human, that much was evident. It had no head but a very long thick neck and an immense chest and it walked with a slow ungainly gait directly into a hail of bullets". This Kelly is almost *hyperreal*—made up of fetishized extensions and representations, particularly ones connected with the physical—his much disputed skull, his authentic and inauthentic portraits, his death mask, and the armour. (305)

This zombiefied reanimation of dead-but-not-yet-dead (that is, not dead at this point in Carey's story) fetishes, as described by Martin, echoes the closing of Paul Kane's "Preface" in the same critical volume. Kane writes, "there is something remarkable out there bearing the name 'Peter Carey'—something we should attend to; something indeed fabulous" (xiii). The phrase "attend to" is a euphemism here: the typical settlement reaction would be that "we" should hunt this "something remarkable" down. Its "ungainly gait" should make it easy to identify and to catch. In Kane's comment criticism is equivalent to hunting. If we follow Carey's example into an unsettled (dehumanized), Kelly-infused landscape, we might all inhabit the reanimated armor-body of Ned that Martin refers to as "national dress" (314), no matter how ungainly our gait or the prose that embodies it. In neither scenario is the hunt over: there is merely the choice to be the hunter or the hunted. Kelly refers to himself as hunted game in the *Letter* when he writes, "I will be compelled to show some colonial stratagem which will open the eyes not only of the Victorian police and inhabitants but also the whole British army and now doubt they will acknowledge their hounds were barking at the wrong stump" (27–28). His long-winded style lands us with an altered cliché ("at" instead of "up") at the end: a cliché that is literally true in terms of hounds, and at least figuratively true in terms of wrong stumps as it took so long for Kelly to be captured. This conception of Kelly as hunted adds a twist to the saying "game as Ned Kelly," meaning "fearless" (Macquarie 766). Kelly himself calls Constable McIntyre "game a man as wears the [police] jacket" (79); McIntyre was the surviving policeman from Stringybark Creek, whose later testimony condemned Kelly (47). The bloodiness of the *Letter* goes beyond hunting, as if Kelly were trying to turn a hunt into a war by sheer force of the "rhetoric of blood" (McDermott xxv).

As a hunted writer, Kelly's text is also endangered. As an arch-complicator of English grammar in the (subsequent) Irish tradition of Joyce and Beckett, he also endangers English writing. He adds this threat immediately following the previous quoted sentence referring to the stump: "and that [Constable] Fitzpatrick will be the cause of greater slaughter to the Union Jack than Saint Patrick was to the snakes and toads in Ireland" (28). Kelly's reference to the saint shows a familiarity with his Irish heritage, but also displays ambivalence in this later quote (also referring to Fitzpatrick): "more fit to be a starcher to a laundress than a policeman...the deceit and cowardice is too plain to be seen in the puny cabbage hearted looking face" (38). Kelly makes a further reference to being the policemen's game in the context of trapping rather than hunting: "...when they could not snare me they got a warrant against my brother Dan..." (29). The word "snare" would tend to be figurative in a contemporary context, but must be taken literally during the colonial era of capital punishment. Colonial poet Ada Cambridge was unsympathetic: "The cowardly Kellys, murderers, and brigands as they were, and costlier than all their predecessors to hunt down, always seemed to me but imitation bushrangers" (Webby 45).

Was Kelly hunting a form, a language in *The Letter*, or was he merely, as Indyk claims, "murderous"? Kelly has illustrious precedents (and contemporaries) in the notion of the writer as a hunter of language. In an appendix to *The End of the Poem*, Agamben writes of Dante as "present[ing] his...search for the 'illustrious vernacular' in terms of a hunt," citing Dante's remark, "we are hunting down language." Agamben repeats this formulation in the note that follows on Giorgio Caproni's late poetry: Caproni, Agamben says, "hunts" "language itself"...his "prey [is] speech" (125). Kelly's use of the vernacular in the *Letter* turns from his agriculturally imbued descriptions of dung and cattle to the bush terms "wombat" and "magpie," but the *Letter* is an expression of his boundedness to those town inhabitants, the police, so he can never fully "range the bush." Perhaps he is learning that freedom isn't readable in Australia, nor writeable, Australia not quite being the West; that "there is no such thing as 'free country'" (Muecke, Honeysuckle 36). Perhaps as much as language itself, Kelly is hunting down a rhythm: one strong enough to transform settlement.

In a perhaps surprisingly pertinent comparison, John Taggart writes of another unsettler, Emily Dickinson, that:

> The freedom to hunt is purchased at a price. Freedom is always freedom *from* something. To hunt, the poet must tear away from all the some-things that would prevent entry into the wilderness...What must be torn away from is all that which is represented by settlement, historically limited and approximate as that term may be, by all the settled usages of grammar and law, at and beyond the frontiers. (176–177)

This is an apt summary of Kelly's position. Kelly wants freedom from the police, but also from "settled usage": from rural poverty and boredom. He leaves the settlement of Greta to enter "the wilderness" of the bush, but also the wilderness of outlawry's black economy. He is undergoing a shift parallel to that of the plough itself (see following chapter): a transformation from an implement of the farm to one of battle, on the way to becoming an icon. He is constructing the myth of Ned Kelly, but he is also losing himself; in Christian terms, Kelly is beginning his Passion. According to Kristeva:

> The poet is put to death because he wants to turn rhythm into a dominant element; because he wants to make language perceive what it doesn't want to say, provide it with its matter independently of the sign, and free it from denotation. For it is this *eminently parodic* gesture that changes the system. (31)

As a letter of complaint to a newspaper editor, the *Letter* is a parody on an epic scale. Kelly's "poem" silences the police; the police poem is the nonparodic hero poem, such as A.B. "Banjo" Paterson's much-loved 1890 ballad "The Man From Snowy River" (220). The police poem is the Ern Malley obscenity trial (see Mead 87–185). Parody is one of the strategies named by Zizek as reinforcing ideology rather than "changing the system." Yet Kristeva's use of parody here goes beyond the parody that is on the level of verbal irony. Rather it is meta-parodic, and seems in her characterization above—of not the merely parodic but the "eminently parodic"—to displace the system, instituting a new one. Regardless, writers are "put to death" in repressive regimes, as much for their unpatriotic rhythms as their semantics. It is the poetics of the police that Kelly excoriates, their simplistic imagery and prosaic, functional language. But if at times the *Letter* is a burlesque, in Kelly's description of the hunt-confrontation that is the incident at Stringybark Creek, the language and the rhythm break down.

Carter also writes of rhythm, of the rhythm of the "pre-mechanized... accent of the work." He suggests that the working poet is "writing back" from an "ethical ground"; that, in his example, the poet John Shaw Neilson (aged six at the writing of the *Letter*) "attend[s] to a counter-pattern" of "land clearing," of the rhythm of the axe or plough. Carter's argument is that Neilson, through salvaging a rhythm for poetry, in some measure makes up for the destruction of the working day (Forest 142). What then, is the rhythm of Kelly's work: the rhythm of stock theft? Bank robbery? Like Neilson's, Kelly's work involved the rhythm of horse riding. A rhythmic analogy could perhaps be constructed for Kelly speeding up and shouting with police chasing him. The rhythms and the work of the outlawed Kelly are also his talking, telling, writing: they are also the rhythms of the (hunting) hunted. Taggart uses the figure of hunting to make a comparison between Dickinson and the twentieth-century poet Charles Olson:

> The poet becomes a hunter by putting on power. Primarily this means a power over language whether, as with Dickinson, over that of another contemporary poet's poem or over the inherited legends and literary detritus making up the wilderness that is language. The act of composition, assumption of power, takes place in the woods of words. In part, this should remind us of Olson's composition by field and its finest realization, "In Cold Hell, In Thicket". To make this assumption is to move consciously and aggressively, to move as a hunter. The poet does this in order to bring about a more powerful composition, literally to bring about composition. (174)

Olson's field is not the radically cleared field described by philosopher Serres (177). In the scenario above, words compose, and are composed in, a wood, a thicket: a metaphorical hell. This description fits well enough the literal scene of the shootings at Stringybark Creek, the climax of Kelly's *Letter*. Despite the blame that Kelly ascribes to Constable Fitzpatrick for triggering the narrative, when he, Fitzpatrick, claimed to be shot in the wrist by Ned's brother Dan (34), it is the killing of the three police at Stringybark Creek that requires the justification of the *Letter*. The "putting on power" of the hunter, and the hunting of a suitably powerful language, can't be separated in the *Letter*. Like the "prey" of Dickinson and Olson, Kelly's "'prey'... is hunted down in the wilderness of language" (Taggart 177); but while the "prey" of Dickinson and Olson is a metaphorical construct, this is not the case with Kelly. In fact, the metaphors fall out of his language as we approach the clearing of Stringybark Creek. Kelly as literal hunter is a different kind of writer. From "I came upon police tracks" (44) up until "remember those men came into the bush with the intention of scattering pieces of me and my brother all over the bush" (63), Kelly's writing is, despite digressions relating to individual police officers, relatively low key and lacking in figuration; some examples that do occur include two unadorned references to being shot "like dogs" (44, 46) and the images of the police "manur[ing] bullock flat with us" (57) and "being shattered into a mass of animated gore to Mansfield" (61). There is humor in Fitzpatrick being "subject to fainting" (52) and in McIntyre apparently telling Kelly that "he intended to leave the force, as he had bad health, and his life was insured, he told me he intended going home" (53). But Kelly's version of the shootings of Stringybark Creek consists largely of plain prose statements such as "we could have shot those two men without speaking but not wishing to take their lives we waited" (45); "[a]s soon as I shot Lonigan he jumped up and staggered some distance" (52); and "I told McIntyre to tell them to give up their arms" et cetera. (57).

Russian Formalist Jurij Tynjanov has theorized poetry and prose in terms of sound and meaning, and his distinctions, that the "principle of construction in prose is the deformation of sound by meaning," and, conversely, that "the principle of construction in poetry is the deformation of meaning by sound" can be usefully applied here as a relative comparison (Steiner 117; translated from the Russian by Steiner). At this moment in the text, where careful narration is everything, Kelly cannot afford to write poetry; cannot afford his "meaning" to be "deformed by sound." The *Letter*'s readers, having been stimulated by pages of poetry, must now understand the clear prose of the events of Stringybark Creek. This was not a place for satire or jokes or metaphor or becoming-animal or even style. The more lurid the preceding pages, the more the plain facts of Stringybark Creek will be defined as reality. There is one curious line, however: "I did not blame them for doing honest duty but I could not suffer them blowing me to pieces in my own native land and... [instead of convicting Fitzpatrick] they would rather riddle poor unfortunate creoles" (56). Here the unusual, unsettled usage of "creole," not commonly used in Australia (it is picked up by Les Murray, however: see Matthews 21–22), is made to refer to Kelly and his gang following a reference in the same sentence to Kelly's "own native land." The "creole" in Kelly's usage is defined by its adjectives: their poverty and lack of fortune, their being hunted; it points further to Stuart Hall's definition of creolization as "forced transculturation," and the "questions of power as well as issues of entanglement" that are entailed (Lionnet and Shih 25). Kelly, then, as a convict's son, is a forced creole, has never settled.

Dickinson writes from a different position; yet she meets Kelly as she "tears away." Taggart writes:

> Once we have torn away from the settled usages...we must remain in motion...If not, the poet risks...becoming the hunted. There is only one possible protection...and that is to stay in motion...acutely and continuously alert...the poet must always be going into exile, must always act alone, and must always know that the title of hunter could be exchanged, with equal accuracy, for murderer...*Power is pitiless.* (177)

Taggart's metaphorical descriptions of Dickinson's hunting poetics remind us that if our interest is in tearing "away from the settled usages," it is not the biographical model of the writer that is the point. Kelly and his gang in their time on the run from the police, and at Stringybark Creek itself, were "in motion," and "acutely and continuously alert," and so is the language of the *Letter*: as must its readers be. Moving from "native" to "creole is just one unsettling example. It is not as bushranger or even cop killer that Kelly does anything that is, ultimately, disruptive of settlement, but as writer. As Kelly himself points out in the *Letter*, he (and his gang) provided employment for the police (26), while Captain Standish remarked on the profits made by local business during what he termed the "unpleasant business" of the Kelly hunt (27–28). Further, the historical space he takes up displaces the primary settlement event of Indigenous dispossession, with that of his own battle with authority. We don't make icons of the leaders of Aboriginal resistance; that one has been made of Kelly marks him as an aspect of settlement. Yet we can read the *Letter* against this. It is ironic that the image of Kelly as writer is more disruptive than that of him as bushranger. It is such reversals, however (Kelly as poet, Dickinson as hunter), that are necessary to avoid the cliché of "settled usages," and to not take the ground of the past for granted. To not be "easy," Taggart argues:

> We have to remain uneasy with such poets. When [poet and Dickinson scholar] Susan Howe writes "together We will hunt and kill for pleasure," there can be no assurance the reader is included in the collective. The play of the poetry is never less than frightening...(175)

The *Letter* is similarly unnerving. We never know when the narrative might once more swerve into violence (or punctuation). Taggart again: "The power of the hunter poet is made all the more absolute when the evidence for the enacting of power has been concealed in a simulated revelation" (176).

What, then, is Kelly's "simulated revelation"? That "Fitzpatrick is to blame" (McDermott xiii)? Or is it the corruption of police in general, the persecution of the Irish (Kelly 64, 71)? That, like earlier letter writers, he is aware that "the self is multiple rather than singular" (Milne 81)? Perhaps rather it is that of (self-constructing) language itself: the hyperbolic, fanciful smokescreen of Kelly's language, a performance by an outlaw son of a convict, and a hunter of poetry. The revelation is not that of the order of the prosaic, but that of the *Letter*'s unsettled epic poetics: a revelation considered further in chapter 2.

Bennelong's "Letter to Mr Philips, Lord Sydney's Steward" (Heiss and Minter 9) has none of the excesses and deformations of sound of Kelly's *Letter*. But neither is it as prosaic—nor banal—as it might first seem. As Heiss and Minter, editors of the *Macquarie PEN Anthology of Aboriginal Literature*, note in reference to the "Letter"'s inclusion, it is "the first known text in the English language by an Aboriginal author" (1); it is also included in the *Macquarie PEN Anthology of Australian Literature* (60). These major anthology appearances (2008 and 2009 respectively) follow literary historian van Toorn's 2006 complaint that the "Letter" is "lock[ed] away: in the National Library, "largely beyond the reach of his [Bennelong's] descendants" (70). The "Letter" is apparently conventional and politely social: yet as van Toorn claims, it is also "what Nicholas Thomas would call an 'entangled object,' a product of intercultural engagement" (54). Bennelong's "Letter," written in 1796, is just the third text written in English considered worthy of inclusion in the chronologically ordered *Macquarie PEN* general anthology. It is worth, then, attending to the "Letter"'s difference from contemporary white texts and from social letters generally. Mead refers to "the *un*settling difference of Indigenous narratives" (400), and, as brief and apparently conventional as it is, Bennelong's letter is the first example we have (Van Toorn notes that while there was a white settler perception that the marked sticks used by Aboriginals, known as message-sticks, were a form of letter also, the sticks' "coded information" functioned rather as mnemonics for, or identification of, the bearer, 211, 20, 212).

At the time the British arrived, Bennelong was an Aboriginal man living the traditional life of his people, the Wangal. He was, therefore, a hunter. Isadore Brodsky, Bennelong's biographer, records that he could "throw...the spear ninety yards" and that, on a trip to Norfolk, he "brought all his spears" (24, 59). The primary game of the Wangal was fish, and Bennelong was known to be an expert spearer of them (Smith 13–14). Bennelong himself came to be hunted by Governor Phillip's men: not in order to be killed, as in Kelly's case, though he was imprisoned. According to Brodsky "*Bennelong*'s reaction was that of a hunted animal" (his italics; 12). Bennelong was also speared by Wangal men, in rituals analogous to hunting: "a spear had passed through his arm and another through his leg" (Brodsky 25). Bennelong's wounds at this time have no relation to settlement, though his later spearing by Carroway, referred to in the "Letter," seems to be an indirect result of his travelling to England (Heiss and Minter 9). Nevertheless, Bennelong's wounds, like those of Kelly, are literal manifestations of the wound as colonial metaphor, characterized by Walter Mignolo as "being out of place" (I Am 183). Bennelong survived being hunted by white settlers, but many thousands didn't: massacres and murders ranged around the country for over a hundred years, while white commentators insisted that Aboriginal people were passively dying out. As Ross Gibson puts it, with deft use of a colon (a significant punctuation mark for this chapter), "This is how the colony was maintained: by sensing but trying not to see, by fearing and knowing but trying not to acknowledge" (111).

Van Toorn refers to the letter merely as Bennelong's "Letter." The longer title, "Letter to Mr Philips, Lord Sydney's Steward" was added for the purpose of anthologizing. We have no evidence that Bennelong could physically write English: like Kelly, he dictated his letter (van Toorn 53). Dictation, then, is a prime example of what van Toorn refers to as a "practice of literacy" (9). If we consider the letter as information, the letter's scribe is a functionary; but considered as an example of poetics, the anonymous scribe is a collaborator. Collaboration is also then a "practice of literacy," what we could even term "joint literacy." We know that the Kelly gang, for example, jointly composed ballads while on the run (Jones 180–181).

Although there is a similarity between Bennelong's "Letter" and Kelly's *Letter* in these terms, Bennelong's text is different in terms of scale and style. English was Kelly's and Byrne's first language; despite the limits of their literacy in making written sentences—and in punctuation, spelling, and capitalization—they would never write something like Bennelong's "Not me go to England no more" (9). Possibly some of Bennelong's grammatical constructions are a synthesis of the syntax of his first language (Eora) and of English words. Bennelong's sentences are all short. The longest is just over two lines long, and that sentence includes five punctuation marks (whereas Kelly's are often unpunctuated and go on for more than a page). The use of the colon in Bennelong's "Letter" is unusually sophisticated in a text by a not conventionally literate writer: presumably they were inserted by his scribe (though by a scribe that allows "Not me go to England no more"). There are seven colons in the 13-line text: enough to say it is a marked stylistic device. In 24 sentences there are only five commas and one semicolon. The most pronounced use of the colon is in this sentence: "I have not my wife: another black man took her away: we have had murry doings: he spear'd me in the back, but I better now: his name is now Carroway." The word "murry" here is not to be confused with "Murri," a Queensland word "for an Aboriginal person" (Mead 430). Bennelong's "murry" is annotated as "meaning bad" in the surviving transcript of the original letter (van Toorn 55). First Fleet surveyor William Dawes, however, writes that "Murry" means "Large. An augmentative in general" (44). Dawes's Eora language notebooks were written just a few years before in 1790–1791. A later example can be found in Louisa Atkinson's novel, *Gertrude the Emigrant*, from 1857, where an Aboriginal woman character says, "then blackfellow move camp, murry quick" (Spender 108). The word, then, is an ambiguous but determined marker of Aboriginal life; Bennelong is not pretending to be English. The excess of colons tends to a parody of punctuation and correctness. They resemble answers to an interrogation: what happened to your wife, your back? et cetera. Though the colons may not be Bennelong's, presumably the structure is. The stop-start rhythm suggests a list or short poem:

> I have not my wife
> another black man took her away
> we have had murry doings
> he spear'd me in the back
> but I better now
> his name is now Carroway

The sentence has a musical quality, produced by the repetition of "now" and the rhyme of "away" and "Carroway." Despite having given up his wife, he keeps the name of "Carroway" at the far end of the sentence, distancing it from his "wife." The movement of the sentence is one of distancing, pushing, politely, "Carroway" (the seducer of his wife and spearer of his back) "away." Remarkably, Carter reports another instance of the colon, in a text derived from Bennelong's speech. A David Collins asks Bennelong "where the black men (or Eora) came from? He hesitated.—Did they come from any island? His answer was that he knew of none: they came from the clouds... (*boo-row-e*)." In Collins's record of the exchange, he becomes the colon-inserting scribe. Carter comments that, "[t]he colon in this passage is eloquent. It is like a caesura, marking both a point of arrest and a sudden leap forwards, as if, pulled up short by Collins's nonsensical questions about islands, Bennilong [sic] at length finds a way out of the conversational impasse. But Collins finds Bennelong's talk of clouds equally unintelligible" (Lie 264). Here the colon seems to suggest something of Bennelong's speaking style; there is a sense here too of distancing, in this case from his questioner, Collins. Also, again, Bennelong is referring to "black men." In the "Letter" he distinguishes between himself and "another black man." These are historic moments of differentiation and identity. In the "Letter" he makes it clear that Carroway, a contributor to "murry doings" is a black man, as he is. In the Carter reference, he is required to differentiate black men from white by Collins. The poetic is mixed up with the prosaic; the literate folds in the illiterate. The literate is not equivalent to the poetic, it may even draw on the less or differently literate to give a sense of the poetic, as Collins appears to do.

The tone of Bennelong's "Letter" is highly polite. An ungenerous reader might call it obsequious, a "begging letter" (Bennelong asks Mr Philips and his wife for stockings, handkerchiefs and shoes). Van Toorn proposes that Bennelong's requests "could be understood as part of a customary Dharug practice of gift exchange between kin. A crucial element of Aboriginal kinship systems is the obligation to give and receive gifts from particular kinfolk" (62; see Heiss and Gibson for the relations between different names of Aboriginal groups in the area). She justifies this notion through an argument relating "kin-based Indigenous relationships" to "European patronage systems" (63). The meaningfulness of the comparison in this case stems from Bennelong's relationship as it developed with Governor Philip. They called each other "father and son" (62), while Lord Sydney and Arthur Philip were "patron and protégé" (63). Van Toorn further elaborates on the value of the stockings, handkerchiefs, and shoes as items for trade and prestige (65). Van Toorn's arguments persuasively lift Bennelong's letter, and his apparent "tactless[ness]" (63), out of the genre of the Western letter of social politeness, yet her own arguments are themselves rather prosaic. I prefer to think of Bennelong the writer, with his attention to stockings, handkerchiefs, and shoes, as paying attention to sartorial style: they are the punctuation of his English-speaking person, as wounds are to his Indigenous person. The accessories assist in the assemblage. Keith Vincent Smith, in his book of Indigenous travels, *Aboriginal Odysseys*, writes that while Bennelong and his companion Yemmerrawanne were in England, "[n]o expense was spared to provide [them] with food, suitable clothing, entertainment and board and lodging" (28). He further describes their being fitted out "with long frock coats of superfine green cloth with plated buttons, breeches, striped waistbands, underwear and spotted 'pepper and salt' waistcoats at a cost of £15.00 each" (30). Might not Bennelong merely wish to continue this practice of English style, at least while in town? Smith also records that "[a]fter one month [of being back in Australia], Bennelong left Governor Hunter's house and removed his fine English clothes to wander naked in the bush" (38). Here we have an active model of entering settlement and withdrawing from it: of assemblage and disassemblage.

Bennelong's clothing requests could be described as an instance of what Erving Goffman calls "breaking frame" (345). Bennelong's reference to the body is in mediated, balancing contrast to the explicit violence of being "spear'd...in the back." This is an experience closer than metaphor. Goffman writes, "it seems that the body is too constantly present as a resource to be managed with only one primary framework" (37), while Milne notes that "'signifiers of presence'—such as references to the physical body in the epistolary act—may eclipse the corporeality of the actual body of the writing subject" (73). Perhaps punctuation, when not purely conventional, can also be thought of as "signifiers of presence," eclipsing the body of the text. Colons, in particular, seem to be deictic, to say "here": two dots (or holes) "here." (Colon is also etymologically related to the body: both senses of the word are derived from the Greek *kolon* meaning limb, Concise 184.) Whereas Kelly's language of excess spills out of his sentences, unable to wait for punctuation, Bennelong's suppressed Eora language is sublimated in punctuation, in a nonsemantic cryptography, a practice that, for Carlo Ginzburg, "introduces in a clandestine manner a materialist dimension to the normative idealism of the text as a field of transparent signifiers." Ginzburg goes onto compare this kind of reading to hunting: "the hunter squatting on the ground, studying the tracks of his quarry" (Cluver 200–201). Perhaps if, as van Toorn suggests, the items requested by Bennelong were trophies, rather than for regular use, the asking is a form of hunting, one Bennelong practiced while in England. This reading allows for a different structural relation to Serres's parasitism: "The king has gone a-hunting and lost his place...hunting is a mistake, for it immediately makes parasitism possible. Someone fills the empty space" (215). Bennelong, described by a contemporary memoirist "General" Joseph Holt as "king of the natives" (Smith 41), lost his place to Carroway. He returned and was himself hunted: both symbolically, and in the vernacular meaning of scared off. Brodsky writes that Bennelong's presentation in England was that of a "flamboyant exhibition of the trophy of the chase" (78). While emphasizing the hunt, this description also suggests that Bennelong may have contributed to the performance.

It is not just through language, or even content, that Bennelong "confounds...propriety" but through style. As Carter argues, "Style is a political matter" (Forest 136). D. A. Miller, writing on the style of Jane Austen, proposes style as an aspect of "extra-territoriality, or...the daring presumption of it" (116). Bennelong's requests maintain a foot in England as a stylish counter to the many English feet in his country. The shifting of style could perhaps itself reverse Milne's notion of letter-writing's "paradoxical" "disembodiment" (73). The abrupt requests for clothing, like wounds or spurts of blood in the text, are balanced with the reassuring politeness of "please" and "thank you." The saying of "please" and "thank you" stands in metonymic relation to English politeness in general. Asking for things can be understood, then, as a pretext for uttering them (Bennelong uses each expression four times in the "Letter"), making the expressions or the asking natural. Serres notes that thanks can be a form of payment in itself, and a form of self-reassurance—that of having been "a good guest" (90).

The letters of Kelly and Bennelong are associated not just through their inclusion in the *Macquarie PEN* anthology, but in the anthology's reception. In his review, titled "Obscuring the Heritage," Peter Craven appears to disparage the "Letter" ("everything from Bennelong's letter to speeches by Marcia Langton," 8), yet in his response to Sophie Cunningham's protest on *Crikey*, he writes, "I agree with her that you can make a case for including Bennelong's Letter and the way it happens to dramatise the encounter of Aboriginal and settler just as you can for Ned Kelly's Jerilderie Letter" (Craven n. pag.; Cunningham n. pag). The phrase "happens to" suggests passivity on Bennelong's part, as if he is an effect of "encounter." Craven excuses the "Letter" on the basis of what it represents, rather than its semantics or its materiality. This normative form of reading ultimately denies the writing of the text. It is an example of what Ron Silliman refers to as, "ideologies of textual transparency that create the illusion of the 'disappearance of the word' in the service of strategies for consuming texts solely for their summarizable 'content'" (Dworkin 54). Silliman is attempting to defend the word itself from prevailing notions such as Merleau Ponty's: "When someone...succeeds in expressing himself, the signs are immediately forgotten; all that remains is the meaning. The perfection of language lies in its capacity to pass unnoticed" (Milne 20).

Charles Bernstein's essay "Artifice of Absorption" also challenges this notion that "[t]he perfection of language lies in its capacity to pass unnoticed." Bernstein's term for such "unnoticed" writing is "Absorptive writing." He writes, "The suspicion about & rejection of absorptive / writing is partly & importantly a response to / attempts to absorb / readers in an eminently palatable, amusing stasis" (Poetics 84). What if a writer fails "to express himself" in Merleau Ponty's terms? Do we then remember the signs? It seems to follow that if we remember anything of the language itself, then the expression has been a failure. Rather than consider the failure or success of Bennelong's "Letter" in terms of expression, it is to be considered a success in Bernstein's terms if it is not absorptive: apart from its abrupt style, it is arguably too repetitive to allow "stasis." We might ask, how convincing an assemblage of Englishness is it? Apart from the repetition of the colons, the "please"s and "thank you"s, there are the repetitions of address: seven

"Sir"s and nine "Madam"s. What is the meaning of this? We might say that an excess of convention unsettles convention, but is this excess the "Letter"'s "meaning"? Or, again, that Bennelong creates rhythms that unsettle the prosaic and the "Letter"'s form. How do we read such a letter in order to unsettle its framing? The inclusion of this "Letter" and other Aboriginal texts in the *Macquarie PEN* goes further than any previous general anthology in unsettling white definitions of literature. Yet little attention has been paid to the poetics of such texts. Van Toorn is an exception: but her primary focus is recognizing the agency as such of, for example, Bennelong (55), in undoing racist assumptions (1–2) and asserting Aboriginal English literacy (9). The significance of texts such as Bennelong's "Letter" has previously been (un)read as historical, sociological, political. A closer, more poetically attentive reading may also produce insights. By this I mean a reading that attends to the textual decisions effected by Bennelong, one that is partisan for Bennelong as an Aboriginal *writer*, and not just as an effect of his circumstances: nor as someone merely using writing instrumentally. Though Bennelong's text is arguably a fugitive text—the original is lost (van Toorn 237), and its ostensible subject matter slight—it is also, ironically, in terms of the historical binary of the city versus the country, dubbed in Australia as "Sydney and the bush," a "Sydney" text (written in "Sydney language" writes van Toorn, citing linguist Jakelin Troy (54). Yet van Toorn appears to have misunderstood Troy; Troy refers to the variously named Indigenous language, such as "Dharug" or "Iyora" [or "Eora"] of the Sydney area as the "Sydney language," of which Bennelong was a native speaker, 9, 14).

If we are to unsettle the reading and critical treatment of Australian literature, such early Indigenous texts must be taken into account, and in doing so we might find more to the writing than seems at first. Van Toorn suggests Bennelong's assemblage capacity in that, following Governor Phillip's various letter writing examples, Bennelong "combin[es] in a single piece of writing several epistolary genres that, in Phillip's letters, remained largely separate and distinct" (59). In a sense, Bennelong could be said to be assembling Australianness, while dissembling Englishness. He is forming us as much as being formed (Muecke, Textual 4). In Delys Bird's terms he is becoming "Australianised" (365); in Mignolo's, he is displaying metaphorical as well as literal wounds (I Am 186).

That the "Letter" is the first known text in English written by an Aboriginal person makes it of poetic as well as historical and political interest. In his survey of twentieth-century Aboriginal literature, *Black Words, White Page*, Adam Shoemaker writes, "I contend that a fundamental relationship exists between the socio-political milieu and Aboriginal creative writing in English" (6), or, as Heiss and Minter phrase it, "one of the persistent and now characteristic elements of Aboriginal literature—[is] the nexus between the literary and the political" (8). I actively read Bennelong's and other colonial texts, written in English by Aboriginal writers, for their unsettling, other-than-semantic intent. However coded, however ironic, all such texts inevitably bear the traces of, the rejection of, and resistance to, settlement. Unsettling is, in a sense, the job of these texts: literally opposed to the job of settler texts. As Muecke puts it, "It could be argued that Aboriginal criticism is political and legalistic by default; it has not 'learned' to depoliticise the aesthetic. Only when, and if, the texts become well and truly mainstream will they cease to be regarded as always political, always in the process of making a political statement" (Textual 58). Of course, many Indigenous texts are semantically explicit in their protest against settlement, just as a number of non-Indigenous texts are. But if the form of such texts allows their inclusion in the English tradition, how unsettling are they? Or if their criticisms of settlement are noted with approval, how unsettling are they? Has their unsettling energy waned? Stephen Slemon notes that, "subjected peoples are sometimes capable of producing reactionary literary documents" (104). Citing Jenny Sharpe, he goes on to assert that:

> resistance itself is always in some measure an "effect of the contradictory representation of colonial authority"...and never simply a "reversal" of power—and secondly, that resistance itself is therefore never *purely* resistance, never *simply* there in the text or the interpretative community, but is always necessarily complicit in the apparatus it seeks to transgress. (105)

Shoemaker writes of Aboriginal poetry being "dismiss[ed]...as propaganda" and defends such poetry in the following terms: "No matter how obvious or how covert the socio-political dimension of this verse, it all expresses and reinforces a distinctive Black Australian world-view, highlighting pride, dignity and survival in the face of loss" (180). Further, as Katherine E. Russo notes:

> [the] widespread definition of Indigenous literature as merely political may be due to the misinterpretation of the Indigenous relation with "community" which is very different from the Western synecdochical [sic] relation to an imagined community or nation for it is a relation of belonging and affiliation. (113)

Bennelong's "Letter" is clearly not a text of "pure resistance": it is easily read as complicit with colonialism, being a social letter of inquiry addressed to Lord Sydney's steward in England, from the very colony named for the

Lord. But if we move beyond these aspects of the text, we find valences of resistance, or at least unsettlings of relations and convention.

My instinct—my ongoing methodology—is to look for the key in the punctuation. For example, the sentence of four colons: "I have not my wife: another black man took her away: we have had murry doings: he spear'd me in the back, but I better now: his name is now Carroway." It is this sophisticated sentence that mentions "murry doings": there is no other lexical indication that the writer is Aboriginal until we read his closing signature of "Bannalong." The polite tone of this first Aboriginal letter almost effectively obscures the remarkable intrusion of a new culture into the genre of the English letter. Though we don't have a record of a responding letter, there are "two worlds" (Milne 59) in Bennelong's letter, or rather three: the England of Lord Sydney's house, and the two worlds that Bennelong lives in: one of "dinner with the Governor" and one of "murry doings." The violence of a spear in the back is an uneasy equivalence to the writing of the letter itself. The apostrophe of the word "spear'd" enacts the spearing, removing the "e": "but I better now." The "I" resembles a spear; is it the spear that is better, or is it that the Indigenous hunter Bennelong identifies with the spear? Such readings may be considered too close or as going too far, but in approaching this closely I mean to emphasize the material, graphical nature of letters, in all senses of the word. For Bennelong, *writing* a new language is, arguably, relatively more material, because more separate from his known culture, less taken for granted. Jennifer Rutherford writes, "[l]anguage takes on a material quality when it is newly found, each word has its own strange dissonance, a misfit between the word and the thing it manipulates" (Kairos 3). I am not, of course, trying to discern Bennelong's unknowable intentions, but rather what acts his text might be performing beyond the polite enquiries and requests for clothing that are its ostensible purpose.

I have been deferring stating what might seem obvious: the theme of colonization and possession. Bennelong's text is literally colonized: with colons. Here, rather than in the "Letter" as a whole, we see an instance of what Slemon refers to as "radical ambivalence": the colons could be said to cooperate or collaborate in practicing literacy. As a slightly different pun on the "colony" itself, that is, Sydney, where Bennelong lives, it has a new set of implications in helping to structure relations between him and his wife and Carroway, turning them into Bennelong's textual colony. The sentence: "I have not my wife: another black man took her away: we have had murry doings: he spear'd me in the back, but I better now: his name is now Carroway" uses colons to separate a series of relations. The first is Bennelong himself, marking the absence of his wife; the second is "another black man" with Bennelong's wife; the third, the "we," is Bennelong and the "black man," but could also imply his people more generally; the fourth is the "black man" and Bennelong together in a phrase separated by a comma—in fact, the "black man" and Bennelong joined by the spear— and then Bennelong, "better," alone; the fifth is the "black man" finally named as "Carroway" alone: "his name is now Carroway." The semantics are enacted by Bennelong's sentence, where "he" is nameless till the last colonized phrase. It is in the "Letter"—in language—that Bennelong can control Carroway, even isolate him. Despite "liv[ing] at the Governor's" and having his wife taken, he makes it clear to Mr. Philips that he is still part of a "we" that has its own "murry" doings; he is still subject to being "spear'd in the back." He makes the abstract "doings" subtly central; it is the third term of the five, and made concrete in the fourth. It is bordered (protected) from the white "doings," or rather the doings of the "black [Eora] man," Bennelong, in the white world: as represented in the other sentences of the "Letter."

Consider the preceding two sentences: "I live at the Governor's. I have dinner every day there." That Bennelong has "dinner" at "the Governor's" emphasizes his guest status. What are the terms of his living there? Is he welcome at all meals? Does Bennelong follow the English meal routine? We don't have the answers, but we have Bennelong's letter, and his own uses of "have": "I have dinner there. I don't have my wife." Like the "having" of his last dinner, the "having" of his wife is now in the past. But "wife" doesn't come around on a daily basis. It is as if Bennelong is parodying the word, Wittgenstein fashion: Wittgenstein questions the uses of "have" by writing "I have a pain" and "I have an apple" (Perloff, Wittgenstein's 20). Bennelong's loss of his wife points to the meagreness of having dinner: it is not the same having at all. Muecke writes of the nuances of the ontologies of having (as opposed to being) of different peoples (Something 176), and it as if Bennelong is demonstrating these two ontologies where he is English and has dinner at a table, and where he is Wangal, and has "murry doings" and a wife.

In the accompanying biographical note to Bennelong's "Letter," Heiss and Minter have written: "Bennelong travelled to England in 1792, and in 1795 returned home in poor health, unable to rebuild relations with his people and out of favour in the colony" (9). (The "Letter" is dated 1796.) A critical reading must resist such notes, otherwise the texts they introduce are already interpreted. If we follow the bleak biographical information in this note, we might think Bennelong is brave but lonely; pathetic and desperate (or demanding) for things like "Handkerchiefs" he knew nothing of a few years before. Bennelong writes, "Not me go to England no more. I am at home now." He seems to mean Australia (or at least the country of the Sydney area), rather than "at the Governor's," or with his people. There is no explicit reference to loss of land, of country: but it is there in the loss of his wife. It is there in the daily dinner invitation. It is there in the request for "anything you please...stockings...some Handkerchiefs...shoes." The notes of "compensation," and of homelessness, have been introduced (van Toorn 69).

More interesting, though, is the autonomy signified by the text as one both writerly and innovative. Bennelong's "Letter" as the first Aboriginal text in English is, by that fact, representative. Like any text it is not just the expression of an individual, but of a milieu; it is intertextual: quoting from history, and from the English language itself. Our awareness of this is heightened both by the historical circumstance of the "Letter," and by Bennelong's use of English. It possibly also quotes from Eora syntax. Certainly it quotes "murry doings," and quotes the Eora word that is his name, given as "Bannalong" at the end of the "Letter" (in both van Toorn and Heiss and Minter) not, as he is officially known, "Bennelong." However, the name appears to be spelt "Bannolong" in van Toorn's transcript (55), facing the typed version (54). This is a further unsettling circumstance in terms of constructing a fiction of and by "Bennelong" (who went by numerous names, Brodsky 11–12). To what extent the structure of the "Letter" and the perspective of its writer is "Black"—specifically Wangal—and what English, is difficult to construct. English perspective itself was beginning to morph into Australian. In Shoemaker's terms, its "distinctive Black Australian world-view" may be "covert," but Bennelong's "pride and dignity" are not. Though a superficial or ungenerous reading may not admit these qualities, an examination of Bennelong's poetics asserts a complex representation of Bennelong's circumstances.

There is something else remarkable about the structure of the "Letter." Though it is ostensibly addressed to "Mr Philips" (referred to as "Sir" throughout), address within the "Letter" alternates toward both Philips's wife and his employer, Lord Sydney (noted by van Toorn 58–59). Both alternations are structured in the same way: Bennelong moves from reference to direct address. In the first instance, he is addressing Mr Philips; he writes, "I hope Mrs Philips very well." This sentence is followed directly by, "You nurse me Madam when I sick." He has used the reference to Mrs Philips to structure a change of address. Does this say something about Bennelong's idea of the structure of language, or is it an effect of his imagination? By the latter I mean that when he mentions Mrs Philips, does he then see Mrs Philips in his mind, before then addressing her? It is as if the name functions as a portal. This structure is repeated with regard to addressing Lord Sydney, when he writes, "Sir, you give my duty to Ld Sydney. Thank you very good my Lord. very good: hope very well all family."

There are numerous ironic aspects to this "Letter." It is ironic that in 1796 an Aboriginal man is writing in English at all, let alone enquiring after the health of Lord Sydney and his family. Further, there is the irony that "wife-taking," "murry doings," and spearing are mentioned in a polite social letter addressed to a Lord's steward in England. There is irony in Bennelong's particular use of English: at times poetic and at times ungrammatical (not, as I show, that these are exclusive terms). Then there is the irony that a writer fluent in only one language is conscious that their use of a second is a relatively reductive and poor articulation, at times merely "a tool of negotiation" (Heiss and Minter 8). Bennelong's "Letter" is more than this. Bennelong might well be proud that he was bilingual, claiming a broader practice of literacy than that available to the many monolingual white settlers who could not write (Ward, Legend 96, 196). When Bennelong states "I am home," he is perhaps proud of the English expression of such a sentiment. Is Bennelong conscious of the impoverished expression here—or is the act of composing the "Letter" so other to speaking Eora to his own people, that he is oblivious? Perhaps the foreignness and novelty of the word "home" has a powerful resonance for him that he associates with the larger meaning in the Eora language. Anthropologist W. H. Stanner has written that, "No English words are good enough to give a sense of the links between an aboriginal group and its homeland. Our word 'home,' warm and suggestive though it be, does not match the aboriginal word that may mean 'camp,' 'hearth,' 'country,' 'everlasting home,' 'totem place,' 'life source,' 'spirit centre' and much else all in one" (Shoemaker 180).

The close of the eighteenth century was a heyday for letter writing; according to John W. Howland, "the 18th century found in the letter a most congenial form for what was human" (Milne 14). But no European had to justify their humanity in the circumstances Bennelong did. Brodsky records an English newspaper report that compares Aboriginals to "beasts of the field" on the occasion of Bennelong and Yemarrawannie's visit to England (64); the description is not unique (see Plumwood 504). Alison Ravenscroft notes the ironic description by Aboriginals of Queensland's *Aboriginals Protection and Restriction of the Sale of Opium Act 1897* as the "Dog Act" (93–94), while Marcia Langton has argued that a Western construction of "wilderness" in Australia as "pure nature…colludes with…the colonial representation of Aboriginal people as merely animal" (Plumwood 506). As Cary Wolfe notes, "the discourse of animality had historically served as a crucial strategy in the oppression of *humans* by other humans" (his italics; xx). Yet when the meaning of what is human is defined by the colonizer,

Aboriginal inhabitants have little chance against the colonizing force or discourse. Kate Soper writes in *What Is Nature?*:

> To view the "other" as endowed with the makings of civilized humanity was, in effect, to construe any manifestation of divergence from its values and behaviour as a wilful, and hence punishable, rejection of the intentions of Providence. When interpreted in this fashion, then, the idea of the equality or sameness of all human beings became a legitimation for the oppression of all those potential members of the "Family of Man," who, by their persistence in heathen rites, bestial practices and rebellious resistance to the civilizing mission, revealed their refusal to comply with the basic rules of kinship. On this logic, any and every vile treatment of the native could be justified, as it was, not only for the colonists of the New World, but through into the high period of British imperialism in the nineteenth century, when whole populations were systematically destroyed in the name of "civilization". (77)

As settlement actions, hunting Aboriginals and criminals were virtually automatic expressions of authority, not always legal. Reading Kelly's and Bennelong's letters against settlement practice rescues their poetics from sentimental readings that are dominated by the images of the writers themselves. Yet there is more to say about who is an animal, and what kind, questions that make up a substantial part of the rhetoric of Kelly's *Letter*. The next chapter examines Kelly's rage against (and with) the pastoral machine.

CHAPTER 2

An Australian Poetics of the Plough

The Jerilderie Letter

Ned Kelly is a major figure of the Australian imaginary. Lyn Innes cites poet Peter Porter's estimation that he is one of Australia's three most potent icons, along with racehorse Phar Lap and cricketer Don Bradman (83). Alluding to Ned in his armor, she goes on to describe him as "Don Quixote and Frankenstein's monster, human and robot all at once" (85). Kelly's potency is undeniable, attracting novelists, painters and poets, as well as critics: but to see him merely as a function of nationalist poetics, is to deny his own poetics, his own vision. Arguably his knightliness allowed him to represent an image of (white male) Australians more generally: as critic for the magazine founded in the year of Kelly's death and known as "the bushman's Bible," the *Bulletin*, A. G. Stephens (1865–1933) wrote: "Every man who roams the Australian wilderness is a potential knight of Romance" (Ackland, Poetry 77).

In devoting a second chapter to a closer reading of *The Jerilderie Letter*, I hope to reposition Kelly within the writing network of colonial Australia, de-emphasizing his role as "content." The text of the *Letter* is remarkable for its use of metaphor and its language generally, for one who was practicing oral literacy. It challenges its ostensible genre and is worth attention for what it does in terms of the page (and it is interesting in this light to compare to printed versions). Further, in reading his work through the plough turned into armor (as romantic an action as that appears), I mean to free the plough from its buried pastoral history, and retrieve its role in poetic discourse. Titus Burckhart writes of it as a sacred machine: "The art of ploughing is often considered as having a divine origin...Symbolically the soil is opened up to the influences of Heaven, and the plough is the active agent or generative organ" (S. Stewart 348). As we will see, Kelly is more interested in ploughing police than paddocks.

A moment of inspiration ensured that Kelly would become an Australian icon: that of appropriating plough moldboards to turn into armor for himself and his gang (Jones 190–191, *not* ploughshares: McDermott xxxiii). The plough that the armor was made from was, according to Ian Jones, deliberately symbolic. Although the armor failed to save them from police bullets, it provides an image that is instantly recognizable. (It has been reused in Sidney Nolan's celebrated painting series of Kelly, and as a dance costume for a host of Kellys in the opening ceremony of the 2000 Sydney Olympics.)

The plough belongs to Australian settlement in an obvious and inevitable way. It is a global implement used in cultivating the land: to break and make ground into pasture, but more often to turn over existing fields for sowing crops and grass. The plough represents culture ("cultivation"), and poetry in particular. The very word "verse," meaning "turn," is derived from the turn of the plough (Concise 1194): making what is now known as a line-break into an agricultural metaphor. The writing hand is therefore comparable to the hand steering the bullock or horse (later tractor) pulling the plough. From the beginning of writing in the West, poetry has had a relationship with agriculture, and the rural. With the Industrial Revolution, and the rise of the cities, the plough becomes less crucial; the line also begins to change. Of course, Kelly didn't turn the plough in the way that the line of poetry borrowed. As deadly as this turn was, the agricultural way is also deadly, not only in the terms of Serres's assertion that the slicing of the earth is a killing (177), but in those of the murder, war, and infection with European diseases, of Aboriginal people, which deliberately, or in the case of disease, conveniently, cleared a space for white industry (Ward, Legend 91–92, Gibson 66–67, Kenny 21, 25, 35).

The settlement years of nineteenth-century Australia are to some extent a beginning again: as Harpur put it, "lo, the unploughed Future, boys!" (14); or, more soberly, in the terms of the *Edinburgh Review*, "by colonisation nations are able to retrieve the past," quoted by historian Richard White (34). White notes that this view belies the dependence of industrialized nations on colonized ones: of, for example, England's factories on Australia's wool (29). An early Australian ballad of a subset known as "transportation ballads" gives a particularly dehumanizing slant on the notion of retrieving the past, in the enslavement of convicts to do the heavy farm-work of pulling the plough. Russel Ward, who quotes it in full, refers to "Van Diemen's Land" as "one of the most popular and typical":

> The first day we landed upon this fatal shore
> The planters they came round us, full twenty score or more,
> They rank'd us up like horses, and sold us out of hand,
> And yok'd us up to ploughs, my boys, to plough Van Diemen's Land.
>   (Felons 30)

Here we have an early Australian representation of ploughing: and already we see a departure—an unsettling—from the metaphor of writer as farmer. The literal animal is displaced from the farming assemblage in order to animalize the convict. As the ballad is narrated by a convict (one of "three daring poachers"), it is not possible to read this in conformance with the farmer-writer concept: the convicts are merely animal labor. So if the convicts are writing the land, turning it into literature, culture, farmland, they are merely scribes: the landowner, by extension, is the author, editor, or publisher. The steering hand, the guiding force, is perhaps the "They," that first "ranked us up like horses, and sold us out of hand." The expression, "out of hand," here means "without delay" (Concise 451). The hand appears to be passive, abstracted: the hand of market forces, or imperialism. Despite the disruption of the poet-farmer metaphor and the evocation of the dehumanizing horrors of transportation, the ballad is written (ploughed) in regular lines or verses; and its message supports not subversion in Australia, but law and order in England. The ballad ends:

> So all you gallant poachers, give ear unto my song,
> It is a bit of good advice, although it is not long,
> Throw by your dogs and snares, to you I speak plain—
> For if you knew our hardships—you would never poach again. (31)

The ballad's message is that the poaching assemblage must itself be undone. Ultimately, the balladeer is as domesticated as a horse, his double load not just the ploughing of Van Diemen's Land (now Tasmania), but of singing the support of the English landowner. As "daring poachers" they were "out of hand: according to a second meaning: "out of control" (Concise 451). Now they have been taken "in hand." Certeau's more general use of the term "poaching" in his definition of the everyday ("Everyday life invents itself by *poaching* on the property of others," Certeau's italics; xii) suggests that the emphasis on the small-scale theft of poaching serves to blur the fact of large scale theft: that by Britain of the Australian continent. The invention of contemporary everyday life in Australia has its roots in both crimes. The enslavement involved in such ballad writing adds poignancy to the concept of free verse. When the history of metrical verse contains such ballads, the later concept of free verse has a greater, more literal emancipatory inflection: not just being able to turn (break the line) when you like, but also not to be chained to the implement, and to not feel the whip.

Knowing that Kelly's father, Red, was a convict in Tasmania adds further resonance to Ned's rejection and use of the plough (Jones 4). Kelly and his gang rejected their lot of subsistence farming for the more lucrative horse dealing and bushranging. The *Letter's* editor, Alex McDermott, writes that "the likes of Ned Kelly expected to have money in their pockets, flash horses to ride, and flash clothes to display. There was more to life, they thought, than the drudgery of farming" (xxxi). This attitude comes across in the *Letter*:

> What would
> people say if they saw a strapping big lump
> of an Irishman shepherding sheep for
> fifteen bob a week or tailing turkeys in
> Tallarook Ranges for a smile from Julia or
> even begging his tucker, they would say he
> should be ashamed of himself and tar-
> and-feather him. (65)

Yet Jones records Kelly as doing some "ploughing for [a] grazier" (71), and quotes a Greta storekeeper saying that Ned "bitterly complained of not being allowed to get an honest living" (72). Either way, in the hands of the Kelly gang, the plough is literally unsettled itself from farm labor and given a more romantic (literally subversive) role. Yet, following the "Van Diemen's Land" ballad, we can also see the refashioned armor as a transformation of his father's shame and suffering, and that of the Irish generally. Though Kelly doesn't mention the plough explicitly in the *Letter*, the reference is implicit in his metaphorical reference to the "yoke." The context is a bitter protest against the English oppression of the Irish, but Kelly is also highly critical of the Irish who assist them, particularly as police:

> a policeman who for a lazy loafing
> cowardly bilit left the ash corner deserted

the shamrock, the emblem of true wit and
beauty to serve under a flag and nation
that has destroyed massacred and
murdered their forefathers by the greatest
of torture as rolling them down hill in
spiked barrels pulling their toe and finger
nails and on the wheel. and every torture
imaginable more was transported to Van
Dieman's Land to pine their young lives
away in starvation and misery among
tyrants worse than the promised hell itself
all of true blood bone and beauty, that was
not murdered on their own soil, or had
fled to America or other countries to
bloom again another day, were doomed to
Port McQuarie, Toweringabbie Norfolk
Island and Emu plains And in those places
of tyrany and condemnation many a
blooming Irishman rather than subdue to
the Saxon yoke, Were flogged to death and
bravely died in servile chains but true to
the shamrock and a credit to Paddys land. (67–68)

Here we see Kelly's inherited culture and education (Jones 14, 22), the Irish identification (1), the violence, and the land. This is the passage that, as Ward points out, has allusions to Frank the Poet's ballad "Moreton Bay": the place names "Port Macquarie, Towngabbie, Norfolk Island and Emu Plains" are all in the earlier ballad, as are the words "condemnation" and "tyranny" (Legend 51). These allusions are mixed in with a land presented symbolically through references to the "soil," the "shamrock," and the "blooming" flowers of "Irishmen." The "yoke" appears as a symbol also. But this is only one version of the Kelly poetic; as we will see, there is much else in the letter that speaks of Ned's actual milieu. Unlike the "two worlds" indicative of epistolary exchange (Milne 59), Kelly's *Letter* is a "one world" view or dramatic monologue. It seeks to make an effect rather than to elicit a dialogic response.

Although Kelly makes no explicit reference in the *Letter* to the plough as armor or implement, the *Letter*'s language is imbued with the culture of the plough and the farm, that is, agriculture. As a son of a farming convict brought up in a rural community, it is to be expected that Kelly's language reflected this. The ground of the *Letter*'s poetics is that of the farm. In a triumphalist poem from 1823, "Australasia," W. C. Wentworth (1790–1872) writes:

> The crowded farm house lines the winding stream
> On either side, and many a plodding team
> With shining ploughshare turns the neighb'ring soil,
> Which crowns with double crop the lab'rer's toil. (n.pag.)

In Wentworth's poem the yield rather than the load is doubled. This is a different style of imperial propaganda than that of the "Van Dieman's Land" ballad. Rather than designed to discourage criminals, it encourages potential settlers. The word "shining" indicates that the ploughshare is new; this reference also contributes to the poem's "prophecy of future greatness [in] one of the first outbursts in Australia of nationalistic pride" (Wilde 14). The word "crown" is a hint at Australia's relation to England; Wentworth also describes Australia as "Majestic" and "Queen of isles." The project of settlement in Wentworth, with its "double crop," is a 100% improvement on expectation. But 50-odd years later we see antagonism to this loyalist sentiment in Kelly's threat of "consequences, which shall be worse than the rust in the wheat in Victoria" (83). Kelly counters Wentworth's "nationalistic pride" with an early version of what Kinsella has termed "anti-pastoral." Kinsella refers to "anti-pastoral" as synonymous with "counter-pastoral" and (Indyk's term) "poison pastoral" (Contrary 132, 153). In Kelly, "anti-pastoral" is constituted by its negativity, by reference to things like disease ("rust in the wheat") and the prophesied "druth" (drought) and grasshoppers (83). The *Letter* further fulfills antipastoral criteria in Kelly's denial of Arcadia and his critique of "the hierarchy of land ownership" (Contrary 132). Kinsella further notes a linguistic distinction between antipastoral as a contemporary genre that uses, or has some relation to, the actual language of farmers, and the traditional pastoral's expression in the more formal language used by "Virgil... or Phillip Sidney" (156).

The ploughing of land and its metaphorical counterpart, the writing of verse, accompany each other in supporting and, arguably, mutually parasitic roles. But the relation, however, natural-seeming, is not inevitable: nor, in Indigenous terms, is it Australian. The naturalization of the plough, like any other imported aspect of European culture (such as hunting with guns), was part of settlement, and poetry played its part in that settlement. Further, these aspects of culture were part of European history, as much as of the European present. As White asserts, "the idea of 'Australia' was a European invention" (Inventing ix). But what of new ideas? In *The Gay Science*, written circa 1880 (that is, contemporary with the *Letter*) Nietzsche defines evil as the new: "being that which wants to conquer, to overthrow the old boundary stones and pieties," in other words, to create new spaces that "advance humanity." In addition, he writes that: "In every age the good men are those who bury the old thoughts deeply and make them bear fruit—the farmers of the spirit. But that land is eventually exhausted, and the ploughshare of evil must come time and again" (32). The figure of "the ploughshare of evil" is one derived from a long-settled, agricultural mythology: Nietzsche's ploughshare is not "shining." The metaphor does not easily make sense in a colonial Australian context. The underpinning concept of "age[s]" is itself one that belongs to a "humanity" that believes in "advanc[ing]." That the ploughshare "must [have] come time and time again" denies the possibility of applying Nietzsche's metaphor to a new culture, indicating the problematic nature of applying settled European figures to a newly established settler culture, in a land and cultural context that is not new, not "*nullius*" (empty) and not European. As Wentworth writes in "Australasia": "With cautious plough to rip the virgin earth, / And watch her first born harvest from its birth" (n.pag.). The anthropomorphic "cautious" is very different to "shining," yet both emphasize newness, or lack of experience. The Australian earth is virgin to plough, but why is the plough "cautious"? There is an ambiguity to the plough in its unsettling of the soil, as its contribution to cultivation and settlement. Ploughing is an ordering as well as a breaking: one associated in literature with the verse tradition. Though its linearity is broken, the image of ploughed fields suggests metrical stanzas. This is an idealization belonging to already cleared ground, not to the newly made Australian paddocks with their trees, rocks and wombat holes.

The ground of prose is the sentence as much as argument or narrative. In the *Letter*, Kelly's narrow page creates an effect of breaking lines: his prose is, like poetry, broken. Kelly's meaning is often challenged by his use of form: both sound and image take over his prose, making for an effect of poetry. It's a tour de force. *The Letter*—however consciously, however aided by scribe Byrne—stretches sentences for pages and breaks them at unorthodox moments. By "sentence," then, I mean the words between full stops rather than a grammatical unit of sense. A sentence in the *Letter* doesn't necessarily start with a capital letter. If we compare the published version against the manuscript, a further problem arises: that of distinguishing commas from full stops. Kelly's use of the full stop, in its sporadic character, and misalignment with capitalization, suggests the sentence as a moving space, if not one that is out of his control. There is no grammatically correct reading to be made, however. A reading of sentences could perhaps be made against the punctuation, but such a reading would deny the meaning of the punctuation, and the argument for a work of broken sentences would still hold.

The plough is literally a "ground-breaking" implement, and it is through denying the plough-as-plough that Kelly writes the *Letter*, countering with what might paradoxically be considered the settlement concept of the groundbreaking piece of writing. Kelly mentions the "ground" three times on the *Letter*'s opening page:

> In or about the spring of 1870 the
> ground was very soft a hawker named Mr
> Gould got his waggon bogged between
> Greta and my mother's house on the
> eleven mile creek, the ground was that
> rotten it would bog a duck in places so Mr
> Gould had abandon his waggon for fear of
> loosing his horses in the spewy ground. (1)

We could say that Kelly is firm about the ground's infirmness. It is not his ground, but the ground generally, or at least the ground between the town and his mother's house. But he does take textual ownership over this ground: how literally should we read this? As a beginning to the kind of text it is (a defence of murder and an attack on colonial authority, with particular regard to the local police), it is both oblique and quotidian, and "very soft." The *Letter* was written for publication in the *Jerilderie and Urana Gazette*. It is a "letter to the editor" conventionally addressed "Dear Sir," and designed to "acquaint" the public of "some of the events of the present past and future" (1); it is a new, redrafted and rehearsed version of a document originally known as the "Cameron letter," addressed to parliamentarian Donald Cameron. It had been read to Mrs Devine (the Senior Constable at Jerilderie's wife; McDermott ix–x), and a version was given from memory to a literally captive audience at the Jerilderie pub (xxiv). The letter preempts Kelly's trial, justifying his behaviour in the light of police provocation. Kelly and his audience may well doubt the ground he is standing on: his grounds for vindication. As he says himself, the ground was "very soft," "rotten" and "spewy." Though this could be a conscious or unconscious admission of the weakness of his case, it also indicates his vulnerability and, further, the corruption of settler society and the bad smell of police behavior, including drunkenness. Despite the *Letter*'s participation in the genre of a "letter to the editor"—and it does, conventionally enough, vent the spleen of the writer—in other aspects of its form it is not conventional at all. As with the "Babington Letter" (Farrell), I am struck by its poetics. On the first page, apart from the repetition of ground as mentioned above, the use of "g" sounds is remarkable. In eight lines, Kelly has ten "g" sounds: all the same hard "g" of ground. The lower-case "g" words support the factual, capitalized nouns of Gould and Greta (all nicely aligned to the left in the published version). If we are to make anything psychologically of the soft ground, this sounding hardness is Kelly's other side.

We might imagine the beginning of a long letter to be more self-conscious and therefore more literary in some way, but these first few lines are not atypical. In this first passage we have the first example of Kelly's fanciful poetic imagery, that frequently employs the figures of local fauna: "the ground was that rotten it would bog a duck in places." If it would "bog a duck," then a "*hawk*er" should not risk it; Kelly is warming up for his animalized police metaphors, of which more later. The *Letter* also contains many examples of assonance, rhyme, and half-rhyme. He writes "had abandon his waggon" and "loosing his horses in the spewy," where the incorrect grammar and misspelling support the poetics, both in terms of sound and semantics. The doubling of the "g" in "waggon" and "o" in "loosing" not only give us more sound for our word, but also give an expanded—looser—sense of losing, and loss. The first line of the *Letter* alerts us to something unusual. Kelly begins his narrative by saying "I wish to acquaint you with some of the occurrences of the present past and future." Though the reference to the future suggests the inauguration of colonial science fiction, it is rather the effects of the *Letter* (or at least its predictions) that are being referred to. It will make things happen.

Kelly denies the possibility of ploughing the ground three times ("very soft," "rotten," "spewy"). It is not ground, therefore, suitable for cultivation. Kelly's repetition of "ground" emphasizes an attention to the affects of climate and to the state of the ground. Kelly may not know the history of the place, being a second generation Australian, yet he is at home in this place, knowing "no division between human intercourse and local environment" (Bate 18). In this sense, the *Letter* begins with an early version of ecopoetics.

In order to read the *Letter* in the terms of verse, we can examine how it actually "turned" in Kelly's original, as McDermott's edition—though it approximates the form of the original, in terms of short lines on a small page—sets the *Letter* as prose, without regard for "breaks." I don't want to overemphasize the need to refer to the archived original. Kelly wrote the letter to be typeset in a newspaper after all, and it is through this contemporary edition that I found and was struck by the *Letter*'s poetics. It is in this form that future readers will find it, or otherwise set in anthologies, such as the extract in the *Macquarie PEN*. Kelly's words on a small page have a verse effect: the more frequent turning adding to the rhythm of the physical act of writing. The pages of the *Letter,* when combined with the rhythm of Kelly's language, exemplify this. We can see how much the *Letter* reads like a poem in the above quoted passage:

> a policeman who for a lazy loafing
> cowardly bilit left the ash corner deserted
> the shamrock, the emblem of true wit and
> beauty to serve under a flag and nation [etc.]

Indentation adds to this effect. The visual aspect of the *Letter* in its book version, though roughly equivalent to the handwritten original in its page size and line length, resembles a poem less because of the large type. The small page of the published version therefore counters any poetic effect, as there is little white space to define the shape of the text. The text of the published *Letter* is, rather, defined against the occasional opposing photo (with accompanying prose caption in much smaller type).

Editing tends to be a settling process, whether of anthology or manuscript. Though McDermott's edition of the *Letter* honors the original in its general presentation, the actual lines are changed: it is a prose setting. However, it was, when I began my research on the *Letter*, much to be preferred to the online State Library transcript, which made no attention to the original's page prosody: the original page "45," for example, which contains the passage, "a policeman who for a lazy loafing / cowardly bilit…," 20 lines long in manuscript, was reduced to six in the transcript. More recently, however, an improved version has been uploaded, which duplicates the lines of Kelly's original, and gives it more white space on the right margin than was possible on Kelly's notepaper. This shows the visual aspect of poetry to be significant: that although page design has a settling effect, it also has a poetic one. Such transcription and editing displaces the writer's own editing, that to some extent manifests the thought process of the writer, erasing the writing practice by eliding the writer's own corrections. But, as I have mentioned, it is not always easy to determine, for example, whether a mark is a comma or a full stop, especially given the *Letter*'s erratic capitalization; and given that the text does not distinguish, for example, between lower-case "a"s or "q"s other than by size, it is not always possible to be sure whether a letter was intended to be capitalized or not. Possibly this indeterminacy reflects Byrne's own uncertainty (whether grammatical or toward Kelly's meaning) or haste at times. My own, following, transcription of the original (from pages 45 and 46) was made before the current State Library transcript was available:

> he would be a king to a policeman
> who for a lazy loafing cowardly

> bilit left the ash corner deserted the
> shamrock, the emblem of true
> wit and beauty to serve under a
> flag and nation that has destroyed
> massacreed and murdered their forefathers by the
> greatest of torture as rolling them
> down hill in spiked barrels

[new page]

> pulling their toe and finger nails and on
> the wheel. and every torture imaginable
> more was transported to Van Diemand's
> Land to pine their young lives away in
> starvation and misery among tyrants
> worse than the promised hell itself All
> of true blood bone and beauty, that
> was not murdered on their own soil, or had
> fled to America or other count_
> ries to bloom again another day, Were
> doomed to Port Mc quarie, Toweringabbie
> Norfolk island and Emu plains
> And in those places of tyrany and con_
> demnation many a blooming Irish_
> man rather than subdue to the Saxon
> yoke. Were flogged to death And bravely
> died in servile chains but true to
> the shamrock and a credit to Paddys
> land

This is practically the same as the Library version: though I read the "N" of "Norfolk" as a capital, for example, the line breaks are identical. To my ear the above reads more poetically than the published version (67–68) in, for example, the "All" following on the same line as "hell"; in the repeated "e" sounds at the end of lines: "Toweringabbie," "bravely," and "Paddys"; in avoiding the repetition of "to" at line endings that in the published version is not so harmonious; in the spacing between "death" and "And bravely," and in the mid-word enjambments of "count_ries," "con_demnation" and "Irish_man," which create an unsettled syncopated effect. Note in particular that the seventh line of the extract is long because of Byrne's insertion of "their forefathers"; that all versions except the McDermott have the misspelled "massacreed" (an oversight I assume, as McDermott repeats other misspellings faithfully): a word that if sounded with the double e slows down the rhythm and avoids monotony, and adds an unsettling scream or screech, and suggests the clash between English and Irish religious creeds; that Kelly's crossed out "d" in "Van Diemand's Land" unsettles the place name, emphasizes the misspelled place where men die (it is "Diemen's," not "Diemen's"), and suggests the demands that both colonization and Kelly himself make, as well as the rough diamond that Kelly is. In Tynjanov's terms, there is a deformation in the published version toward meaning, toward prose. Though some of these examples point to a poetics of error, or a poetics of illiteracy—both unsettling notions to the literary paradigm—the turn of both the original and the published texts creates distinct poetic effects. The Text Publishing edition of 2008, with its front cover photograph of Kelly's helmet, announces the context or vision of the *Letter*: it is written under the sign of the plough, transformed not back into swords but armor (i.e., defence, not attack); and it is through the slit of the helmet that Kelly was able to see and presumably speak. Kelly's story, then, as told in the *Letter*, unfolds through this opening. Though we as readers also see his story through this slit, the cover with its black slit where Kelly's eyes would be (and which has instead the words of the title: "THE JERILDERIE LETTER") is also our view of Kelly, the author; but the armor is empty, the outlaw gone. As the *Letter* continues on page two, we have further reference to the seasons, to mosquitoes and also to horses, that dominant feature of Australian colonial poetry. The sentence following: "he was stopping at my Mother's awaiting finer or dryer weather..." predicts the metre and internal rhyme of Paterson's "Clancy of the Overflow": "I had written him a letter which I had, for want of better / Knowledge" (6). We can already begin to see what an unsettling textual ride the *Letter* is. It unsettles the genre of the letter, the pastoral, the sentence and even the ballad. Kelly continues:

> the mosquitoes were very bad which they
> generally are in a wet spring and to help
> them Mr John had a horse called Ruita
> Cruta, although a gelding was as clever as
> old Wombat or any other Stallion at
> running horses away. (2)

To say the mosquitoes were bad is a moral metaphor, and in the context of Australian poetry points to the emblematic mosquitoes of the "bad" poetry of Ern Malley. This is perhaps a strained reading, but reading Kelly in terms of grammar is also a strain. Badness and mosquitoes are "what we've got, rather than what we long for" to adapt Pound on American poetics (Quartermain, Disjunctive 15). The unstrained reading in terms of the grammar of the above is that Mr John had a horse to help the mosquitoes, though we assume Kelly means the horse was to help John. Whether Ruita Cruta helped John in stealing horses, or whether this is Ruita Cruta's own sideline is not clear from the sentence. Though the sentence is an effect to some extent of the limited literacy of Kelly's (or Byrne's) writing, a strong identification with and respect for animals, and horses in particular, comes through in the *Letter*. Horses like Ruita Cruta are characters in the *Letter*, as much as humans like Mr John: which adds to the fable-like quality of the *Letter*. As Giorgio Agamben notes, a "fable...is, according to the etymological root, something that has essentially to do with speech" (81); a fabulist however, is also a liar (Concise 345). Serres also comments on fables, asking "What would fable be without metamorphoses? Men must be changed into animals with a wave of the magic wand" (99). The making (and wearing) of the armor is in itself an instance of the metamorphic approach of Kelly, which recurs in the *Letter*: men frequently become animals; and animals, like Ruita Cruta, become men. For Vico, this points to metaphor: "every fable is a metaphor in brief" (White, Tropics 205), yet Deleuze and Guattari contradict this claim, arguing that the "becoming-animal" in Kafka (47) is the end of metaphor, that "[m]etamorphosis is the contrary of metaphor" and "it is no longer [after Kafka] a question of resemblance between...animal and...man" (22). This argument counters the settled, civilized idea of the human. In the pre-Kafka Kelly, there is still metaphor, but also metamorphosis; animals take on human qualities and vice-versa. It is just one of the elements of the *Letter* that makes it an often sarcastic, systemic attack on settlement. Kelly is in this sense an Australian alternative to Whitman, who wrote "I too am not a bit tamed.... I sound my barbaric yawp over the roofs of the world": if in a spirit of celebration rather than anger (65). Yet Whitman was not, like the outraged Kelly, "a widows son outlawed" (83).

The metamorphic examples in Kelly are those of the rural farm animals he is familiar with: horses, dogs and cattle. When he strays to the bush for wombats and magpies, or unsettles his rustic repertoire with exotic baboons, "Guerillas" and lions, he becomes ironical and metaphorical. With the exception of the indigenous wombat and magpie, the others are literal "conjunction[s] of two deterritorializations": a definition given by Deleuze and Guattari for metamorphosis (35). Yet the wombat and magpie are also deterritorialized by being placed in the context of English. In the *Letter*, where the "curs" become "dung" and the gang is predicted to be shot like dogs (44), "metamorphosis turns...[a] becoming-animal into a becoming-dead"

(Deleuze and Guattari 36). This is not quite how it turned out: the gang's wearing of armor was not a becoming-animal, but a becoming-knight, or becoming-machine. They were antisettlement assemblages roaming the land. As Deleuze and Guattari point out, Kafka's metamorphosis takes place in a room (35); yet inhabiting a room need not imply "any settled stance," as in the case of Dickinson (Rasula, This 5). A room is nevertheless, a relatively settled space, compared to the spaces traversed by the bushranger.

We can accept McDermott's (and the publisher's and the State Library's) claim that Kelly is "the 'true' author of the Jerilderie Letter" (xxv), but that does not mean that Byrne, being no doubt influenced by and educated in "Nedspeak," did not contribute to the *Letter*'s composition, nor that Ned did not ask Joe's opinion on a choice of phrasing, nor Joe offer one. Jones claims that, "[t]he two voices blend, creating a composite portrait" (165): the text demonstrating, in other words, "the give-and-take of oral expression" (Ong 130). I assume the punctuation to be Joe's: the image of Kelly saying "full stop" or "comma" contradicts the drive of the language as he ranges over his bush material (though it could also have been added later). Kelly is relying on the local knowledge of his readers to make meaning of the *Letter*: he writes as if we know who the stallion Wombat is, as much as we know Ruita Cruta's "beat which was from Greta to the seven mile creek." Wombat, this "clever" horse (2), is Kelly's first use of an indigenous metaphor, suggesting perhaps "clever" as a wombat, though perhaps also fast and stumpy-legged. Here he imports the poetics of horse-naming: both in terms of metaphor, and of sound, such as the rhyme "Ruita Cruta." The theme of horse-theft is introduced rather subtly. If Kelly as horse thief introduces the horse Ruita Cruta as the first horse thief in his narrative, then we might reasonably suppose an amount of identification between him and the horse. If the mosquitoes are bad and the horse is clever, this is also to an extent self-portraiture: Kelly being described by the *Argus* newspaper as a "clever, illiterate person" (McDermott xxi). An alternative reading of Kelly, counter to the "murderousness" of his semantics, might be made via Margot Norris's theory of "artists 'who create *as* the animal ... with their animality speaking" (she includes Neitzsche and Kafka in her list) are "biocentric": their "organic vitality prevails over ideas and systems" (Rasula, This 77).

Kelly accesses the pastoral and military image complexes in his portraiture of Constable Hall and Hall's hangers-on in four successive figures. His fascinated entanglement with the police goes beyond that of the average criminal. Deleuze and Guattari note both Kafka's and Proust's fascination for servants and employees, for theirs is not the "language ... of masters" (26). Yet in the *Letter* the police have no language of their own, they have only the master's language; hence Kelly's contempt and the paradoxically distracting and resulting "interest...in the possibility of making his own language" (Deleuze and Guattari 26). In the first figure, Kelly writes, "he [Hall] was as helpless as a big guano after leaving a dead bullock or a horse"; in the second, "I straddled him and rooted both spurs into his thighs he roared like a big calf attacked by dogs"; in the third, "he stuck to it [his revolver] like grim death to a dead volunteer." The fourth applies to "two blacksmiths...looking on": "I could have spread those curs like dung in a paddock" (12–13). The first two images are evidence of Kelly's familiarity with cattle: in the first the metaphorical bullock is dead; in the second the calf is under attack. If the latter image is based on reality then the attacking dogs are wild dogs, or dogs that have turned from their training. The third image appears incongruous at first, however poetic, yet typifies Kelly's tendency to mix the animal with the human, and momentary violence with death. The fourth image is typical in its casual rural violence. It can be read as a warning to those like the blacksmiths who assist the police. According to Kelly, they "got ropes tied my hands and feet [while] Hall beat me over the head with his six chambered colts revolver" (13). Kelly would spread them like dung as a farmer does to fertilize the ground before ploughing (an image he returns to).

Kelly's language is typical of someone belonging to an oral culture. His metaphors "use concepts in situational, operational frames of reference that are minimally abstract in the sense that they remain close to the living human lifeworld" (Ong 49). Ong details a number of attributes that distinguish oral thought and expression from written, several of which resonate with the text of the *Letter*. One of these attributes is "additive rather than subordinative." This accounts for Kelly's paratactic tendency to include more than one subject in a sentence and the cumulative style of his narrative. When read as additional, his style isn't as ambiguous. Ong notes that an additive style of writing is typically structured with the word "and" (37). The following is from the *Letter*; the first "and" begins a sentence:

and

McCormack being a policeman over the
convicts and women being scarce released
her from that land of bondage and
tyranny, and they came to Victoria and are
at present residents of Greta and on the
29th of March I was released from prison
and came home Wild Wright came to the
Eleven Mile to see Mr Gunn stopped all
night and lost his mare both him and me

> looked all day for her and could not get
> her Wright who was a stranger to me was in
> a hurry to get back to Mansfield and I gave
> him another mare and he told me if I (7)

We can see here how the narrative continues on an equalizing plane, without subordination, using the word "and" to sustain and structure the unpunctuated text. Another characteristic given by Ong is "aggregative rather than analytic": "closely tied to reliance on formulas to implement memory," as well as the "baggage" of "redundant" epithets (38). Kelly relies on descriptive formulas that he has for, for example, Van Diemen's Land, for England, and for police. He also uses "traditional expressions" (39) such as "bravely died in servile chains" (Kelly 68). Ong then notes that an orally influenced text is typically "redundant or 'copious'" (39). Again, Kelly gives his audience plenty of time to get his drift; his copious style with its redundant phrasing and repetitive narrative is what Ong refers to as oral "continuity": it "is in a profound sense more natural to thought and speech than is sparse linearity," adding that such "writing...affords...the opportunity to interfere with and reorganize its more normal, redundant processes" (40). The *Letter*, however, is an experiment for Kelly, and therefore doesn't quite fit Ong's fourth characteristic of "conservative and traditionalist" (41). The *Letter* calls for change rather than conservation but it is a change that invokes the past to justify itself.

There are further features that make the *Letter* a typical oral narrative. It is "agonistic" in tone, and replete with "verbal tongue-lashings," "[e]nthusiastic descriptions of physical violence" and "exquisitely gory detail" (43–44). Ong's observation that an "interlocutor" or "listener to stimulate and ground thought" is "virtually essential" gives further support to the role of Byrne in the *Letter*'s composition. Ong elaborates:

> But even with a listener...How could you ever call back to mind what you had so laboriously worked out?...Your thought must come into being in heavily rhythmic, balanced patterns, in repetitions or antitheses, in alliterations and assonances, in epithetic and other formulary expressions...Mnemonic needs even determine syntax. (34)

Here we have the oral basis for Kelly's style and poetics generally. Yet Kelly's *Letter* clearly has ambitions beyond that of memorability and rhythm. Its scope is larger than that of a ballad. It is not the "voice" of the *Letter* that is significant, but rather its oral or speech poetics. Kelly's invective against Hall and the blacksmiths uses country language against the town-dwellers.

He uses the earthiness of farm vernacular as if in contempt for their mediated existences. Yet his claim that "I could have spread those curs like dung in a paddock" is doubly abstract: not only is it in language, but is expressed after the event. Kelly's language can also be called bullshit: a "spread[ing]" of "dung in...paddock[s]," through the bush and in towns. Shit as language, with the qualification of bull, insists on the animal in us, the trace of shit in the milk we drink, of the earth. It emphasizes fertilization, but also skepticism. Skepticism is a recurring attitude in the world of the *Letter*, not just towards speech and the law, but also toward possession of animals: once stock went outside the fence, rich landowners would have them seized: "If a poor man happened to leave his horse or bit of a poddy calf outside his paddock they would be impounded," requiring "poor farmers...to leave their ploughing or harvest or other employment" to get them back (23). Kelly is explaining a situation exploited by the rich, and eliciting sympathy for the poor; yet the left plough suggests one that a passing bushranger might exploit.

Kelly's use of shit imagery appears to be as reflex as his use of animal and death imagery, suggesting both his fertile imagination and his verbal diarrhoea. He marks his territory with speech, with language; yet for Kelly, this territory is his constituency or audience—readership—more than it is ownership as such. Shit as a substance is transitory: it is between us and the earth; it resembles the earth and returns to the earth from our bodies, until finally our bodies return to the earth also; and it is the same for animals. Kelly's cycling between the earth, humans, animals, shit, and death displays the ecology of the *Letter*.

Kelly is a master of the image, and of the hyperbolic image in particular. He typically combines the fanciful with an attention to detail: "And when Wild Wright and my mother came they could trace us across the street by the blood in the dust and which spoiled the lustre of the paint on the gatepost of the Barracks Hall" (13). Like the earlier "it would bog a duck in places," this description isn't necessarily hyperbolic; it may well have been literally true, but it is all part of Kelly's stylistic tendency to pile up imagery and incident, without allowing a listener, or an absorbed reader, to stop and question the veracity of the narrative. Figurative language is always, in a sense, exaggeration—it is not literally true—so when colorful but nonmetaphorical language is mixed together in the extreme figuration of the *Letter*, it all tends to participate in the hyperbolic. The etymologies of "hyperbole" and "exaggeration" point to "excess" and to "heap up": Kelly's narrative has an excess of blood and shit and violence and death, and like the tragedy it is, bodies imaginatively and literally heap up (Concise 490, 334): and even more so in Kelly's biography. The deaths of the gang and

Kelly himself are not part of the *Letter*'s narrative, but their ends are well known. I have mentioned Kelly's death mask already; the photographs of the gang (Dan Kelly, Steve Hart and Joe Byrne) that are included in the published version are captioned with their fates. All were shot by the police (17, 66, 80). There had been plenty of real life justification for Kelly's language of excess, yet his style is also "a way of calling language into question by apparent, declared excesses of language" (Barthes, Criticism 90). Kelly is at war with the language used against him as well as those using it. That he can suddenly turn the barrage off for the light bathetic irony of "which spoiled the lustre of the paint on the gate-post of the [police] Barracks Hall," shows remarkable finesse.

Kelly returns to the fabulous when he writes (of the police) "the ignorant unicorns even threathen to shoot myself But as soon as I am dead they will be heels up in the muroo" (27). The figure of the unicorn (repeated 72) represents the incongruous and useless: neither horse nor cattle. I couldn't find the word "muroo" in a dictionary, but there is a possible variation found in Harpur. He refers to a "copse of tough maroo" in his poem "The Kangaroo Hunt": his notes to the poem state that "Maroo is an aboriginal name of a sort of brush iron-wood" (487, 509). "Muroo" might then be that unsettling "in-between ground...the province of the poet" that Carter writes of (Lie 3), or what Simone Weil imagined when she wrote: "To be only an intermediary between the uncultivated ground and the ploughed field...between the blank page and the poem" (46). Weil affirms the image of the poem as ploughed ground, but characterizes the poet only as necessary rather than authoritative or controlling. Perhaps whether we think of Kelly, or the unicorns, as intermediaries is an insignificant distinction, but he—nor it seems the police—was never so modest.

Kelly returns to the shit-fertilizer theme even more aggressively when he refers to the police: "they knew well I was not there or I would have scattered their blood and brains like rain I would manure the Eleven Mile with their carcasses and yet remember there is not one drop of murderous blood in my Veins" (40). His use of "manure" as a verb in relation to "carcasses" is both authoritative and innovative. The thematic consistency and the use of the simple rhyme of "brains," "rain," and "Veins" obscure the complexity of this image, as does the "not murderous" paradox. In using the word "drop" in such close proximity to "rain," Kelly evokes the comparison of rain to blood, naturalizing the preceding—apocalyptic—image of "blood and brains" "rain[ing]." The onomatopoeia of "drop" emphasizes hearing: "The drop is the phoneme" (Serres 189). He returns to the theme of hearing later on, when he writes, "I am called the blackest and coldest blooded murderer ever on record But if I hear any more of it I will not exactly show them what cold blooded murder is..." (42). It is as if all he can hear is the blood buzzing in his ears. This manuring image works differently to the previous "spread those curs like dung in a paddock." The curs (blacksmiths) are first compared to dogs. Though cur can also mean "surly, ill-bred or cowardly fellow," the primary meaning of "worthless, low-bred or snappish dog" (Concise 232) is consistent with Kelly's metaphoric-cum-metamorphic style. Though this perhaps complicates the image of Constable Hall as a "calf attacked by dogs," such complication is not uncharacteristic of the *Letter*. Later, Kelly will refer to himself and his gang as dogs: the police "would shoot us down like dogs" (44) and again "like a dog" (46); he also refers to the police who arrested him in an earlier incident as "five curs" (48). In his figuration of the blacksmiths, however, the dogs are turned into shit, or rather, the blacksmiths are briefly dogs, and in a turn from metaphor to simile, they are "spread...like dung." In the latter police image, "they" are "like rain" that is "manure[d]." They are not changed (though apparently slaughtered in some way); they are still blood, brain, carcass, but they are literally treated as, or like, shit. There is something very evenhanded about Kelly's rhetoric. For just as the police and the blacksmiths and himself and his gang are compared to dogs, so the image of being manured comes to apply to the Kelly gang: "the Police might come to our camp while we were all away and manure bullock flat with us on our arrival" (56–57). Though his threats imply that if anyone hunts him they will become fertilizer, Kelly acknowledges it goes both ways: dog eat dog. His metaphors indicate that the killing associated with possessing the earth, stops us noticing the killing *of* the earth: "the slaughtered body of the giant ground" (Carter, Lie 2). Five images of Kelly's own blood follow quickly after the above. It is as if the (admittedly aggressive) pastoral imagery is being left behind for that of war, the hunt, or the butcher shop:

> ...those men certainly made
> my blood boil as I don't think there is a
> man born could have the patience to suffer
> it as long as I did or ever allow his blood to
> get cold while such insults as these were
> unavenged and yet in every paper that is
> printed I am called the blackest and coldest
> blooded murderer ever on record But if I
> hear any more of it I will not exactly show
> them what cold blooded murder is but
> wholesale and retail slaughter, something
> different to shooting three troopers in self

defence and robbing a bank. I would have
been rather hot-blooded to throw down
my rifle and let them shoot me and my
innocent brother... (42–43)

In the *Letter*, Kelly continually makes reference to the corporeal, insisting on being more than an image, name, or voice. Esther Milne writes that "the material body or physical infrastructure of communication can sometimes provide the vehicle for particular fantasies and dreams" (89). Her examples are those of romance and sexuality, while Kelly's fantasies are of violence and power. But Milne's point is that the form of the letter allows for "the disjunction between the actual, physically located, corporeal bodies and those bodies that are constructed or imagined in the epistolary act" (89). The repeated mention of blood emphasizes the fact that despite being wanted by the police, and having killed three police himself, he, Ned Kelly, is still alive. This bloodiness is seen by McDermott as Kelly's signature, asserting that Kelly's authorship (rather than Byrne's) is confirmed by a quote from a contemporary of Kelly's speech:

> The Reverend John Gribble... described how the outlaw... put his gun next to his glass and announced, "There's my revolver. Anyone here may take it and shoot me dead, but if I'm shot Jerilderie will swim in its own blood." It is this extremity of threat, and the rhetoric of blood in particular, that specifically echoes the Jerilderie Letter. (xxv–xxvi)

In the midst of all this blood, Kelly suggests a shift in occupation from the "wholesale and retail horse and cattle dealing" mentioned earlier in the *Letter* (21) to that of "wholesale and retail slaughter." His humor is gone: the irony is grim. There has been a shift in tone and rhetoric. The earlier reference is an ironic use of euphemism for horse and cattle theft. But despite the allusion to butchery, there is no grey area here: except in terms of war, which is in effect what Kelly is declaring.

As the *Letter* approaches the climax of Stringybark Creek, Kelly becomes less controlled. The *Letter* becomes a bloody rant, and the figures become hyperbolic. Kelly then finally tells his version of what happened at Stringybark Creek. This is the hunting scene, elaborated in the previous chapter. He also mentions for the first time—though not by name—the other members of the gang (44). As McDermott notes, "Ned consistently attempts to shield associates from judicial scrutiny" (57). Whatever his conscious or unconscious motivations, the *Letter* is Ned's story, though occasional sympathetic reference is made to his brother Dan. At this point in the narrative the addressee of the newspaper editor appears to be forgotten. Though Kelly's words "attempt to shield" Dan (and Joe and Steve), it is his actions, rather than his words, that doom them.

Distributed between the pages of the published *Letter* are photographs of the narrative's characters, and of the Stringybark Creek site. The photo of Kelly himself is on the left page facing the cover page, introducing and authorizing his story. The photos have a settling effect: historicizing the narrative, providing a human image for the fabulous shape changes of the police given by Kelly. After the Stringybark Creek narration—and before his historical tirade against the English—comes his most inspired, excessively adjectival, and metaphorical summary of the police: "a parcel of big ugly fat-necked wombat headed big bellied magpie legged narrow hipped splaw-footed sons of Irish Bailiffs or english landlords" (63). In *True History of the Kelly Gang*, Peter Carey has Ned regularly use the word "adjectival" as a curse or insulting adjective, for example (referring to Commissioner Standish): "the b- - - - - d's adjectival face" (165). Kelly's description of the "parcel of" police in the *Letter* is an example of what Thomas Conley, in *Toward a Rhetoric of Insult*, describes as the "simplest way to intensify and insult...*accumulatio*...i.e., to pile one abusive term on another" (13). Conley also notes that "animal terms are a standard part of the insulter's arsenal" (72). It is the language and the sustained nature of the insult that makes it Kelly's own, rather than any conceptual originality. In just this one example, Kelly employs a number of traditional modes of insult, or what Conley calls "stock topics of Roman invective": "1. Embarrassing family origin...3. Physical appearance...5. Gluttony and drunkenness [implied by 'big bellied']...6. Hypocrisy for seeming virtuous [relates back to '1']...18. Stupidity." Others from Conley's list, such as "12. Cowardice in battle...15. Cruelty to fellow citizens or allies" and "16. Plunder of private or public property" (37–38) are all alluded to by Kelly at other times. Kelly's style of cumulation was not unique either, as we see from this example from Ward: "W. Craig records an amusing story of an old hand at the diggings who was robbed by a newly arrived Scotsman:...[a] 'chuckle-headed, porridge-eating, lime-juicing son of a sea-cook'" (Legend 107). What Kelly inserts in his satirical description are the local references of "wombat headed" and "magpie legged," and a greater piling up of terms; both Kelly and "the old hand" are though, it seems, inspired by racism imported from the British Isles.

The human–animal relation (particularly the police-animal relation) is never stable in the *Letter*. Kelly moves from the comparison of the police to local fauna to that of "a baboon or Guerilla." The punning of "Guerilla" is apt, considering the "little war" being carried on between police and

Kelly's gang (69). The illustrative photo shows two men, that McDermott describes as "[l]ooking more like bounty hunters," adding that "[p]olice search parties were often mistaken for the outlaws by local farmers and other police, and fired on accordingly" (70). The *Letter* then turns on the public, Kelly threatening to "exterminate them without medicine" if they assist the police. But just two sentences later, the public as implied vermin figure has shifted to that of universal object: "If I had robbed and plundered ravished and murdered everything I met young and old, rich and poor" (72). This democratizing characterization sounds like a line from a fable (or the Bible), yet the use of "everything" is presumably vernacular (or slip of the tongue or pen) for "everyone." By the following sentence we are definitely back with the human, threatened with a torture beyond the one described: "by the light that shines pegged on an ant-bed with their bellies opened their fat rendered and poured down their throat boiling hot will be cool to what pleasure I will give some of them" (74). The violence promised sounds fantastic, until we remember the burning of the gang's bodies at Glenrowan Inn, after the inn was set fire to by police (Jones 229, 243). We are in the context of human violence, with a level of torture that goes beyond the pastoral. As a language performance, though, we are witnessing a maelstrom, and it isn't over yet. Kelly threatens further extermination (74) before making a humorous bathetic image of a particular policeman: "Brooke. E. Smith Superintendent of Police," an "article that reminds [Kelly] of a poodle dog half clipped in the lion fashion" (76). This ludicrous and atypically town-based image is enough to undermine Smith. What place could such a man have in the Australian bush? It is not Smith that illustrates this facing page, but Captain Standish, "in charge of the hunt for the Kelly gang" (77), who fits the poodle description well enough, and to whom Smith is swiftly compared:

> Smith Superintendent of Police
> he knows as much about commanding
> Police as Captain Standish does about
> mustering mosquitoes and boiling them
> down for their fat on the back blocks of the
> Lachlan for he has a head like a turnip a
> stiff neck as big as his shoulders narrow
> hipped and pointed towards the feet like a
> vine stake And if there is anyone to be
> called a murderer Regarding Kennedy,
> Scanlan and Lonigan it is that misplaced
> poodle. (76–78)

He asks if they "think [Standish] is a superior animal to the men that has to guard him" ("for fear of body snatchers"!) (78). In yet another remarkable moment of condensed contempt and imagination, Kelly also evokes the reality of poverty and the necessity of making do. He suggests that someone making a living off the land cannot simply grow crops or breed livestock, but must do everything imaginable, save everything, from growing turnips to rendering mosquito fat.

A new tone, anticlimactic and melancholy, enters the *Letter* as it reaches its conclusion. His final threat contains no reference to the police, farm animals, blood, or shit; but there is a return to the antipastoral, and a suggestion also that Kelly will come again:

> I give fair warning to all those who has
> reason to fear me to sell out and give £10
> out of every hundred towards the widow and
> orphan fund... neglect this and
> abide by the consequences, which shall be
> worse than the rust in the wheat in Victoria
> or the druth of a dry season to the grass-
> hoppers in New South Wales... I am a widows son
> outlawed and my orders <u>must</u> be obeyed. (83)

In this reckoning scenario the violence is suddenly muted. Here we have Kelly as natural disaster, wiping those with "reason to fear" from the earth. It is not merely an unsettling but literally a de-settling image, on both sides of the Victoria–New South Wales state border: perhaps making a broader threat, but also making Kelly's present location ambiguous. The reference to the "widow and orphan fund" might at first seem sentimental and/or philanthropic, though we know his mother is a widow, but Kelly's explicit self-identification as "widows son" makes the earlier reference ironic. The word "rust" rhymes with the underlined "<u>must</u>." The underlining fails to be emphatic after the extremes of emphatic language in the rest of the letter. The rust is rather a trace, emphasizing the absence of the plough, and the continuing unsettled and unsettling presence of Kelly.

According to Jacques Attali, "Nothing essential happens in the absence of noise" (3); and when Serres writes, "... if a pen ever left a rustling noise on the blank silence of its field," he reminds us that the ploughing of a field is not a silent activity. In Serres's vision, agriculture is by no means opposed to war, but is a war on the earth: "The blade of the plough is a sacrificial blade, killing all the plants to make a clean space. Everything that grows here is excluded... It cuts up space" (177). Clearing is what Carter calls "the *sine qua non* of progress" (Lie, 6). The Australian version of the battle with the land displaces the battle between settlers and the Indigenous inhabitants. As Historian Rod Macneil writes:

> The deculturation of Aboriginality enabled the process of colonisation to be constructed in terms of an opposition between settler and land, rather than as a contest between settler and indigenous peoples. Thus the removal of Aboriginal people from their lands could be equated with the clearing of forests and other features of the landscape that impeded the progress of colonisation. (56)

The plough as a signifier of growth and life is, therefore, linked to destruction. The plough, in the context of colonization, is as much a warring implement as a sword. Kelly's *Letter* is an unsettling mixture of goodwill and scorched earth policy. Though Kelly continually draws on the agricultural for his language and logic, he suggests devastation is the proper alternative to an unfair society. It is a stump, or vernacular, speech that reduces everything to a stump, then burns the stump out. It is not a nation-building text. It unsettles Kelly's image, creating for him another marginal position: that of writer. This image is one that is difficult to settle, considering his bushranging fame and his metallic dress: these aspects (as well as the horses and Joe's listening ear and writing hand) constitute Kelly as unsettling assemblage.

CHAPTER 3

Unnecessary Inventions

Jong Ah Sing's *The Case*

The Case. Written 1867?–1872; published in transliterated English version Moore and Tully 2000; excerpted in essay by Shen on Chinese Australian autobiography, 2001.

In this chapter I read the unsettling poetics of a unique diary, written by Jong Ah Sing (c. 1837–1900), a Chinese gold-miner arrested after a knife fight at the camp where he lived, near Dunolly, Victoria, in 1867. *The Case* was written sometime between 1867, when Jong was arrested for assault (Moore and Tully 62–63), and 1872, the date on the book. It was donated to the State Library of Victoria in 1880. It is listed as "Diary [manuscript]" on the Library catalogue, but the words "The Case" appear on the title page. Though the original remains unpublished, I italicize the title because it appears as a finished work, taking the form of a small handmade book. In the preface to Ruth Moore's and his own "translated" edition of *The Case*, Jim Tully writes that it is "not a diary but a...personal exoneration [written] to seek freedom [from Yarra Bend Asylum] and justice" (ix). In their Introduction, however, the book is referred to as "reminiscences" (1). (Moore and Tully have argued that Jong's name should be Jong Ah Siug, as he writes his name as Siug more often than Sing in *The Case*—an argument supported by Siegel, in his statistically based, linguistic analysis of Jong's book. However, he cites the counterargument that Jong may have transcribed his name incorrectly, and that Siug is not a Cantonese name (311). I have retained Sing, for these reasons, as well as to conform with his name as catalogued by the State Library of Victoria.)

The Case, as a document produced in an asylum by a Chinese goldminer, raises the question of "outsider writing." Yet outsider writing is not a category that exists in Australia's mid-nineteenth century. Not only had "outsider art" not been coined as a term, arguably there was no inside in Australian letters at this time. Though poets like Harpur (1813–1868) and Henry Kendall (1839–1882) have retrospectively been canonized, isolated writers do not make a scene or a literature. In reading the long colonial era of Australian literature, the question of outside and inside is more aptly examined in literal terms, and in terms of homelessness and shelter. Early nineteenth-century commentator J. P. Townsend writes that, "In the first stages of settlement masters and men alike sheltered from the elements in bark huts or 'gunyahs,' adapted from those of the aborigines" (Ward, Legend 81).

The Case came into being because of a knife fight over a black hen and the subsequent legal proceedings. Like both Kelly and Bennelong, Jong was involved in a wounding incident. In 1867 he was charged with striking fellow miner Sheteen with a tomahawk and stabbing another miner, Ah Key, with a knife. These weapons are presented as illustrative drawings on page 15 of *The Case*. Jong also sustained "twelve or thirteen wounds," which were believed to be self-inflicted (Shen, Dragon 20–21). Jong was judged insane at trial, and eventually transferred to Yarra Bend Lunatic Asylum. (He was later transferred to Sunbury Asylum, where he died in 1900 without having been released, Moore and Tully 62–63.) The testament, or diary, that the otherwise unknown Jong wrote after being sentenced to life in an asylum, is an assemblage, an intact "desiring machine" in Deleuze and Guattari's terms (81). An insane asylum is an enforced refuge; it is a home, in the thinnest sense, but it isn't settled, isn't home. In an essay on the history of Australia's asylums, Stephen Garton records a view of the 1860s that "most were little better than prisons" (65). Yarra Bend was itself an unsettled place to live, according to Richard Bonwick, who, in "The History of Yarra Bend Lunatic Asylum, Melbourne," records the recurring problems of overcrowding (in 1870 it was the eighth largest asylum in the world, housing 1,043 patients); feuds between medical administrators; and the ongoing debate regarding the closure of Yarra Bend and the building of a replacement in Kew (46, 41–43, 47, 36). He writes, "One can only speculate on the debilitating effect on the Yarra Bend Asylum of being under constant scrutiny [by Boards of Enquiry] and seeming imminent closure" (44), noting "the lack of surviving original documentation...prevented a clear picture of the day to day running of the asylum...The thoughts of the so-called lunatics also remains largely a mystery" (5). *The Case* offers us an insight into the thoughts of one of those patients.

The mode of writing in *The Case* invents a way for Jong to write in English. Invention is a key trope in a new nation, yet Australian settlement aspired in many ways to continue the old. As a nationalist key entered Australian culture, the new became primarily that of new stories, images, and diction, rather than new genres or forms. In other words, to adapt Wallace Stevens on understanding poetry, new forms (and non-Anglo-Celtic cultures) were resisted almost successfully (350). Yet in texts such as Jong's, new forms were produced, though they await recognition. While Jong was writing outside a literary paradigm, let alone a modernist one, there is a sense, reading his text, of discovering, retrospectively, newness and inventiveness. In an essay on Pound, referring to his modernist formula "make it new," Bernstein states his own preference for "invention" over "innovation," and adding that the "inventive" was not a "progressivist or developmental" poetry, but "one...based on dissatisfaction with the previous inventions" (Task 45). Bernstein's confidence in the "it" corresponds with Pound's: they know what "it" is that is dissatisfying. Perloff's confidence, however, seems to be directed elsewhere: in her 2010 book on conceptual poetics, *Unoriginal Genius*, she commends appropriation as poetry "by other means," thereby suggesting an end to invention, changing our understanding of the "it" by abandoning the "new" (Unoriginal 11). This can affect how—or what—we choose to criticize, research, and frame poetic investigations. Without necessarily reframing *The Case* as poetry, we can recognize its poetic features, and its potential for informing intentional poetic works of the future.

Historian John Fitzgerald, in his preface to *Big White Lie: Chinese Australians in White Australia*, claims that "Chinese voices are not difficult to find in Australian history...I have often come across documents dating from the late 19th and early 20th centuries written about Australia, some in English, many more in Chinese" (x). Nevertheless, the publishing and anthologizing of nineteenth-century Chinese Australian writing in English is rare. The *Macquarie PEN* includes just one example: that of Taam Sze Pui, also a gold-miner. Like Jong's, Sze Pui's text is also autobiographical; unlike Jong's, it is written in clear and simple English. Although thousands of Chinese have lived in Australia in the period since the 1840s (Fitzgerald 13), there is little evidence of creative writing from this earlier period. Fitzgerald mentions a novella from 1909–1910 (63), but anthologies such as *The Penguin Anthology of Australian Poetry* and the *Macquarie PEN Anthology of Australian Literature* include no Chinese Australian poets earlier than the contemporary poet Ouyang Yu (345, 1281). According to Deborah L. Madsen, there is no mention of "Chinese-Australian literary production" until Elizabeth Webby's *Cambridge Companion to Australian Literature* (2000) consisting of "a brief paragraph devoted to [contemporary novelist] Brian Castro." Madsen points to the White Australia Policy and "anti-Asian prejudice" as accounting for "the erasure of writers of Chinese descent from the national literary canon" (158). Madsen's concern, too, is with contemporary (or "modern Anglophone" 160) writers, that is, largely with a diaspora later than that of the nineteenth-century gold rush.

The Case unsettles Australian literary history through its "ethnic [and] racial difference" and as an example of "a minority language and culture," representing a challenge to "an obsessive monoculturalism and monolingualism" (Mead 401). This is, however, merely to begin framing the complex and highly original work created by Jong. *The Case* tells the story of the knife incident and of Jong's life in the asylum, but it is not the kind of straightforward, poignant story of hardship favored by publishers or anthologists. Jong was to, some extent, the typical asylum patient, as defined by Garton: a single male rural laborer between 25 and 55, arrested after a violent incident. Garton doesn't mention Chinese inmates specifically, noting, rather, that they were "often of Irish descent" (67). Moore and Tully record a Chinese incarceration rate in Yarra Bend Asylum of 1.7 percent, adding that "the proportion of Chinese in the population was between 10% and 7%" (53). They write (of Chinese patients) that "it seems likely that, once committed, their release was improbable because of communication problems and cultural differences" (56), observing also that "It is doubtful if the European authorities were capable of understanding or assessing apparent aberrant behaviour in Chinese" (55).

Jong's writing, presumably learned in the asylum, is also aberrant: it is grammatically unorthodox, repetitive, and written in a hybrid language of English words and Cantonese syntax (1). It is visually striking, written all in capitals. Its visuality, or to use Perloff's more active term, "visual prosody" (Dance 110), emphasizes its materiality; the maps of the diggings and diagrams of the asylum that form part of the text further supplement *The Case*'s visual poetics. The basic unit of *The Case* is the phrase, rather than the sentence, making it an atypical example of life writing (at least of the nineteenth century). The phrase structure is made explicit by the use of invented punctuation. Jong uses what might be described as a triple-line hyphen to join words together as part of a phrase. He also ends lines with a mark resembling a giant comma, or right parenthesis. *The Case* has never been anthologized as such, but Yuanfang Shen devotes her first chapter to it in *Dragon Seed in the Antipodes*, a book on Chinese Australian autobiography. In 2000 *The Case* was published as *A Difficult Case*, in a "readable English" transliteration by Moore and Tully. Shen, and Moore and Tully, in demonstrating their concern with *The Case*'s biographical and historical significance, largely treat its poetics as a barrier to truths and usefulness, rather than as a contribution to a remarkable assemblage of a new kind of English, and of a new kind of poetic text.

Jong's *The Case* is similar to Kelly's *Letter*, in that they were both written to effect their respective authors' freedoms. Both texts failed in this aim. To adapt Mead, it is an example of "the *un*settling difference of... the plural knowledges of the multicultural" past (Mead refers to the "present"; his italics 400–401). As Shen writes, "Australian historians have not often attended to the scant but important testimonies left us in fractured or unorthodox writings like Jong's diary" (19–20). Similarly, Australian historian Jan Ryan complains that "the Chinese are not there in our grand national histories and the token fragments that are included retain familiar stereotypes of Chinese as a homogenous 'race,' a detached entity, with a separate and alien identity. By such inclusion they are excluded" (71). There has not been much attention paid in the literary context either. No Chinese nineteenth-century writers are referred to in the recent *Cambridge History of Australian Literature*, though there is a reference to Chinese nineteenth-century autobiography in the context of Shen's work (325): as well as indexed references to "Asiaphobia" and "Chinese, Australian antipathy."

An argument for the literary significance of Jong's *The Case* therefore unsettles the white plus Indigenous paradigm of the history of Australian literature. Its significance for my purposes is that of its poetics: not of its testimony, nor for what "this extraordinary discipline of pain [might] tell us about the early Chinese digger's life in colonial Australia" (Shen, Dragon 20). Rather, I am interested in how Jong's inventive practice unsettles notions of Australian writing in the nineteenth century: his inventive use of punctuation and compositional structure in particular, as well as the visual nature of Jong's text, the synthesis of Chinese and English effected in the language, the repetitive, indirect style of narration, and finally, its construction as a small handmade book. Shen writes that *The Case* "consists of sixty-three pages of verbal document and five maps carefully and accurately (if crudely) drawn" (19). The inclusion of the maps, as well as Jong's use of English, supports Shen's argument that Jong thought of himself as a "settler" (Sojourners n. pag.). Jong was born in Zhingshan, near Canton, in "about 1837," and came to Australia in "about 1855," aged 18 approximately, as part of the Chinese migration to Australia during the Victorian gold rush (Moore and Tully 4, 62). This Chinese migration constitutes what has been called "the diaspora par excellence" (Reid xv); also qualified as a "trade diaspora" (Faist 12). One critic of diaspora, Victor Ramraj, distinguishes "immigrant writing" from diasporic writing, asserting that the latter "diverges... in its preoccupation with the attachment to the homeland," whereas "immigrant writing... focuses more on the current experiences in the adopted home."

He further categorizes "exile writing" as that which is concerned with the circumstances of exile, rather than the "*émigré*'s or *émigré*'s community's relationship with the dominant society" (228). In his survey of examples, Ramraj's reading of these differences is almost completely dominated by a concern with narrative and thematic content. Though he mentions an example of a text written in "both Standard English and Guyanese Creole," this aspect is not examined any further (223). Jong's text problematizes these categories. His concern is with his current situation, yet writes his attachment to his culture and identity (if not his homeland), through syntax and through visual and narrative style, rather than narrative content. The first phrase of *The Case* is "CHINAMAN≡NAME": a bold short poem in itself.

Perhaps it is more useful in Jong's "case" to make a distinction between the diasporic text, and the displaced or displacing text, since *The Case* displaces English, Chinese, and conventional punctuation. Diaspora is a potentially powerful term in the context of unsettlement: it is retrospectively available as a reading for the arrival of all settlers in Australia. Although its use may appear to neutralize colonial intentions, it also undermines the purposeful narratives of individuals like Captain Cook, of Empire, and of "discovery." It undoes the claimed right to the land, as well as, perhaps fruitfully, class and race divisions between different kinds of settlers. I am not suggesting that it become a primary model, but it is one that could provide new ways of thinking settlement and unsettlement. The notion of diaspora in relation to Australia must also, of course, take Indigenous diaspora into account. The notion that Aboriginal people were displaced within Australia is a convenient lie that erases the fact that many Aboriginals were dispersed from their different countries, to the countries of others; conversely, they were confined to parts of their country (Cooke 31). I note, too, that "dispersing" was a conventional euphemism for Indigenous genocide (Godwin 113).

Shen writes that *The Case* "is a typical example of hybrid writing. Jong did not translate Chinese into English, but transposed Chinese concepts into English words, and forced English words into Chinese syntactical structures." A simple example given by Shen is "day day night night," the Chinese being "riri yeye," meaning "day and night": Jong has transposed the Chinese disyllabic repetition and rhythm into English monosyllables. Another example given by Shen is "my body my Chinaman" ("wo shenwei zhongguoren"), which is translated as "being Chinese" (22). Shen describes Jong's narrative style, with its "long, winding introduction," as "more Chinese than English," and adds it "suggests that Jong received a reasonably good education in China" (23). Of this indicative Chinese style of "indirection" or "detour" Francois Jullien asks, "Does not detour—which is anything but gratuitous—exert a certain power, which is all the more forceful for its discretion?" (7).

According to Carrie Noland, in her introduction to *Diasporic Avant-Gardes*, "It may be...that a detour through the expressive practices of another people is the norm rather than the exception...the forms most closely associated with a diasporic population are sometimes the result of fruitful combinations of many influences" (8). Noland's formulation suggests a diasporic agency for texts like Jong's, despite the enclosed situation of the writer. Jong's text can be described as structurally indirect, if we assume that the point of the text is narration, yet the tone of *The Case* is emphatic, "forceful." Its poetic force is one of cumulation, a characteristic effect of parataxis. The introduction of Jong's text does not seem to me to be "long, winding." Shen appears to be referring to narrative style, rather than writing style. The writing style of the introduction is not distinct from the remainder of the text. It consists of, for example, short, direct, phrasal expressions, such as "UP≡COUNTRY," "WEEKS≡WEEKS," and "MY≡MOUTH≡STOP." The paratactic progression and the capitalization combine to produce an emphatic, if disjunctive, even sculptural, and relentless style. Jong so rarely isolates single words it may be he does so in error: even in headings he has "BOOK≡TOP," and as page numbers, "NO≡74." We might then, conceivably, read each phrase as a qualification of the first term. Shen asserts that Jong's "presentation of the text" is "highly conventional by both English and Chinese standards." Yet she is referring to the structural presentation of text in a book, and not the presentation of the text on the page. Shen writes that the title page "functions as an abstract of the 'book,'" but does not remark on the unconventional nature of the handmade book itself. By referring to it as a "book" in quotes, she rather deprecates it, though she adds that "Jong's diary is probably the most complete manuscript produced by a Chinese in Australia" (23). Yet it is the handmade nature of this book that points immediately to its unconventionality. If we hypothesize a manuscript in pages, subsequently typeset, such a document would not possess the striking visual poetics of *The Case*: instead it might look like Shen's representation of the text. Shen goes on to quote the fight scene from *The Case*, providing an English transliteration on facing page 25 (23–26). Here are some samples from that extract:

> My stop my yard my see name Sheteen 2 mates been him yard
> Sitdown a the my gate catch my black fowl kill,
> My fowl my last months of February 1867 been Mesded new house
> Buy 4 chicken 4 shilling half pound quarter pound 1 chicken,
> My that 4 chicken my week week my buy 1 shilling clean wheat
> Feeding big 4 chicken 3 pound 2 pound 1 fowl sometimes,
> My last night my tell Sheteen kill my fowl tell my no kill
> My no freedom Sheteen what for kill my fowl,

Sheteen kill fowl that knife my last day my take go bush sleep bush
Him go see my him we my take knife go home putdown him tent,
My no speak Sheteen my go in my tent putdown bason rice
Go out from Sheteen charge for what kill my fowl,
...
Step my head step my too much
My jumping up my gate high jump kick Sheteen arm knife
Sheteen let go knife fall down ground,
My that gate that high jump 2 feet high my last
My care nannie goat eat my vegetable make that high jump,
My been high jump top jump down ground stoop ground
Catch knife,
Ah Key see my stoop ground catch knife Ah Key catch hatchet
Chop my head two time,
...
Talking Nugget calling Ah Than assistance him,
My cursing Sheteen you call nugget you catch tools no stop
...
My body stream blood stream supple 2 tied no line

With the assistance of Shen's explanation, it seems that, according to Jong, things happened quite differently to the court's interpretation: that Sheteen started the conflict by killing Jong's black hen, and that Ah Than and Sheteen both struck Jong first. The goat reference is interesting. Shen interprets the lines referring to the goat like this: "I jumped up the gate with a high jump and kicked Sheteen's knife arm. / He let the knife fall to the ground. / I had jumped 2 feet up that gate like the nanny goat that had eaten my / vegetables." In Jong's version, the reference to the goat is a paratactic digression. In Ong's terms, the mode is "additive," but there are no "and"s: statements merely accrue. To explain the goat reference, Shen makes it into a simile, introducing a metaphoric element that is not quite there in the original. It seems to be more a citation of memory than a comparison or identification as such. Jong is writing a document some time after the original events happened; as Tully states, it is not a diary, which records events on a daily basis (ix).

Jong's occupation of gold-mining manifests in the word "nugget": apparently an insult. Possibly this was the only English word used in the original verbal conflict. In a curious instance of networked language, Jong refers to his English use as "my little language," a phrase used by Jonathan Swift, and cited by Susan Howe (Quartermain, Disjunctive 228). Jong complains further that the court interpreter did not represent him properly, perhaps due to their personal relations or because the interpreter didn't speak Jong's dialect: a common problem in cases involving Chinese (Shen, Dragon 27).

I discovered Jong's text through reading Shen's chapter. It seemed strange that Shen wrote nothing about *The Case* being poetry, despite the apparent verse form and the text's rhythm and repetition. Even her own interpretative, facing text, is set in verse form. Shen's text uses normative syntax; it is in sentences. Jong's text—as represented by Shen—is punctuated by commas; Shen's own version is punctuated by full stops. What appears in Shen's article to be a transparency of process, with her own text assisting readability, is shown rather to be an extreme mediation of Jong's original. While Shen acknowledges Jong's synthesis of Chinese-English syntax, there is much else that is unique about Jong's text: its visual aspect, its structure, and its punctuation are all erased by Shen. Though I can't reproduce Jong's text typographically, this is a closer approximation than that offered by Shen:

MY≡STOP≡MY≡YARD MY≡SEE≡NAME≡SHETEEN 2≡MATES≡BEEN≡HIM≡YARD
SITDOWN≡A≡THE≡MY≡GATE CATCH≡MY≡BLACK≡FOWL≡KILL)
MY≡FOWL MY≡LAST MONTHS≡OF≡FEBRUARY≡1867 BEEN≡MESDED≡NEW≡HOUSE
BUY≡4≡CHICKEN 4≡SHILLING HALF≡POUND QUARTER≡POUND 1≡CHICKEN)
MY≡THAT≡4≡CHICKEN MY≡WEEK≡WEEK MY≡BUY≡1≡SHILLING CLEAN≡WHEAT
FEEDING≡BIG≡4≡CHICKEN 3≡POUND 2≡POUND 1≡FOWL SOMETIMES)
MY≡LAST≡NIGHT MY≡TELL≡SHETEEN≡KILL≡MY≡FOWL HIM≡TELL≡MY≡ NO≡KILL
MY≡NO≡FREEDOM≡SHETEEN WHAT≡FOR≡KILL≡MY≡FOWL). (25)

What is lost in the transfer to type is the striking appearance of a page of capitals, all with the heavy serifs added, that have the estranging effect of an English calligraphy. The serifs indicate that Jong learnt English from a typed text. The marks that join word in phrase clusters "≡" are an approximation of what looks like a triple hyphen (on page one, and occasionally thereafter, Jong uses a four bar sign or quadruple hyphen); the large right parenthesis is thicker and resembles a fingernail paring in the original (more so in the enlarged reader's copy offered by the State Library), and perhaps is more accurately thought of as a giant comma than a parenthesis (there are no left parentheses). Shen has not completely disregarded Jong's poetics, however. In her representation, she respects Jong's lines, and has retained the giant comma's placing, albeit reducing the mark to a conventional comma. Jong has invented two punctuation marks and composed completely in capitals to create this unique work. His handwriting is modeled on a serif font, also remarkable (but not unique: as we will see in later chapters). The appearance and material significance (serif lettering, new punctuation structures) of *The Case* make it a proto-concrete work, or assemblage. As an invention *The Case* was useless, excessive, unable to contribute to the structure of Australian settlement literature. As a secret, yet publicly archived, Chinese text it was automatically—preemptively—anti-Australian; as a hybrid Chinese–English it bordered on offensive. It influenced no one. Only belatedly can it be seen as a "startling...Chinese perspective" (Shen, Dragon 32).

In *Uses of Literature*, Rita Felski argues that "linguistic experiments can accentuate rather than block involvement, using the musicality and expressiveness of sound to trigger inchoate yet intense associations or a sharpened auditory and sensory awareness" (73–74). Felski sets up an opposition between sense and sound that is not apt for *The Case*; she seems not to have considered the enchanting possibilities of the visual. Her reference to "linguistic experiments" suggests experiments in expression, and *The Case* is experimentally expressive in its merging of English and Cantonese; yet it is the invention of new punctuation marks and its visual style that are for me its most compelling aspect. The "music" of *The Case* bears further consideration, however. Its peculiar structure suggests new possibilities of cadence; and given the "expressiveness" of punctuation in twentieth-century poets like William Carlos Williams, and, in particular, e.e. cummings, we can retrospectively read an abstracted expressiveness in Jong's punctuation. How do we measure the prosody of unfamiliar marks? That is perhaps a new question.

The Case points to the possibility of Chinese English in grammatical terms: a possibility that besides Shen's reference to "hybrid writing" does not seem to have been considered by Australian critics. As Madsen's contemporary term of "modern Anglophone" suggests, the writers she cites are Chinese Australians writing in English, not in Chinese English; she refers to "cultural hybridity" and "a hybrid cultural production of Chinese-Australianness," but not to the possibility of a hybrid language (166–167). The construction of Jong's narrative is a remembering, or to use Kathleen Stewart's term, an "unforgetting." Stewart proposes

> that this kind of re-remembered attention...Far from reducing remembered events to illustrated ideas...use[s] them to interrupt the very progress of master narrative codes and to displace the certainty of concept with a densely textured interpretative space that follows a logic of digression and accidental adjacency. (80)

Stewart resists the reduction that might result from reading for an "illuminating" narrative. Retrospectively finding a place for the Chinese in the writing of the Australian nation is ultimately a settlement action; what Stewart (in a North American Appalachian context) rather suggests is the taking of such narratives "seriously as graphic theoretical models in themselves" (80). Taking Jong's narrative seriously involves an appreciation of his poetics: the literal "graphic" nature of *The Case*, its phrasal structure, punctuation, and its Chinese-Englishness. The hybridity of *The Case* is complex. As Ong notes, "Chinese character writing itself is hybrid (mixed pictographs, ideographs, rebuses, and various combinations, often of extreme complexity, cultural richness and poetic beauty)," adding that "even alphabetic writing is hybrid when it writes *1* instead of *one*" (87). (Jong uses Arabic numerals as words throughout *The Case*.)

In order to highlight the extent to which Jong has created an impressive and integrated Chinese–English assemblage, I will briefly compare *The Case* with its most obvious successor: that of Pound's *Cantos*, featuring his "inventive" use of the Chinese ideogram (Typhanopoulos and Adams 59). Pound's "protohypertextual" (Perloff, Dance 128) example is seen as a major event in Western literature; its influence is still being discussed; and it is the primary case of the dispersal (and consequent transformation) of Chinese language within English poetry. *The Cantos* can also be described as a diasporic text, as it enacts and mimes diaspora in its parataxis and proliferation of languages.

After discovering Ernest Fenollosa's work on the Chinese character, Pound went on to exploit select characters for their graphic and semantic possibilities within the frame of his long poem in English (Nicholls 694). This is not what Jong is doing with English exactly; yet, in his hand, English has a new graphicity. Pound's practice exemplified his credo of "making it new," where "it" is the form of the canto, as well as the-poem-in-English, and the Chinese character recontextualized: or, in Deleuze and Guattari's term, "reterritorialized"; Jong reterritorializes the Chinese aesthetic approach of the calligraphic, as well as producing, in *The Case*, a Chinese space for (his) English, or "little language."

Pound's translations have been heavily criticized by Sinologists, though, as Guiyou Huang notes, they have also been affirmed by Chinese critics (Tryphonopoulos and Adams 61). Reviewing the recent critical edition of the jointly credited (to Fenollosa, whose original idea it was, and to Pound) *The Chinese Character as a Medium For Poetry*, Peter Nicholls notes Eric Hayot's objection, that the ideograms in the *Cantos* "all mean the same thing, namely that an English idea finds its authoritative and absolute representation in Chinese" (695). Again, this is not quite what Jong achieved in reverse, but in a sense it is what he is trying to do: to express an "authoritative and absolute representation" of Chinese ideas in English. But whereas Pound is inventing a visual idea in his use of ideograms in *The Cantos* (the idea is "visualizing history," according to Nadel 163), Jong is transferring—and transforming or reterritorializing—a preexisting visual idea or practice in his representation of English in *The Case*. On page 74 is Jong's one inclusion of a line of Chinese characters in the English text: the line apparently begins with his name and hometown, but Tully writes that "a confident interpretation [of the complete line] has not been obtained" (122). Uncannily enough then, Jong's native language functions as indecipherable code. Codedness also occurs in the *Cantos*: Pound, who not only presented ideograms to an English audience, due to error presented one upside down (Nadel 155). Jong is not attempting to present anything of Chinese history, but rather is insisting on personal history, which comes inflected with attributes of Chinese language. *The Case* is concerned with experience; *The Cantos* with knowledge.

Pound invented a new bricolaging model of the long poem, assembling different national languages as well as the languages of nonliterary discourse, such as that of economics. Jong's invention constructs what Jonathan Monroe calls (in reference to the prose poem) a "genreless genre" (280). *The Case* is not a prose poem; it is not composed in sentences. Yet it is not verse either. It has an explicit assemblage aspect also, the maps, emphasizing Jong's desire to present his "case" in visual terms. Considering Jong's maps, as well as drawn objects (such as the hatchet), *The Case* appears to have a more direct relation to concrete and other forms of visual poetry than do Pound's influential *Cantos* (or, for that matter, Mallarmé's "Un Coup de Dés"). Yet Ira B. Nadel argues for "the importance of 'visual history'" to the *Cantos* (151), and reports that *Cantos LII–LXXI* were to have included a map of China (drawn by Pound's wife, Dorothy) as endpapers, but that both Pound's publishers (Faber and New Directions), citing paper restrictions and incomprehension respectively, declined to publish it (159). Jong's maps of the diggings and the Cochran and Donnolly (Dunolly) townships on pages 52 and 53 are dominated by words (there are also maps of the Chinese camp, the diggings, and a plan of the Dunolly hospital, 3, 15, 71). The maps include little by way of representative drawing as such: just graphic lines and words (the hospital map, though, includes a drawing of a fence, possibly of palings; the camp map includes a drawing of what looks like a cut-down burnt tree, but it is difficult to determine the dimensions). Nadel's summary of Pound's visual practice in the *Cantos* is also apposite to Jong: "By using visual signs Pound is able to bring another dimension to the poem, one that compliments language and event by the visualization of experience" (165).

Spacing, word size, and orientation add dimensionality. Ian Davidson writes in *Ideas of Space in Contemporary Poetry* that:

> Ideas of space...have changed, and that change, is reflected in the poetry. Rather than space being envisaged as a pre-existing surface or container within which the material of the poem is arranged, the space of the poem is now produced by the writer and reader in the act or performance of writing and reading. Perspective is no longer fixed, as it was for much earlier graphically based concrete poetry, but shifts according to viewpoint. (144)

Davidson concludes with a comparison to the three-dimensionality of architecture. Writing about maps as an analogy for poetry, Davidson assumes the use of "symbolism," noting also that "the subject position can be various" (61). Jong eschews symbolism in his maps. There are, however, pronounced shifts in perspective, both from reading words that orient in different directions and in, for example, the shift between words and the depiction of the hospital fence (which in itself is not from one perspective).

Jong's word assemblages can be read as contemporary textual reproductions of sites, and in the case of the town and diggings maps, products of memory. Jong's maps emphasize the drawing (or tracing) of his experience in *The Case*'s narrative. The subject(s) is (are) always changing position. It tells of one act after another:

AH≡THAN≡BEEN≡AH≡HIM≡TENT CATCH≡1≡STICK 2≡FEET≡LONG≡SOMETIMES GO≡UP≡MY≡TENT GO≡IN≡MY≡GATE≡INSIDE)
AH≡THAN≡SPEAK≡AH≡HIM TALKING≡LAST—DAY GO≡TELL≡MEN≡CATCH≡HIM VERY≡GOOD)
MY≡BEEN≡MY≡TENT BEEN≡BEDSTEAD≡BUNDLE≡GOLE BUNDLE≡AFTER BEEN≡WRITING≡GOLD≡MARK HEAR≡LOOK≡MEN GO≡IN≡MY≡GATE)
MY≡VERY≡QUICK≡CATCH≡BAG≡BIG≡GOLD SMALL≡BAG≡GOLD ALTOGETHER≡GOLD PUTDOWN≡TROWSERS≡TOCKET)
MY≡VERY≡QUICK≡GET≡UP GO≡TABLE CATCH≡1≡BASON≡RICE... (24)

As the words in the narrative, the letters in the maps are capitalized and serifed. But the maps are not designed to read like a conventional English text, in that words are not placed in a left to right order. For example, the words "COCHRAN≡TOWNSHIP" and "DONNOLLY≡TOWNSHIP," written in larger script at roughly 45- to 50-degree angles, represent the main streets of their respective towns; they bisect a list of names of shops, in smaller script, such as "**PUBLIC☰HOUSE**," "**CLOTHING☰STORE**," for example, which run along, and are perpendicular to, the name of the town (52). In terms of page orientation (based on the page number at the top, as written by Jong), the lists on the left are upside down, branching off the town's name; another list branches to the right, conventionally right side up. Jong's maps emphasize the settling of the area with English words. There are no symbols representing settler culture, such as crosses for churches, for example, and a road is represented by the word "road." A hill is represented by the word "hill," circled. Jong's word-rich maps suggest a strong relation between them and the narrative text. Rather than illustrating and supporting the narrative, they become part of it and encourage a reading that moves around the sites that Jong lived in and refers to. Davidson notes Deleuze and Guattari's idea that "the map contains within itself potential 'lines of flight'; it contains ways of escape and ways of living within the condition described by the tracing. Yet," as Davidson adds, "the map will always contain the tracing, which is in some ways a precondition" (65). The weakness here is in the very analogy, as Davidson intimates. For Deleuze and Guattari, maps are "performances" that can "free...up 'blockages' and permit...flows": in other words, "journey," in its verb sense. Yet for Jong, mapping refers to terrains that he has been excluded from.

In *The Production of Space*, Henri Lefebvre suggests that Chinese characters have a relationship to space that "Western conceptual tools" lack (32). Many of the texts in this study refer to everyday and imaginative spaces, in particular Brennan's post-Mallarméan work, and the drawings of Charlie Flannigan (discussed in chapters 6 and 8). As Brennan and Flannigan do, in their distinct ways, Jong not only represent the spaces in his text, but also attempt to spatialize the words themselves. Jong gives them a dimension tending to that of Chinese characters, or in Lefebvre's terms, undoes the "contrast" (42) between "representations of space ('conceptualized space')" and "representational spaces ('space as directly *lived*')" (38–39). Jong's map of the town tends to the generic: using, for example, the word "**STORE**" rather than the name of the store. If he has learned to write English in the asylum, this might indicate that the English names were relatively abstract for him at the time. Further, his use of punctuation constructs and delimits space more directly than words. Jong's invented punctuation, then, suggests the need for Jong to invent a conceptual, textual space within his lived space, and possibly, according to the psychiatric assessment included in Moore and Tully, in order to control a hallucinated space (141).

The language of Jong's narrative is strikingly consistent in its tone, structure, and diction. *The Case* is a model for a language as well as a work. Yet its language has never been used in other texts; even if *The Case* had been made public, what could be more useless than a hybrid language based on Cantonese, as Australia approached Federation (the joining of the states as one nation in 1901), and the initiation of the White Australia Policy? What could be more abstract? Even now, its language and poetics are apparently considered useless by Jong's editors, as if a barrier to the story of his life, and to those of other Chinese "settlers." It is in fact, as much the oral features of the work, for example, the amount of semantic redundancy, that obscure the story, not just the graphic style. Jong's language is a new language—an event yet to be felt in Australian letters—and, as Pound observed, "a new language is always said to be obscure" (Quartermain, Disjunctive 57). In *Disjunctive Poetics* Peter Quartermain points out the common limitation imposed by readers "supposing that a poem addresses itself to one frame of reference only" and that "any ambiguity...serves to intensify and render more complicated a 'central theme'" (87). The multiple frames suggested by Quartermain need not be semantic only: and in Jong they can be read as addressed to the frame of visual poetics, and to those of an inventive grammar, syntax, and language distinct from "settled usage."

With both Pound and Jong, there is more to their uses of the Chinese character and the Roman alphabet than semantic meaning. In *Toward the Open Field*, Melissa Kwasny writes of "Pound's conception of the poem as an ideogrammatic field" (247); and it seems clear that Pound uses ideograms in terms of their graphics in distinctly different ways. "Canto LXXVII," a "Pisan" canto containing 19 ideograms, has an Explication (62–63). It lists the ideograms in the order that they appear in the canto with an explication in English. Some of these are also explicit in the text, such as the first, the meaning given of which is "middle." The word "middle" also occurs next to the character; it is also in the middle of the page. As an ideogram bisected in the middle, it can be read as illustrative (49). But not merely illustrative: as Jerome McGann notes, Pound "use[s] decorative materials that distinctly (and deliberately) recall the tradition of ornamental books passed on...by William Morris and the late nineteenth century in general...Because Pound is 'quoting' those traditions...the illustrative materials function at an abstract and cognitive level as much as they do at an imagistic level" (Textual 107). In relation to the ideograms in particular, then, Pound can be read as appropriating Chinese for a Western tradition of ornament, as well as quoting from the Chinese as instances of language (tradition), as much as he is quoting a particular word for its semantic function. According to McGann, for Pound ideograms are not images but "the *idea of an image*...and function *phenomenologically*" (107; McGann's italics). McGann argues that Pound rejects the model of semantic transparency: "the Chinese characters are an index of the kind of attention all scripted forms demand." The use (meaning) of the ideograms is not that of the ideograms alone nor that of contributing to a greater meaning of the *Cantos*, but, as McGann notes, to "reeducate Western readers in the use of their own languages" (146).

Here what we might call visual meaning can lead to incorrect conclusions regarding semantics, as Hugh Kenner notes of the "middle" character in particular, which, rather than being an "ideograph proper" (227), is a phonetic compound (229). The two that follow in the canto are, however, more graphically complex, and explicated by relatively more abstract concepts: "precede" and "follow" (Pisan 62); appearing on the page as "what precedes [character] and what follows [character]" (50). These ideograms are not illustrative, contradicting even the presentational logic of the "middle" ideogram, due to the complicating English semantics. That is, they both follow an English phrase, but only the second refers to the meaning of "follow": the first refers to the concept of "precede." To the reader not literate in Chinese, the two ideograms both have what might be called a blank prosodic effect, as well as a blank semantic effect. A reader coming to Jong for the first time may also experience blankness in these terms: it is the visual poetics of *The Case* that are most prominent, and the significant visual aspect of the *Cantos* can be missed in the rush to read (or resist) its semantics and phonetic prosody.

Jong's practice is of course completely distinct from Pound's. Yet there is a further way of reading *The Case* in terms of discussions of contemporary poetics. Jong is writing in a second language, what Perloff has termed "exophonic" writing. She defines this practice in the context of twenty-first century poetics, likening it to the constraints of the avant-garde group Oulipo, and referring to such writing as a form of "translational poetics," distinguishing it from the "multilingualism" of Pound's *Cantos*, as well as from more recent examples (Unoriginal 14, 16). In Perloff's scenario, writing in a second language is seen as appropriating a language, rather than invention: "Inventio is giving way to appropriation, elaborate constraint, visual and sound composition, and reliance on intertextuality. Thus we are witnessing a new poetry, more conceptual than expressive..." (11). Perloff's theory brings "exophonic" writing into the contemporary context, and makes it possible to read works like *The Case* as conceptual as much as historical.

Settlement requires the speaking of English as if no other language was necessary. Appropriating English suggests a contrary, unsettling agenda: and one that links Jong to Indigenous writers. Certeau universalizes this notion when he refers to all speaking as performing "appropriation, or reappropriation," making a linguistic distinction between "performance" and "competence" (xiii). Certeau's reading gives a different slant to the operation of oral poetics and to performativity itself, as if all speaking is a momentary construction rather than a prerehearsed practice.

The visual aspect of *The Case*, its verbal style, and the remoteness of Jong's situation all contribute to an emphasis on the aesthetics and the conceptual nature of the work over the narrative. What is most apparent is the wordness of Jong's text: the word as word, rather than semantic vehicle. This is an effect not only of the form of the word but the word combinations, assembled in chains or strings that are not those of English syntactic units. This is also unsettling in terms of sound, suggesting a rhythm based on words rather than feet or accent, and distinct from the line-based prosody of free verse.

In order to get Jong's story across, Shen, and Moore and Tully, dispense with Jong's painstaking achievement in order to remake it as "readable" (Moore and Tully 1). I don't mean to negate the work of these critics: their work has made my own reading possible, and despite my emphasis otherwise, I don't mean to dispense with the semantic meaning of Jong's diary. The interpretations of *The Case* in Shen's essay, and in Moore and Tully's historical study, have been invaluable, as has the historical context that Moore and Tully's work in particular provides. There is much more that could be written about *The Case* as a literary work, and again, the criticism of Shen, Moore, and Tully means that some of the groundwork has been done. There is also, of course, the new "translation" by Moore and Tully to consider, and the relation between it and Jong's text: one quite different to that between a translation from one distinct language to another.

Reading Jong's text, I can't avoid reading the triple hyphen as somehow equivalent to the equals sign ("≡") associated with Language poetry. The equals sign suggests the democratic equivalency of all language. As editors Bernstein and Bruce Andrews write in their introduction to *The L=A=N=G=U=A=G=E Book*, language writing is "writing...that takes for granted neither vocabulary, grammar, process, shape, syntax, program or subject matter" (ix). It emphasizes the material word in order to critique the consumption of language as if it were a commodity (xi). Whether or not Jong thought of "≡" as a sign of equivalence, he uses it as an explicit connector that structures the work both semantically and rhythmically. The phrase "MY≡BODY" could be a concrete or conceptual work in itself, pithily summing up the relation of and identification with the self and the body. The longer chain "MY≡STOP≡TREE≡GROUND≡HERE" suggests an attention to and identification with place; it is expressed in the syntax as much as in the unqualified semantics, and resembles Indigenous philosophy rather than settlement sentiment: of experience and guardianship rather than ownership (Benterrak et al 147).

Retrospectively then, *The Case* could appear to present a kind of ecologically inflected Language text. Further, it can be read as networked to a range of nonverse options in contemporary poetry, in particular that of concrete poetry, as well as other forms of visual poetry. These are not marginal, nor minor, practices of poetry, but interact with and constitute the contemporary as much as verse (or poetry in lines) does. In order to assess *The Case*, we need to consider it in terms of a holistic, material practice of writing, one that gives weight to each mark (the triple hyphen, for example) and not just the semantic word. Ong asserts that writing began "not when simple semiotic marking was devised but when a coded system of visible marks was invented whereby a writer could determine the exact words that the reader would generate from the text" (83). This definition follows Ong's claim that "It is impossible for script to be more than marks on a surface unless it is used by a conscious human being as a cue to sounded words, real or imagined, directly or indirectly" (74–75). Words or characters from a language other than that of a writer's intended audience will tend to be abstract. In the case of *The Cantos*, Pound "determined the exact words...generate[d]" through his explication; the characters cannot be sounded by a reader that doesn't know Chinese, and given the explication, the characters are then semantically redundant. Yet they are more than "marks on a surface." A blank, or rather silent, effect is not equivalent to no effect. Ong himself mentions the paragraph mark: though it is "not a unit of discourse" nor suggests a sound, it is meaningful, it is not just a mark (122). Later in his argument Ong concedes that "punctuation marks...though part of a text...are unpronounceable, nonphonemic" (147), and as their qualifying terms of "paragraph" and "punctuation" affirm, they are not "just marks." Reading without semantic meaning still takes time, and all marks take up space. The ideogrammatic examples incorporated in the *Pisan Cantos* text (61, 69) have a visual prosody that those that merely seem to accompany the text as a form of illustration, lack (74, 75). In the act of reading punctuation there is no determined sound referent; yet, as Jurij Tynjanov argues, there is "metrical energy" in that absence (Steiner 189–190). An "oral rendition" is arguably possible in performance (Brody 8). Tynjanov refers to marks as representing silence, whereas in (and after) Mallarmé, blank space is claimed to represent silence (see preface to "Un Coup de Dés," and the poem itself, 121–145). Concrete poetry critic Craig Saper rejects this notion, however. He writes, in reference to the iconic concrete poem by Eugen Gomringer, "silencio," or "silence" (consisting of the word "silencio" written 14 times in a block, with a blank space in the center) that:

> Instead of repeated words describing a pre-existing blank silence, the poem also demonstrates that our concept of silence as blank space arises only from the surrounding words. Silence is born after writing. This interpretation does require our engagement with the design of the poem, which no longer mimetically illustrates the simple and banal idea that silence equals blank space. (313)

Jong appears to protect his text from white space by running his text to the right margin: or, on every second line, placing a giant comma-like mark, to hold it. The text is relentless: there are no conventional stops any more than there are conventional sentences; they demand an escape into textual space. Yet Jong has his own blank space on page fourteen of *The Case*. It precedes the map of the diggings on page 15, and follows references on page 13 to making and eating dumplings, and not sleeping, and taking opium: "MY≡TAKE≡MY≡OPIUM≡SMOKE." It is tempting to read this blank page as a zoning out. It is not completely blank, though, as it is numbered "NO. 14" in Jong's hand; and the paper is lined, not merely white. Here the sound quality of page numbers becomes a question: page numbers are pronounceable and phonemic, but are they pronounced, sounded by readers? This (relatively) blank page disappears in Moore and Tully's version. After the text on Jong's page 13, they insert the maps from his pages 52 and 53 as one map (of the district), before the map of the diggings on Anderson Hill on Jong's page 15 (74–76). Yet the original page 14 does have a conceivable (nonprosodic) function, as a transition between the text and the map. The more emphatic visuality of the map serves as a reminder that we already know how to read (the visual aspects of) a map, and that we read nontextual aspects with some sense of rhythm, but not of textual narrativity or phonetics: a road, for example. (We may construct a narrative of travelling from or to somewhere represented on a map, but this narrative is extra-textual.)

Both Pound's and Jong's works bear a resemblance to the later advent of concrete poetry, "a distinct genre of visual poetry," as Claus Cluver asserts, noting that it "uses its material functionally and not symbolically" (278). He also cites Gomringer, however, who warns that "it should not develop into a form of poetry set apart from the main tradition" (274). The advent of concrete poetry means we read Pound and Jong (and Mallarmé and Dickinson) differently. The present influences or "revis[es] the past" (Cluver 268). It is easy to construct genealogies of concrete poetry, but such a genealogy is an invention of the present: even an obvious precursor such as Apollinaire is considered by the Brazilian concrete poets "as a point of reference, rather than a strong influence" (Drucker 40–41).

Ong notes that concrete poetry is "the product…of typography." Though he refers to it as a "minor genre" he acknowledges the meaningful link made by Geoffrey Hartman between concrete poetry and deconstruction (Ong 127). There are further strong links between concrete poetry and the poetry canon. Johanna Drucker notes the importance of both Chinese language and the work of Fenollosa and Pound for the visual in Western poetry, though she considers this latter influence "ill-informed" and based on "an impression of Chinese language" (58). Brazilian concrete poet Augusto de Campos claims Pound as a "direct precedent" (376); while Bernstein records that, despite Pound's didacticism, he was interested in "opaque texture." Bernstein notes that Pound's interest in the page follows Mallarmé (Introduction n. pag.), whereas Craig Dworkin asserts that the work of Howe follows Pound (153). In the American tradition, then, Pound initiates a cycle that allows for a new reading of Dickinson by Howe and others, of what Marta Werner calls Dickinson's "textual revelations" (301). Such readings reassemble poetry histories in a fashion less settled than that implied by terms like "canon formation," which suggests solidity, establishment, settlement.

Perloff frames concrete poetry as crucial in fully understanding the contemporary moment in poetry. She refers to Eliot's *The Waste Land* and Pound's *The Cantos* as collagist precursors to contemporary conceptual appropriative writing, and then traces this "poetics of 'unoriginality'" back to "the concretism of the 1950s and '60s," adding that "the concretist program is best understood as a revolt against the transparency of the word" (Unoriginal 12–13). Perloff describes Howe as being "born under the sign of Concrete poetry," implicating Howe's practice in a meshed relation between collage and concrete poetry (12).

The notion of marks on a page evokes those made by a hand, as well as those by a typewriter key or inkjet. Though, in their different ways, Dickinson and, more literally, Jong, are more confined writers than Kelly and Bennelong, both are concerned with the "phenomena of freedom" (Werner 5) as determined in the handwritten text. As Werner writes, "The authority of calligraphy is antinomian: print never can appear in its likeness" (50). According to Ong, manuscript culture is "closer to the give-and-take of oral expression. The readers of manuscripts are less closed off from the author, less absent, than are the readers of those writing for print"; there is "dialogue" (130).

Perloff doesn't mention Dickinson in relation to concrete poetry, but given Howe and Pound's placing we might infer that Dickinson, as read resistantly, antitransparently, has been recuperated via the archive for a place in the Concrete panorama. Resisting "the regularizing effect of type" in her editing of Dickinson, Werner writes that she "stayed by all vagrant spellings, stray marks, and disturbances...in the belief that they will lead me ever deeper into the process of Dickinson's thought-passage" and refers to the "instantaneousness and force" of Dickinson's "'Accidentals'—dashes, flying quotation marks, underlinings, and other flourishes" (50–51). In *The Case* we don't have any drafts, or errant pages; we have the one careful book. Jong writes over Western typography, imposing his own structure and inventing marks that are outside typography. His writing freedom is ironic: he is free to mime the rigidity of type in his lettering, to put his words in chains using bars: "≡."

Inventing punctuation seems like another useless move to make. In the late nineteenth century, punctuation was under threat: "lighten[ed]" by Whitman in successive editions of *Leaves of Grass* (Schmidgall xxv); banned by Australian poet Mary Gilmore from her Spanish poems (430); replaced by Brennan (Barnes 46). In the twentieth century Stein would call commas "servile" (131), and Adorno semi-colons "gamey" (91); punctuation is "washed away" in Breton (57). Yet Jong, Dickinson, with her "dashes [and] flying quotation marks," and later, cummings, avoid punctuation's "settled usage." What is the use of inventing a new kind of writing, a new kind of language that isn't read? What is the use, Jong might ask, of diaspora, if it means dying in an insane asylum: not in a "new home," not in a home at all? The use of his text can only be contemporary: identifying such useless texts may identify methods or allow readings that "undo" settlement and history (Schlunke 178).

Yet there may be a lesson in Jong's production of *The Case* as a unique, highly resistant, nonreproducible, nondispersable, inimical work. It can only be self-identified: can only "speak" (or make noise) as if it desires to be a community of one. It has successfully resisted anthologizing, it further resists the definition of "migrant writing" and "autobiography." It has been "translated," but the original text has not moved since 1872. As a one-off book, it seems destined to reside in a library, and is in a sense a site-specific work, like the literally concrete poems of Ian Hamilton Finlay (Cutts 35). It has waited out its unreadability. One hundred years after Jong's death, critics like Shen and Moore and Tully are finding *The Case* a worthwhile text to explicate. Meanwhile the critical tools have also been developed to begin to read this work, whether as "exophonic" or appropriative writing, or in terms of visual prosody (Perloff); in terms that resist the dematerialization of language and parataxis (Silliman and other language writers); through theories developed from visual poetry (Cluver, Willard Bohn); theories of space, textual criticism, and archival work that read the page as a page rather than as a hoist for a message, that recognize the freedom of handwriting and resist the hegemony of typography (Davidson, McGann, Werner and Howe); or that account for the "non-semantic" (Forrest-Thomson 132). These theories themselves draw on criticism associated with concrete poetry and works such as "Un Coup de Dés," as well as the histories of the avant-gardes.

According to Mead, a shift is occurring: the once "useful" poetries that "underpinn[ed]" settlement are now used up. The hunt is on for new, formerly useless poetries, perhaps poetries in Perloff's terms that are "by other means": other languages and genres (like diaries) that may, if not constitute a new "model of a national Australian literature," at least foster new reading and writing networks of the historical and the contemporary that attend to different literacies, including that of the visual. Yet as exciting as the potential for rereading and reconstructing Australian texts with new interpretive tools may be, in concluding this chapter I return to Stewart, whose work in cultural poetics is specifically related to an ethnography of marginal American culture. Adopting her phrasing, the task, rather, is to take *The Case*: its structure, language, punctuation, et cetera, seriously as a graphic theoretical model in itself and to locate the critical task in the midst of these inventions. An Australian literature that takes *The Case* seriously as a living poetic model, rather than merely finds ways to interpret it, apply theories to it—settle it—would no longer be a settlement literature, at least as we know it. This would be to recast Jong's work as an invention for the future, rather than consigning it to the categories of historical interest and frustrated petition.

CHAPTER 4

Open Secrets

Dorothea Mackellar's Coded Diaries and Norman Harris's "Letter to Jim Bassett"

I Love A Sunburnt Country: The Diaries of Dorothea Mackellar. Written 1910–1918, published ed. Brunsdon 1990.
"Letter to Jim Bassett." Written 1927, published eds. Heiss and Minter, 2008; reprinted Jose ed., 2009.

The British were not the first travellers to learn the Aboriginal secret of the land that became Australia. The Dutch and the French had already been there (Dyer 2). Trade had also been going on between Aboriginal people and the Macassans (of what is now Indonesia) before the British arrived, and settlement began in earnest (Walsh 6). The country soon became, however, Britain's dirty secret: of the disposal of its criminals (or poor, or Irish) and treatment of the original inhabitants. This secret is what we might call an "open secret," a concept theorized by D. A. Miller in *The Novel and the Police*. In a chapter titled "Open Secrets, Open Subjects," he asks "Can the game of secrecy ever be thrown in?" (220). This is a crucial question for unsettlement, leading to further questions: whose secrets are deemed the most important, for example? Barthes considers that all writing "holds the threat of a secret": "Writing... is always rooted in something beyond language, it develops like a *seed, not like a line*, it... holds the threat of a secret, it is an *anticommunication*" (Writing 20).

In this chapter I discuss two texts: one by a beneficiary of British colonization, poet Dorothea Mackellar (1885–1968); the other by a resistant

Aboriginal activist, Norman Harris (c. 1898–1968). Mackellar is remembered for writing the colonial theme poem, "My Country" (1908), in the early years of Federation. The title of her diaries, *I Love A Sunburnt Country*, is the poem's best-remembered line. Her life writing, however, is not so well known, nor is the fact that she created her own code to keep aspects of her life secret (though the diaries are referred to on the "official" Web site dedicated to Mackellar, dorotheamackellar.com.au, there is no mention of the code). In a very different mode, yet also secretive, Harris's "Letter to Jim Bassett" gives expression and evidence to the Indigenous experience of the early twentieth century. His "Letter..." has been anthologized several times.

The "anticommunications" of Mackellar and Harris are directly implicated in the notion of secrecy as it relates to settlement, and therefore are, in a sense, meta-commentaries. They challenge the secret-keeping of settlement: playfully or melodramatically in the case of Mackellar, militantly and sorrowfully in the case of Harris. Miller argues that "the fact the secret is always known—and, in some obscure sense, known to be known—never interferes with the incessant activity of keeping it" (206). Miller summarizes here the hypocrisy of corrupt colonial government, of patriarchy, of any oppressive regime. He adds, "The paradox of the open secret registers the subject's accommodation to a totalizing system that has obliterated the difference he would make—the difference he does make, in the imaginary denial of this system" (207). In other words, the problem is how to speak out about something everyone already knows, yet appears to ignore? Miller's scenario is not of a complete denial of reality by the oppressive regime, but of the invulnerability of a system that only admits oppressive reality in the form of a secret, "tak[ing] secrecy as its field of operations" (207). The business of settlement, then, is a subject not to be discussed other than in the terms of nation-building, progress, and so on. In psychoanalytic terms, to reveal the secret of Aboriginal dispossession, imprisonment, and genocide is only to "re-veil" it, to re-cover rather than discover it (Sacerdoti 174). It is not the speaking of the secret that is unsettling: speaking can always be silenced. Rather it is the practice of coding, the speaking of silences, and the invention of obscure forms that deny power's reception and re-veiling.

If Kelly—and Bennelong more so—had reason to resist the coming nation of Australia, writers after Federation in 1901 were in a different position: that of living in a nation that appeared to be settled, in the sense of "finalized." Of course, if such events are to be events they must be celebrated; and in poetry, this celebration takes place in, for example, the "ideologically-infused topoi" (Ackland 20) of Mackellar's famous poem, "My Country," published when Mackellar was 22. In its title it enacts settler identification and possession. Even the poem's present tense "I love a sunburnt country" (Kinsella, Penguin 127) betrays this "ideological-infusion," serving to justify a country without history and, therefore, as Katherine Russo notes, enacting Indigenous displacement (31). According to the Mackellar Web site, "The last line of verse three, 'And ferns the warm dark soil,' was originally, 'And ferns the crimson soil.'" The displaced term, "crimson," was perhaps considered too florid, too excessive: however consciously, it also evokes the spilling of blood.

But there is more to Mackellar as a writer than the poet of this patriotic lyric; she also wrote a secret diary, using an invented code. To read language as code or noise is unsettling. In diverting from the everyday English of her *Diaries*, Mackellar's text could be seen as setting up a binary between code and language; but both are codes. Another opposition that is in play is that of the retrospective dailiness of the diary, written as if they have just happened. The editor of the *Diaries*, Jyoti Brunsdon, describes the "unforgettable moment [of] the discovery of the diaries," and notes that a "second [moment] came when I turned a page to find much of the entry for the next day in code." Brunsdon goes on to describe the process of deciphering Mackellar's code and provides a key to the coding (15–16). Dworkin, in *Reading the Illegible*, writes of the settling effect that decoding can have on visual texts:

> There is a strong temptation to recuperate the resisting and unsettling potential of "noise" as a "message" which can be absorbed into the very code it challenges, so that it can then be safely consumed by traditional hermeneutic strategies as simply another part of the message's "meaning." (49)

Brunsdon describes discovering a secret (i.e., the secret of coding itself) and proceeding to undo it, and thereby re-veiling the coding. In Brundson's reassembled version, the coding is dispersed in narrative and relegated to the text's literally obscure past. How might this noise of code be communicated like a "disease," as Dworkin recommends? Code (no more than spacing or punctuation) is not what Veronica Forrest-Thomson refers to as the "non-meaningful levels of language" (xiv); rather, despite its literal obscurity, code accentuates meaning by highlighting its hiddenness. Coding a portion of her recorded thoughts and actions became an everyday activity for Mackellar, and suggests the possibilities of thinking code as a prosodical disease, and further suggests a sounding or visual disease communicated to the readers of the diary where communication is not that of the semantic, of story, but a form of affect, of communication itself.

The secrets that Mackellar deals in are at times "open" ones, especially with regard to her own behavior, yet they do allow her to reserve a secret subjectivity apart from the open secret of her everyday subjectivity. That is, while what constitutes the everyday Mackellar, known by her friends and family as a daughter, "socialite" and unmarried woman poet, her active construction of a secret text that contradicts the public texts of her verbal discourse and settlement verse, allows the existence of an undetermined, secret, and unsettled, potential Dorothea Mackellar who is out of the reach of the everyday.

Rita Felski determines "three key facets" of the everyday: "time, space, and modality." She elaborates: "The temporality of the everyday, I suggest, is that of repetition, the spatial ordering of the everyday is anchored in a sense of home, and the characteristic mode of experiencing the everyday is that of habit" (Doing 80–81). From this initial point of definition we can see how the everyday in Felski's terms is something that, while ordinary, is also something that is unavailable to those whose lives are less ordered, whether through privilege, or homelessness. Though the everyday has a negative history, as Felski notes (79), the uncoded aspects of Mackellar's life are far from being completely mundane, as Brunsdon's label of "socialite" implies (27). Moreover, Mackellar had a rich fantasy life involving private theatrics with friends, particularly Ruth Bedford. It is this life that Brunsdon refers to as secret (25, 27). On November 30, 1910 Mackellar encodes, "**Pining to act!**" yet the record of the acting itself (for example, two days later on December 2) is not encoded, and Brunsdon mentions omitting "acting" among other everyday activities (30). It appears that Mackellar is more concerned to hide her desires, and their intensity, rather than her actions (69). There are, then, several layers to Mackellar's life, making the application of "everyday" rather complicated. Consider the dates October 17 to October 28, 1911, while Mackellar was in hospital recovering from an operation. Brunsdon suggests that this was "most probably, a procedure designed to arrest excessive menstrual bleeding" (90). On October 17 Mackellar is "Abominably tired," but "Red roses came for me" (92). This redeeming incident is Brunsdon's cue to oppose the page of diary entries on the left with a reproduction of a painting titled "Roses" by Tom Roberts. The equivalency isn't completely banal: the roses in the picture are mostly not red. The painting is one of several images that, along with apposite graphics that suggest the early twentieth century, add a visual element to Mackellar's edited diary, presumably to enliven the everydayness of the typeset prose. Yet read in this way, the images are a titivation of a mundaneness that is Mackellar's editor's construction. The visual aspect of the illustrations displaces the original visual aspect of Mackellar's code: the

Diaries are in fact, recoded by Brunsdon as an acceptable, historicized settlement text, with predictable visual accompaniment. The dominant note is nostalgia; the images might derive from any sentimental Europeanized context from the early twentieth century.

On October 18 Mackellar writes, "Of the day there is nothing memorable, but massage began in the evening…" The entries have been abridged by Brunsdon, who "omitted many passages devoted to lunches, teas, dinners, plays, books, hair-washings, weather reports and acting" (29–30): here is Mackellar's everyday. Brunsdon's list presents the everyday as repetition, an aspect linked to women: "the key to women's experience of extrasubjective time, cosmic time, jouissance" (Felski 82). Felski further characterizes domestic activity, menstrual cycles, and pregnancy as women's link to the concept of repetition. Mackellar was not subject to housework, or pregnancy as far as we know, but she suffered particularly from menstruation. According to Brunsdon, Mackellar used a swastika to represent menstruation "in ever-increasing frequency" prior to the operation (90). (Note that this signification is pre-Nazi.) Felski suggests that distaste for repetition is a modern Western phenomenon; in an Indigenous culture the kinds of everyday repetition represented by "lunches…hair-washings, weather reports…" would be validated as ritual (83).

As Felski notes, the concept of home is a fraught one within theories of everyday life. She writes of Lefebvre's perception that "Being at home in the world is an affront to the existential homelessness and anguish of the modern intellectual"; and cites Adorno: "'Dwelling, in the proper sense, is now impossible…It is part of morality not to be at home in one's home,'" adding that "The vocabulary of modernity is a vocabulary of anti-home." Felski notes further the gendering of the home, and feminist theorizing that distances women from the home. Her own position is more nuanced, arguing that "The everyday significance of home clearly needs to be imagined differently." She points to, "in de Certeau's terms, an active practicing of place," and to the "active produc[tion]" by women of the home's "familiarity," and of the "leaky boundaries between home and non-home," and home's "conflicts and power struggles" (85–87). These struggles are represented in Mackellar's text, which reflects such "leaky boundaries" as much in the relation between its descriptions and encryptions, as in the semantic content.

Robert Menzies, who, as Australian prime minister, presided over the latter phase of the Stolen Generations (a retrospective description of government policy that resulted in Aboriginal children being taken against their will and placed in white foster care), defined home as "where my wife and children are." How many Aboriginal men of Menzies age could say the same thing during the "Menzies era"? Menzies' formula follows a complacent theory that equates home with "a house" ("and garden"):

> ...one of the best instincts in us is that which induces us to have one little piece of earth with a house and a garden which is ours to which we can withdraw, in which we can be among our friends, into which no stranger may come against our will.
>
> If you consider it, you will see that, as in the old saying, "the Englishman's home is his castle," it is this very fact that leads on to the conclusion that he who seeks to violate that law by violating the soil of England must be repelled and defeated. National patriotism, in other words, inevitably springs from the instinct to defend and preserve our own homes. (408)

Menzies conflates Australia with England, and denies the killing and dispossession necessary for such a conflation. Though written as a message to (Anglo) Australians as inspiration (or propaganda) during World War II, Menzies' text can be read as a reactionary reversal, a belated (and disguised) defense for settler attacks against "invading natives." In the recent critical anthology titled *Halfway House: The Poetics of Australian Spaces*, Jennifer Rutherford outlines the problem of home and house conflation. She writes, "it goes without saying that in the Australian context, space and its poetics cannot assume the innocence with which Bachelard [for example] imbues the house" (Undwelling 114). In making her argument, Rutherford uses such terms as "unhousing" and "undwelling," and reads the "trope of unhousing in white Australian literature [as a] negative form of his [Bachelard's] idealization" (123).

Perhaps Mackellar practiced unhousing in a different way, treating a house like a theater, and using theater as a pretext for escaping the house. All writing is in a sense preedited: Mackellar, like Brunsdon, also practiced omissions. In one instance, the phrase "Of the day there is nothing memorable," stands in for that day's "nothing." The abridged entry for October 19 consists of one decoded line: "**R. came back straight from the train**" ("R." being the married man Mackellar is involved with. I bold the text as per Brunsdon for all originally coded entries). October 20: "A better day than yesterday—which was *vile*." October 22: "Felt very cheerful. **I can't help being glad that R. loves my figure**." On October 25, Mackellar is "hustled...into bed" by Ruth "with various nurses, and hot water bottles...[and receives] Massage in the dark..." The next day she is "Very limp" and "***can't stop him making love to me now***," then on October 28 she is limp again: "R. came. Was studiously distant and cheerful till the end when—**when**

I lay limp and scarcely realized how close things were. Afternoon...I wrote to R. on the balcony...and wept bitterly..." (92). With all the "R"s and water, and limpness and darkness, Brunsdon's use of Roberts's "Roses" takes on a related poetic quality. The delicate style and use of pink and white in the paintings seem more fitting to the narrative than the more vigorous bloody image of "Red roses." The coded text is vivid and romantic, melodramatic even: not so everyday. Yet this reconstruction is to take Mackellar too much at her word. Because the edited, typographic version makes it seem more natural than it really is, as if a painting (or a patient) really is like roses, "passionate yet compliant" (Felski 83). Yet Mackellar was being quite careful in her construction of these scenes, written hours—perhaps days—after the events that they describe.

Brunsdon's emphasis on the semantic, over the material fact of coding, results in a loss. Rather than give us more of Mackellar the writer, Brunsdon constructs a banal portrait of, in this instance, the overwrought love affair. Not that this is false: it relies on Mackellar's own construction. Brunsdon refers to the *Diaries* as a jigsaw puzzle that she attempts to solve (18, 30). This is a settling, settlement action; the published version is an assemblage that reflects Brunsdon's framing of Mackellar's narrative. Rather than elicit the multiple stories of the text (Bush 206), Brunsdon constructs the singular story of a romance. The narrativizing of Mackellar is also reflected in the work of later scholars. In "Finding a Place for Women in Australian Cultural History," Jane E. Hunt, who cites the *Diaries* as a biographical source (226), mentions nothing of the coding, perhaps wanting to counter the marginalization (221) that the use of code might evoke.

The *Diaries* are more than simply a missing piece from the jigsaw of settlement literature: their value is the critique they offer of the settlement model. Mackellar's code points to the many things that could not be said or written in the early years of Federation, of which Harris's "Letter" provides a more shameful example. In terms of poetics, rather than reading Mackellar's code as a closing action that needs to be reopened, her diaries—in contrast to her verse—can be read as open or experimental forms (see Davidson 100). Read in this way the diaries counter Mackellar's verse and unsettle her position—and her poetry—in the Australian canon. In writing this I am not proposing that a new canon of unsettled texts displace the canon of settled texts, as this "paradigm," in Mead's terms, "break[s] up" (400). Rather that Mackellar should retain our interest as a reading (and writing) resource, both for the *Diaries* themselves, and for the unsettled relation between the *Diaries* and her poems. These texts, though formally unalike, are explicitly networked in having the same author; the point of the unsettled text, however, is that it can be considered alongside other unlike texts: network implies the work of the critic, rather than the predetermined alignments allowed by genre, time, theme and so on.

Mackellar's coding in the *Diaries* disrupts the expression of the linear life. It resists the notion of life writing as a kind of prose lyric—and makes the construction of life writing as assemblage explicit, in that the coding makes the retrospective nature of writing up the diary apparent, and distances us from its intimacy. The entries quoted above were written in hospital, and therefore outside of the everyday as associated with home; yet for Mackellar, who travelled often, it is the diary-keeping itself, and the coded secrets, that are the consistent, everyday repetition. In Fremantle, January 12, 1912, she writes, "It was warm and **I wore Robin's red roses** and was gay" (103). Touring Egypt a month later: "**I wasn't well and the hurrying hurt me**" (109).

There is visual prosody in the relation between Mackellar's code and her English, and even in Brunsdon's edited version between bold and regular text. The sense of change in moving between everyday English and invented code is one that disrupts the semantic. Though for Mackellar the code has a practical purpose, it also perfectly expresses Mead's "dissatisfaction with... the overly settled idea of the "ordinariness" of ordinary, or everyday language" (5), if not dissatisfaction with her life. "Society," as Susan Sontag writes, "contains no mystery" (Photography 59–60). In the diaries, Mackellar's coding disrupts the assured, conversational, and everyday qualities of the typical entry. A paradoxically heightened consciousness of "language" presents itself, consciousness of the word as made up of letters: a materialist poetics. To translate this—to break the code—is to lose the poetics. Theologian Henry Corbin contends that "instead of seeking a secret *in* or *under* the text, we must regard the text itself as *the* secret" (Rasula, This 103). Brunsdon settles the question of Mackellar's artifice by dealing with the code in the introduction, as if it does not belong in the body of the text. Mackellar's code has been typeset in Brunsdon's introduction, but it challenges quotation: not all the symbols have equivalents in Microsoft Word. Brunsdon replaces Mackellar's code with deciphered, bolded English: the boldness of the type reveals what boldness of life the writer was hiding. The code itself, however, is completely elided as a (poetically) useless invention, or rather one that has served its purpose. For Brunsdon, the secret of the text is the semantic message behind the text, with the secondary meaning of what it might tell us of Mackellar's life and milieu. The convenience of such code is that it appears to offer a means to interpretation: once the deciphering is complete, the critical work appears to be done: an assumption Barthes warns against. It is "vain," he writes "... to suppose that [a work] has a final secret, to which, once discovered, there would be equally nothing to add: whatever one says about the work, there always remains something of language, of the subject, of absence, *just as there was at the moment of its inception*" (Barthes's italics; Criticism 87). This situation is what makes the work literature: "Literature cannot be mastered, nor does it give up its secrets" (McQuillan x). The code is the secret and secretive aberration of Mackellar's oeuvre. The actual coding, rather than what was encoded, tells us something of her poetic, inventive, secretive, and performative nature, enriching our sense of both Mackellar as a poet, and of Australian colonial poetics generally.

Maurice Blanchot implies that secrets are not part of the everyday: that the everyday "belongs to insignificance, and the insignificant is without truth, without reality, without secrets." For Blanchot, it is the lack of secrets that makes the quotidian ungraspable (Shaviro 112). The quotidian, the normal, has no desire to be grasped; it is "non-negotiable reality" (Felski 77): it "separates" (a root of "secret," Concise 950) (certain) people and actions from itself. Yet there are those who can be seen as crossing from the realm of the quotidian to that of secrecy. These are the agents of the quotidian, the duplicitous ones of the "folded paper," the "diplomats" (Concise 270; Nietzsche 226). Such an agent may "pass" as a representative of the quotidian and yet fold a secret within. It too may be an open secret. In Georg Simmel's remark that "The secret is one of man's greatest achievements... The secret produces an immense enlargement of life... The secret offers, so to speak, the possibility of a second world alongside the manifest world," we see the privileged nature of the secret (Bru 135). As well as the world kept hidden by the code in the *Diaries* (though, ostensibly, a text, as a whole, written for its writer to read only), Mackellar had a further shared secret world in her acting out plays, or closet dramas.

In a discussion focused on women poets of the Victorian era, Susan Brown defines closet dramas as "drama that, either by intention or default, finds its performance in the minds of readers within their 'closets' or private rooms"; her own examples she describes as "being on the boundary between poetry and drama" (89). Though Mackellar and Bedford are clearly Australian examples of this practice, they did not act in "private rooms" indoors only: according to dorotheamackellar.com.au, they would drive out in the bush to act out their stories.

Brown's definition of the closet drama in terms of reader's minds allows us to think of scenes from the diaries as also being versions of closet drama, replayed in Mackellar's mind as she writes up the scenes, and played in her *Diaries*' belated reader's minds also. Writing, with reference to George Eliot's dramatic poem *Armgart*, of "breakdown in the female body," Brown suggests this breakdown "functions... as a metonymic shorthand or literary code for the effects of the psychic division which results from the internalization of the social censure of female ambition" (93–94). Eliot's heroine Armgart's lines "As letters fallen asunder that once made / A hymn of rapture" are read by Brown as "Her language evokes a disintegration of self, a castration, and even a crumbling of language" (94). This description evokes not just Mackellar's coding as a hiding practice, but, as in the case of the swastikas, an inexpressive lexical despair. Armgart's self-dramatization is also one that readily corresponds to Mackellar:

Oh, I can live unmated, but not live
Without the bliss of singing to the world
And feeling all my world respond to me.

Brown notes, "Such a relationship to the world is rooted in the assumption that she has a privileged relationship to nature" (94), aptly describing Mackellar's attitude in "My Country." Yet there are different ways of thinking about this privilege: having the bush available as a setting for play-acting is also a kind of privilege, though one that might appear to be ironic in its "relationship to nature."

While not explicitly using the term "closet drama," Miller evokes the closet in constructing scenes produced by reading Austen, performances that conform to Brown's definition (4–5). The point of the metaphor of the closet is that we can hide inside ourselves, take our closets with us. The *Diaries*' code performs a kind of closeting: not only of Mackellar's affair, but at the level of the "letters...asunder." The *Diaries* are the closet of Mackellar's everyday life story, yet at the level of the letter, there is a queer reversal: alphabetical letters don't hide queer coding inside; rather, the code has been contrived to hide the normative letter (or in the case of the swastikas, which have no letter equivalent, normal bodily function).

In the published version, the use of bold type tends to what Ron Silliman calls a "strateg[y] for consuming texts solely for their summarizable 'content'" (13). The editing enacts this strategy, but not completely, because the content of the published diaries is the hiding by Brunsdon (by eliding the code) of what was hidden by Mackellar, as much as revealing the hidden (the semantic behind the code). The bold type announces a differentiation (an exclusion), but is an effect that fades with familiarity as we follow what has become emphasized: Mackellar's narrative. No consideration is given to coding as poetic material in its own right. The visual poetics, including prosody, are ignored. Once deciphered, the text is treated as prose (14, 84).

Here are the first two coded entries of the published version: "Florence came frightfully worried. **Her pretty maid Cayley has just had a child**" and "Sat on the lawn and **smoked to keep the mosquitoes away**" (34). This is from a diary written in January 1910. Mackellar was 24 and living a life of both "privilege" and "restriction" (Brunsdon 15, 16). The published text, then, is to some extent unsettled, the bold type interrupting what Silliman calls "textual transparency" (Dworkin 54) and Charles Bernstein "absorptive writing" (Poetics 84). In thinking of this as an unsettled text, I am not referring to the semantic content but to Brunsdon's representation of the content. In this instance, however, it seems that there is a direct correlation between the content that Mackellar finds unsettling and its representation as code. Though the propriety of the above entries (referring to unwed childbirth and smoking) has changed since 1911, other entries refer to Mackellar's relationship with "R":

Thursday August 10
After dinner we talked. **He was worried about me, and I told him something of what was in my heart, for indeed there has been a great change in the last two days**. A relief, but rather exhausting... (59)

Friday August 11
Got up earlier than usual... Felt quite reasonably well. Evening: Mrs Arthur Feez's and Mrs W. Collins' dance. A very nice one, and I loved it—what I had of it. Broke down at the 12th dance. Rather a stirring night. **He was upset because I love him**, and it upset *me*, and **I nearly kissed him, which would have startled things** a good deal. I never felt like that before—rather desperate—and yet not as miserable. Only he wouldn't believe me when I told him so. (84)

Mackellar's coding of specific phrases is, as we can see, very particular. She doesn't encode her feelings or R's reaction. Once we know of the affair, there are plenty of implications of it in the uncoded text: yet no evidence. Mackellar's secret tends toward being an open one.

Mackellar's original diary unsettles reading through unsettling (veiling) semantics. Yet if any act of "reading is an act of decoding" (Wolfreys viii), reading Mackellar's ostensibly straightforward "My Country" also involves decoding. Russo, for example, refers to the poem's gendered aspect as "far from innocent and [functioning as] a metaphor for the relation between the masculine Australian settler and the conquered country." The poem suggests that "streams," "skies," "mountains," and "ferns" are naturally accompanied by "cattle" and "paddocks." There is no suggestion of a history of settlement, and therefore no questioning of its origin. The poem ends, "Though earth holds many splendours / Wherever I may die / I know to what brown country / My homing thoughts will fly." The lines of "My Country" are those of someone who travels the world, representing Australia, like one of Nietzsche's diplomats, with diary "folded" to hide the unsettling code itself rather than what it might reveal. Though Mackellar's "homing thoughts" may refer to Australia, as a writer her fixed position, her need for familiarity (Felski 85), is writing itself: that is, the unsettling, unpatriotic fact of writing, that it is ultimately only true to itself.

Mackellar is, officially, a settlement poet. She was described as "the first genuine Australian songster" in the *Commonweal* (Brunsdon 12), a description that rivals one of Harpur as "Australia's 'first authentic poetic voice'" (Wilde 104). In her coding, however, Mackellar resists her implication in the settlement project, inventing an alphabet outside English, a writing that is outside the established categories. Her invented code could be considered useless in terms of settlement: deceptive, sly, serving only a private purpose. Alternatively, it can be read as an innovative form of diplomacy, affirming (settler) community by avoiding scandal. Further, it is symbolically diplomatic, in that it practices the re-veiling of the open secret (if in egoistic miniature): of the lies told by the state. The popular sentiments of "My Country" have effected for Mackellar a relation to Australia's national culture, a home or settled structure that the poem helps produce. The *Diaries* with their coded entries, by contrast, are unsettled, homeless texts; they provide the possibility of producing an alternative, unsettled Mackellar that is not at home, where, as Brunsdon says, the "restriction" is too great (16).

The visual emphasis of the code's bold type in the published version evokes, like Jong's lettering, a concrete quality, but this is explicit in the original. Here is a sample, where a dash (–) represents "A" and so on:

```
 – A    |  E   /\ G   \/ H   \ I   / O
 = S    || T   +  U
```

Mackellar's code includes two punctuation marks: a small star represents an exclamation; a small cross a full stop. There is no differentiation between upper and lower case letters, so I follow Brunsdon in presenting the deciphered letters as capitals (16). In the coding we see another aspect of the everyday: that of order, or pattern, the pattern of Mackellar's life. Lorraine Sim, following her subject, Virginia Woolf, argues for the "central" meaning of this pattern (11). Mackellar's code patterns her everyday as well as encrypting aspects of it. Paradoxically, the code has an order that the Roman alphabet lacks. The code has a 1:1 relation to the alphabet; the alphabet has no such relation to another system, despite being partly derived from earlier alphabets.

Questions regarding what makes a text concrete poetry are part of the generic territory. "What makes me read this text as a Concrete Poem?...What do I do when I read it as a Concrete Poem?" Claus Cluver asks in an article, "Concrete Poetry: Critical Perspectives from the 90s." Such questions, he admits, "are not easy to answer but seem crucial in assessing the status and achievement of Concrete poetry...Among the many lessons I have learned...from Concrete Poems is an understanding of the signifying potential of all the material aspects of the text" (279). These "aspects" are what might be called, in Forrest-Thomson's terms, "the "non-semantic" effects...contributing toward the 'total image-complex' of the poem" (Bernstein, Poetics 11). Cluver writes: "Everything concrete is nothing but itself. To be understood concretely a word must be taken at its word. All art is concrete which uses its material functionally and not symbolically" (278). Defining Mackellar's text as concrete poetry is a conceptual reading not easily settled. The code is "material [used] functionally," but can it be said to consist of words at all? When the cipher obscures the Roman grapheme or letter, the text can only be "read" as a line of (nonsymbolizing) symbols. In Mackellar's original, there is no clear demarcation of words. If we accept the definition of "concrete," the boundaries of the text itself remain undefined. Is it only the code that is "concrete"? What of the pages of (edited, at times fragmentary) everyday description? The bolded type in the published version is functional, yet also in a sense symbolic, in that it symbolizes what Mackellar thought should be hidden. In editing Mackellar's diaries, then, Brunsdon becomes implicated in concrete procedure. The *Diaries* challenge Cluver's definition, demonstrating that the functional and the symbolic are not always easily separated. It is a doubly unsettled text: there is the original version that we can imagine in English, having been shown the code; then there is the published version with its bold text that we can imagine as cipher, and read, with the knowledge of the absent code, aware of a visual and intentional impoverishment. Mackellar's text is an assemblage: a personal diary that appears to participate in (desire) concrete poetry. As a work by a nationalistically implicated poet, the *Diaries* are interesting for the way in which they are constituted by an internal, textually explicit exclusion and othering. We can think of this as a process of punctuation: the main body of the text punctuated by bolded (coded) examples, just as the *Diaries* may be seen to punctuate—or puncture—Mackellar's nationalistically inflected oeuvre.

There are levels of the secret that make those that are less urgent seem like analogies or metaphors of secrets, rather than secrets as such. Peter Middleton, in *Distant Reading*, notes that "word puzzles...offer consolatory answers." Despite the personal nature of Mackellar's entries, though they may or may not mask, "deeper unknowns," they do mime "the verbal secrecy of...governing institutions" (184). Middleton is referring to Britain's "governing institutions" specifically: institutions that had a strong influence in Australia during the 1910s, the period covered by the *Diaries*. (Particularly during World War I: Mackellar's brother was killed at the end of the war.) Felski theorizes the everyday in a contemporary context where "no sanctum of the ordinary...escapes the tentacular grip of late capitalist consumer culture" (90); it is a more successful, more comprehensive tyranny than colonialism. Though Mackellar's—and Harris's—texts are both more "consumable" as products of life writing, this is not the point I want to make, but rather that there is an ordinariness to their exceptional-seeming, respective poetics. The coding of Mackellar's *Diaries*, and the questioning and what might be called the creative spelling in Harris's "Letter...," have the ordinariness of habit (Felski's third "facet," 80). Though Harris is rhetorical in style, albeit with opposite intent to "My Country," or Menzies' house and garden manifesto, it is the unemphatic ordinariness of habit in the two writers that potentially "escapes" the colonial.

The association of the everyday with the ordinary and the nonintellectual (Felski 79), belies, in the context of colonialism, its privilege; not having to intellectualize can be an effect of privilege. Though of course Aboriginal people on reserves had mundane, everyday activities to perform, what constituted the settler ordinary in early twentieth-century Australia was often out of reach, as Harris's "Letter..." and its attendant "Questions" attest. In other words, to produce a reading of the everyday is to produce a reading of settlement, as if the conflict between settlers and Indigenous peoples is over, and everyday life can begin (or resume for those who see Australian life as basically a continuation of English life). Thus, according to Ross Gibson, the White Australia Policy was not just to keep non-European migrants out:

> The newly federated nation, confronted with the paradoxical opportunity-and-threat of maturity in the complicated world, could not "let go" of its fixation on Mother England. The legislature demanded that similitude with England be the defining characteristic of its populace. Hence the White Australia Policy. This insistence was a way to avoid the mourning...(166)

Yet as Harris's "Letter..." attests, the conflict was far from over. Making a distinction between the everyday and the "ordinary," Sim writes that, "illness, celebrations and falling in love are a part of ordinary experience and life but are not typically a part of everybody's everyday life" (2). This "everybody", however, cannot be taken for granted in colonial Australia; while the ordinary lows and highpoints that texture Woolf's everyday may be similar to those of Mackellar, they are in stark contrast to that of "girls [that] were tied with chains to get punished" (Harris 27).

Western Australian Norman Harris's "Letter to Jim Bassett" is included in two recent *Macquarie PEN* anthologies of literature. The text contains many of what would conventionally be considered spelling errors. This indicates contemporary editing practices that allow the reader to negotiate spelling and grammatical differences: differences that evoke the writer, their time and culture. As Walter Ong writes, "when other dialects of a given language besides the grapholect [such as 'English'] vary from the grammar of the grapholect, they are not ungrammatical: they are simply using a different grammar, for language is structure, and it is impossible to use language without a grammar" (105–106). Penny van Toorn further argues against the "cultural progress" model of Indigenous literacy, adding that there is a "multitude of ways to practice literacy" (9). Grammar aside, in a review of the *Macquarie PEN Anthology of Aboriginal Literature*, Kevin Brophy describes Harris's writing as "worthy of Jonathan Swift" (n. pag.). The "Letter..." is an example of an editor's assemblage, as a note from Bain Attwood and Andrew Markus attests (124). The "Letter..." as published by Heiss and Minter consists of a letter as such, with the additional text, "Questions within the meaning on the Act"; Harris also signs the "Questions," as if a letter or contract (25–28). The "Act" referred to is "The Acts of the Parliament of Western Australia Aborigines Act 1905." Attwood and Markus describe this act (and similar acts determined by other Australian states) as "discriminatory legislation" that deprived Aboriginal people of the right to travel or work as they wished, to own property, and even to have custody of their own children (8). The "Letter..." itself does not begin with a conventional address, but commences, "We have been looking out for you for some time now..." The addressee is first referred to in the second paragraph: "Now, Jim, we are trying to get some of the natives and half-castes together..."

Harris evokes a sense of community, but there is a double (if overlapping) sense of community here: of Jim's belonging with Harris's "we," and of belonging to the group of "natives and half-castes," that is, of friend- or comradeship, as well as racial identity. Regardless of whether Harris and Bassett share an Indigenous language, they are forced to write in English to correspond, a situation noted by Mudrooroo (Russo 55). Harris goes on to enumerate some of the prohibitions and exclusions faced by Indigenous people: "He is not alowed in a pub, not to have a gun, not to camp on revers" (25). This theme of "negative community" here coincides with a formulation by Serres in relation to culture: that its constitution follows the exclusion, the expulsion, of whatever belonged before. In other words, non-Indigenous community is constituted by Indigenous exclusion (179). Certeau's definition of the everyday is also pertinent: that it "invents itself by *poaching* in countless ways on the property of others" (Certeau's italics; xii).

British settlement, and its attendant modernity, destroyed to a great extent the precontact, ordinary existence of Aboriginal people. Bennelong lost his everyday in 1788; one hundred and forty years later, Aboriginal people like Harris still have no "taken-for-granted backdrop" to their lives (Felski 80). Further, the racist assumptions that drove the establishment of Aboriginal reserves enforced a particular form of everyday, as if it could be no more than the mimicking of what Lefebvre characterizes as the "current social degradation" of the lower classes of Europeans (Felski 79). Although there were and are class differentiations to be made regarding the Australian everyday, it is in terms of Indigenous and non-Indigenous relations that the inflection of power is most apparent, and most fatal. Race as a concept is inadequate here: the conflict relates rather to land appropriation. (The racist treatment of the Chinese, for example, is of a different order.)

Harris's "Letter..." strikes the tone of a secret agent at the close when he writes, "Burn this when you are finished with it or send it back to me" (28), corresponding to WH Auden's contemporaneous espionage-inflected line in *The Orators*: "Better burn this" from 1931. (Auden's poem might also be thought of as closet drama.) Harris's text is as incendiary as Henry Lawson's

> We'll make the tyrants feel the sting
> O' those that they would throttle;
> They needn't say the fault is ours
> If blood should stain the wattle! (400–401),

written in the context of the 1891 Queensland shearers' strikes. Harris wants to keep his agency secret, as being identified as an Aboriginal activist could have further negative consequences (Attwood and Markus 17). While Simmel's "second world," may be seen as an "enlargement" for Mackellar, for those forced from the "manifest world" to occupy an unchosen "second world," such as the Indigenous Australians referred to in the "Letter...," the second world is a reduction. Alison Ravenscroft writes of Aboriginals at the Cherbourg Settlement in Queensland as "playthings": forced to dress up and act for the amusement of the Whites rather than for themselves (122). The circumstance of Harris, who was preoccupied with very real prejudice and the necessity for resistance, puts emphasis on the italicized phrase of Nietzsche's *"Better be careful*—There is nothing we like so much to impart to others as the seal of secrecy—along with what is under it" rather than its more smug explanation (197).

Harris writes to elicit help in exposing the more serious state secret of the cruel treatment of Aboriginal people. While such treatment might well be called an open secret, the titles of John Pilger's history *A Secret Country* (1989) and Henry Reynolds's *Why Weren't We Told?* (1999) indicate the level of ignorance regarding, for example, "massacres and punitive expeditions" (Reynolds 4). The other aspect of Indigenous and settler relations, also to an extent an open secret, is the "civilisation whose sophistication is barely acknowledged by a white society still tied to stereotypes of its own invention" (Pilger 29). The paradoxical openness and entanglement of these secrets is summed up in a 1927 quote from Aboriginal activist Fred Maynard about living conditions for Aboriginal people: "The public did not learn about it because there was a 'hush' policy." Yet Maynard is quoted from a letter originally published in the *Sydney Morning Herald* (Attwood and Markus 71).

The "hush policy" cited by Maynard is an effect of the social control that Miller labels "the police" (vii). Actual police (and other government officials) were involved in the literal violent actions of killing people and stealing children (Pilger 53, 66; Gibson 54–73). Miller, however, uses the term "police" figuratively in an argument derived from Foucault, deemphasizing police as persons, and allowing for the term to circulate as a controlling, repressive process. Miller's further theorizing of the open secret suggests the difficulty of agency "in the face of a secret everybody knows" (195). In terms of the open secret, then, Reynolds and Pilger inevitably become complicit, despite the implicit titles of their books, and the explicit nature of their contents. Reynolds's title implies that we have only been told now, and only if we read his book; Pilger exposes the secrets of white Australia by writing a (further) book about them. Yet in a sense they merely reassemble the secret. This raises the question of how any knowledge can become universal, become other than a secret?

The other side of Harris's secret is "why"? Why do white people behave so deviously and mysteriously? The whites consistently act as if Indigenous people can read their minds, performing exchanges with them for their own benefit. As the Yolngu of northeast Arnhem Land, in the Northern Territory, wrote in their 1963 Yirrkala Bark Petition to the Australian

Parliament: "...the procedures of the excision of this land and the fate of the people on it were never explained to them beforehand, and were kept secret from them" (Heiss and Minter 50). Deborah Bird Rose attempts to explain how such deceptions appear from an Aboriginal perspective. She writes that non-Indigenous people (or "foreigners") appear to Indigenous people to be outside the Aboriginal "moral order" (188). She reports the Yarralin perspective of Aboriginal lawman Hobbles Danayarri and his attempts to theorize non-Indigenous destructive behavior, asking: "can conquest be located within a moral universe"? (189).

The act of conquest was so much a part of settler culture that moral and ethical contradictions appeared to go largely unexamined. The motives behind settlement behavior might be described, then, as a "foreigner"'s open secret, inaccessible to Indigenous people. Miller writes that "secrecy would seem to be a mode whose ultimate meaning lies in the subject's formal insistence that he is radically inaccessible to the culture that would otherwise entirely determine him," adding that the subject cannot "resolve the double bind of a secrecy that must always be rigorously maintained in the face of a secret that everybody knows, since this is the very condition that entitles [them] to [their] subjectivity in the first place" (195). Miller's conundrum approaches that of Harris's in that although Harris asks "Questions" of the settler sphinx, he cannot reveal that he is asking the "Questions," but must veil them by sending instead to a trusted friend. It is through this secrecy in relation to the settler culture that he produces his (secret) subjectivity in relation to settler culture. Miller further writes of "indeterminability in the safety of silence" (195), suggesting that secrecy has no sound and that its silence is one of "Questions" unasked, of indecipherable codes, of being your own secret "police." The codes of the settlers were as indecipherably silent to the Indigenous people as the codes of the Indigenous were to the settlers. In Harris's case, his "Questions" were a means of constructing a secret between himself and Jim Bassett.

In his survey of twentieth-century Aboriginal literature, *Black Words, White Page*, Adam Shoemaker "contend[s] that a fundamental relationship exists between the socio-political milieu and Aboriginal creative writing in English" (6); or, as Heiss and Minter phrase it, "one of the persistent and now characteristic elements of Aboriginal literature—[is] the nexus between the literary and the political" (8). This is not surprising, as the first motivation for Aboriginal writing in English was the writing of "letters and petitions to colonial government" (Attwood and Markus 10–11). This is in contrast to the job of settler texts, Mead's "kind[s] of poetries that best support that previous model of a national Australian literature." Like many Indigenous texts, Harris's "Letter…" is semantically explicit in its protest against settlement (non-Indigenous protest tends to be against authority, corruption and Federation, rather than against settlement as such). Nevertheless, as in Bennelong's "Letter," there are appreciable poetic aspects. Shoemaker, however, largely evades both poetics and aesthetics in defending Aboriginal poetry against the charge of "propaganda" (180). The political nature of Indigenous texts does not necessarily reflect the politics of the Indigenous writer either, as Jennifer Jones argues throughout her *Black Writers White Editors*. Jones provides examples of editorial depoliticizing of texts, as well as the emphases of politics deemed more suitable (24–30).

My poetic readings of ostensibly prosaic texts have a double aim: that of unsettling the excluding community of the Australian poem, and of unsettling the assumed cultural hegemony of the pragmatic (that is, the prosaic). Late nineteenth- and early twentieth-century writing had of course already unsettled the prose and poetry distinction by the time of Harris's letter. Whether Harris is or is not one of Mead's "poetic artificers," the poetics of his "Letter..." are relatively complex, and this complexity is further enhanced by the editorial, perhaps providential, combination of the letter with the "Questions." His text has the effect that, "the fibre lines between poems and other linguistic domains begin to appear active, lit up" (Mead 6). Felski writes about enchantment, of the error of "equat[ing] innovative form with mental states of knowingness, irony, and distance." It is the "seduction" of "yielding to the grain of the voice" of Harris that brought me to perform a reading of his text. I am, in Felski's terms, "claimed" by it. This "yielding" is not separate from "intellectual pleasure," nor from Harris's political meanings, nor from the creative critical state that veers from "knowingness, irony, and distance," though this is perhaps another irony (71–76). I emphasize poetics rather than semantics in order to demonstrate the possibilities of insight that can be gained from "plural styles of reading" (Spivak xxix).

Stephen Collis discusses plurality in the context of (serial) poetry's relation to anarchy, citing Jean-Luc Nancy's "ontology of relational space." Collis claims a relation between the serial poem and the Greek etymology of anarchy: "*an-arche* is 'without origin.'" He writes, "in Nancy's ontology, there is no authority in origins, only relations," and he adopts Nancy's terms of the "singular plural" for the serial poem, quoting Nancy to the effect that singularity "assembles" "the togetherness of singulars" (111–113). We might read Harris's "Letter..." as a serial poem and as an anarchist text, in that we cannot determine whether the singular pluralities of the "Letter..." or of the "Questions" were written first, and in that the "Questions" challenge the origins of settler authority. Collis argues that the form of the serial poem is "*radically* open" (his italics; 114); to categorize Harris's text as having "no origin" suggests something of Harris's displacement in the English language.

While Nancy's phrase "the togetherness of singulars" suggests that a text might be a community unto itself, my interest is in establishing a community of texts from both Indigenous and non-Indigenous writers, without eliding this distinction. Such a diverse assemblage does of course imply a plurality already, and risks an oversight of the plural nature of individual texts. Each text is, however, an assemblage within a greater assemblage, and though, as a community, this diverse collection of texts might be said to be anarchic or without origin, in terms of settlement, their origins derive from challenging the origin of settlement, and of settlement's denial of "plural knowledges."

How, then, does Harris's writing—what we might call its "poetic literacy"—argue for inclusion in the "community" of poetry? I don't mean to reduce Harris's urgent and real political claims to an analogy, but I want to recognize that his "Letter…"'s contribution to Australian literature is more than historical. I imply here the open secret of reading pleasure. As Miller writes in the context of reading fiction, "We too inevitably surrender our privileged position as readers to whom all secrets are open by 'forgetting' our knowledge for the pleasures of suspense and surprise" (Novel 206). As Derrida suggests, also in relation to fiction, literature is a space, along with the university, where there exists "the right to say everything publicly, or to keep it secret" (McQuillan viii). This is a space that Harris could not enter at the time of writing, yet his text can, retrospectively, be allowed in.

There is, as Brophy suggests, pleasure in reading Harris's "Letter…" for its poetics, its irony and tone. I begin with Harris's first sentence: "We have been looking out for you for some time now but I don't think that you are much of a swimmer and I know that you haven't got a boat and now that the lakes are running you can't come per road or by water and perhaps not by train, so I don't expect to see you this winter" (25). By noticing the length and the lack of punctuation, we might miss the way that the rhythm of the sentence relies on the assonance of the "er" sound. They constitute three instances of half rhyme, roughly equally distributed: "swimmer," "water," and "winter." These three are further linked by the assonance of the "i" in "swimmer" and "winter," and the consonance of the "w" and the "t" in "winter" and "water." This community of like words, once established, suggests the belonging of two further "er" words: the unusual use of "per" instead of "by," which points to the repetition of "per" in "perhaps." Instances where unconventional or misspellings contribute to the "Letter…"'s poetics are numerous. Harris's "other literacy" produces rhyme and assonance, as well as resonances of meaning a more conventional text would not. For instance, he writes "prohibiterd," again using the "er" sound, enclosed between two uses of the word "Perth": "I suppose you know Perth is prohibiterd around Perth for natives and half cast it was in Saturdays pappie…" Here we get three "er" sounds in quick succession, but then the writing pulls back from the fourth that could have been "paper." The term Harris uses is both more colloquial and meaningful: "pappie" for newspaper is close to "papa," and suggests both the newspaper's implication in colonial paternalism and the construction of Indigenous infantilism. Harris then makes an expressive, misspelled pun on "discussed": "Last year in Parliament House they disgust where they should give halfcasts a vote or not." The misspelling of "halfcasts" also aligns it with "disgust," enforcing Harris's disgust for the term, as well as evoking Parliament's disgust for half-castes: and the ambiguous sense of "half cast" out of society. In another rhythmic move, Harris truncates Aboriginal into the colloquial "Abo" for rhyming purposes: "Now you see yourself where is the Abo. got a fare go." Since this rhetorical question leads directly to a statement detailing where an Aboriginal cannot go, the spelling of "fare" suggests a ticket an Aboriginal can't buy. The full stop after "Abo." acknowledging abbreviation, literally stops the "Abo." The disallowance cited by Harris, "not to camp on revers [rivers]," suggests both the reserves where Aboriginal people were sent to, and the reverse that Aboriginal people were suffering under settlement; whereas Harris's use of the word "Proctor" for Protector is, with its disciplinary and religious connotations, a more accurate term than the euphemistic official one (25). More crucially, in the list of "Questions within the meaning on the Act" (that has given Harris "a headache thinking about," 26), and elsewhere in the "Letter...," Harris continually spells "there" as "their," supporting the statement-question "The country belongs to him [the native]"? (27), affirming that it is "theirs." In a final example, "as" also becomes possessive as "has."

There is a persistent knowledge of dispossession in Harris's text, with its particular practice of literacy, that is not—and could not be in this fashion—produced by standard English texts. Harris has a flair for phrasing, and an ironic, and at times grim, sense of humor that may be read in expressions such as, "their was hell to pop over that," "In the North has you know they were never given wages just work for a kick in the sturn and a little tucker such has it is," and "What dose their food consist of, I bleave Billy Goats"? (25, 26, 27). The extent that Harris's language is style or accident (like the unpleasantness of the food in "dose" for "does," and "bleave" in relation to "Billy Goats" as synthesis of "believe" and "bleat") is difficult to discern, pointing to the lability of language, which, in a settlement context, could be said to support the "un"settler.

Throughout the "Letter...," Harris expresses a concern for the welfare of Aboriginal people in Western Australia. As a farmer, he embodies a contradiction to Chief Protector of Aborigines A. O. Neville's paraphrased pronouncement that "it was no good giveing natives land because they would not work it" (26). Harris writes, "How are you getting on with your cropping, we haven't started putting any in yet. I was doing some rolling before that rain it settled the burn, although I set it alight last Sunday I may be able to plough it in" (27). In fighting for Aboriginal community he is no supporter of settlement, settlement being dependent on the exclusion of Aboriginal people from the land; yet Harris has what might be called a plural relation to the land, one that includes the adoption of white settlement practices. He isn't agitating for his own rights, or for those of farmer's, however.

In Harris the use of question marks is notable. In the "Letter..." they are not used: for example, "thats rotten what do you say Jim," and "thoes who dont pay what do you think ought to be done to them" (25, 27). But whether the questions listed in "Questions" were punctuated by Harris or added by an editor, they mark the nonrhetorical nature of the "Questions" themselves, the "Why?," "Who?," "How?," "Is?" and "Do?" that Harris asks in relation to the treatment of Aboriginal people. The repetition of question marks points to the humdrum of the everyday. Bob Hodge and Vijay Mishra cite evidence, however, that according to a popular satire of Australian culture, "asking questions is the one thing a true Australian never does" (137). Even the "how are you" that commonly substitutes for a greeting in Australia often expects no answer. The everyday that Harris refers to questions that of settler culture: "Does children have to work?," "Why shouldn't a native have land?," "Why is he a prisnor in any part of the State?" The exceptional inclusion of statements within Harris's list of questions are given more force because they are exceptions: "He can be arrested without a warrant" and "I bleave girls were tied with chains to get punished." Question marks complicate the notion of silent punctuation. Not only does the question mark affect the inflection of the word preceding the mark, but also the word following which commences the next question. In other words, punctuation is implicated in Harris's prosody, an aspect of poetics defined by Charles O. Hartman as "the poet's method of controlling the reader's temporal experience of the poem, especially his attention to that experience" (13). In terms of poetics there is a distinction between the "Letter..." and the "Questions." The latter is more emphatic and less personal, more of an activist's assemblage of evidence; whereas the former is more personal, more intimate in its address, and more complex in its thinking through the political situation of Aboriginal people. Harris's text as a whole performs question marks. The unsettling questions that his and Mackellar's texts ask relate not just to the construction of Australia's nationalist colonial poetics, but also to our understanding of the relation between colonial and global poetics, and the histories of genres such as concrete and prose poetries, networked as they are with other forms of writing, such as letters and diaries.

CHAPTER 5

Boredom

Charles Harpur's "Note to the Song of 'Good Night'" and Mary Fullerton's "Bromide"

"Note to the Song of 'Good Night.'" Written 1850; in Mitchell 1973
"Bromide." Written 1945, unpublished

Australia was never meant to be fun. It was designed to be a prison: a convict settlement where England's victims were sent "to pine their young lives away in starvation and misery" (Kelly 67). Historian Russel Ward records the high level of drunkenness in mid-nineteenth-century Australia, but suggests that this was a result of the "loneliness of bush life, no less than the brutalities of the system," rather than boredom (32–33). Andrew McCann, however, writing on the fiction of Marcus Clarke (1846–1881), claims that, "In the nineteenth century practices of spectatorship, and of culture-consumption more generally, were closely connected to a sense of ennui and boredom" (331).

In writing of boredom in the context of settlement, I am not merely examining a deflating negative mood as a counter to jingoism, nor am I concerned with the unsettling nature of boredom as such, as expressed by Hegel: "the frivolity and boredom which unsettle the established order" (Svendsen 61–62). Rather, I am concerned with how boredom affects texts and how it punctuates them: leading, in Harpur, to a dramatized running down of voice and, in Fullerton, to an emphatic underlining extended to the point of abstraction. Harpur and Fullerton, then, enact a formal dissatisfaction with the semantics and formalities of British verse as replicated in the bulk of Australian poetry, not least their own.

The two texts under discussion in this chapter stand somewhat to the side of their authors' canonized oeuvres: a short prose text written in 1850 by Charles Harpur (1813–1868), who claimed for himself the title of Australia's first poet; and an unpublished game and set of instructions from 1945 by Mary Fullerton (1868–1946), included in a letter to her sister Emily and the novelist Miles Franklin, a year before Fullerton's death. Both writers have established reputations as colonial poets. There are chapters devoted to them in recent critical histories: on Harpur by Paul Kane, and on Fullerton by Ann Vickery. Harpur's is an assemblage of scenes in discrete paragraphs, a prose poem of collaged diction; Fullerton's is a literary diversion: a found, archive-assemblage of complementary or networked lines. I examine their punctuation and establish an implicit network between these two texts by reading them both as responses to boredom: through an explicit connection to alcohol, in Harpur's case, and to sedatives in Fullerton's.

Harpur wrote voluminously, and published regularly, in order to establish himself as Australia's national poet. Fullerton is a more complex case, having been less prolific and publically less prominent, in part an effect of using pseudonyms, and of becoming an expatriate. Her oeuvre is more complex, having published both memoir and a work titled *The Australian Comic Dictionary of Words* under the pseudonym Turner O'Lingo (Vickery 117). The dictionary, like much of Harpur's verse, satirizes settlement, but ultimately neither offers a challenge to the settlement of English literature in Australia. I don't mean to disparage the normative poetry of Harpur or Fullerton, but rather to unsettle their (relatively recently attained) canonical positions through an examination of exceptional texts. Both works suggest—complexly—the boredom of the English version of Australian life; Fullerton's game, titled "Bromide," further suggests the boredom inherent in English literature. Harpur dramatizes boredom with poetry, in writing what appears to be a prose poem, and narrating a becoming-animal that must be saved by God from drink. Fullerton's "Bromide" is an entertainment for her friends in Australia, yet its name suggests the opposite of entertainment or stimulation.

Elizabeth Perkins, editor of the large volume of *The Poetical Works of Charles Harpur*, writes that:

No historical account can supply the kind of record of the political struggles of the [eighteen] forties and fifties that is found in Harpur's verse. Without necessarily sympathising with Harpur's point of view, the reader finds that a poem...elaborates or neatly sums up the principles which underlay opposition to or support of a government proposal or public practice in the colony. (xxi)

Harpur is exemplary as a poet who supports Mead's "previous model of Australian literature." Nevertheless, plural knowledges of writing can be found in this one, uncharacteristic text, "Note to the Song of '"Good Night.'" In this "Note" Harpur performs his "dissatisfaction with...the overly settled idea of the "ordinariness" of ordinary, or everyday language" (Mead 5). Although, arguably, Harpur's verse also does this (his vocabulary is wide and occasionally startling), it does not perform dissatisfaction to the extent that the "Note" does. The "Note" plays out the "drama" of life and spirit, a conflict also perceived by Brennan. In his "Literature and Melodrama" chapter of *The Oxford Literary History of Australia*, Robert Dixon records Brennan's formulation:

"The true thinker," Brennan argued, "perceives in the world a continued drama" between life and spirit; life consists "not merely of high movements and hours of insight, such as give birth to poetry, it consists also of days, weeks and calendar months of dullness and mediocrity." (79)

In other words, boredom. Nietzsche, in the *Gay Science*, also refers to this state of affairs:

For the thinker and for all inventive spirits, boredom is that disagreeable "lull" of the soul that precedes a happy voyage and cheerful winds; he has to endure it, must *await* its effect on him—precisely that is what lesser natures are totally unable to achieve! To fend off boredom at any price is vulgar, just as work without pleasure is vulgar. (57)

Nietzsche's formulation could be said to oppose Brennan's. Brennan writes that "high movements and hours of insight...give birth to poetry," whereas Nietzsche, in writing that artists and thinkers, "do not fear boredom as much as work without pleasure; indeed, they need a lot of boredom if *their work* is to succeed," places more emphasis on the boredom itself (Nietzsche's italics; 57). In her book on *Boredom*, Patricia Spacks writes, "Persistently it has associated itself with ideas of victimization and entrapment...Almost always it suggests disruptions of desire: the inability to desire or to have desire fulfilled," adding that "boredom in its verbal renditions usually masks another condition" (x). Neither Harpur nor Fullerton verbalize boredom as such, though in Harpur's text there is both the sense of "entrapment" and of "another condition" being masked: layers of masks—of the animal, of alcoholism, of frustration. In any case, in 1850 "boredom" as such had not yet been coined; Spacks writes that though there were "bores" in the eighteenth century, "the first citation of the noun *boredom* belongs to 1864" (13). A century later Fullerton ironically titled her quoting game "Bromide," writing in the accompanying "rules," that it was "an in-bed sedative exercise." As well as a sedative, a bromide can be a "bore" or "trite remark" (Concise 115), and is almost an anagram of boredom. Unlike Harpur who seeks pleasure and finds despair, Fullerton actually seeks boredom and finds pleasure. In the accompanying letter she writes, "I think it's a beauty for the right people." That a bromide is a "trite remark" further ironizes the name, as the game is made of quotes from literature.

We can compare Harpur with Spacks's example of Samuel Johnson's *Rasselas*, where the "prince's situation in the Happy Valley...dramatizes boredom's ravages." In Happy Valley, Spacks notes, "'Every desire was immediately granted'": "The concept of the Happy Valley makes vacancy and tediousness inevitable, since the granting of all desires...devitalizes experience...Rasselas compares himself with a beast, noting that, 'I am, like him, pained with want, but am not, like him, satisfied with fullness.'" Spacks summarizes this condition again in terms of desire: "The unfulfilled desire that creates boredom is the desire for desire" (46–47). Johnson's solution in the novel is that Rasselas and his companions "admit...fancy" into their desires: "desires," as Spacks writes, "that they know cannot be satisfied" (49). The policeman featured in Harpur's anecdote expresses a simplified version of this. However fast the racehorses go he wants them to "*go faster.*" He admits they are already "first rate!," but he requires the impossible "fancy." At the close of the text, Harpur seems to propose to himself the impossible condition (requiring God's help) that he give up drinking. If he can maintain a sober state, he may then be satisfied: by not satisfying himself. Drinking would then become the impossible desire that might relieve his boredom. He could then recover agency, able to feel "active" rather than "acted upon" (Spacks 34). The writing of the "Note" is itself active. Was Harpur at that moment bored with verse? The "Note" read on its own terms, as a vow to stop writing such notes, can also be read as: I must settle down and get on with writing the verse that will make me the nation's poet. Mead claims that poetry "has an afterlife in subsequent and changing cultural contexts" (1). This changing context may give a text new life as poetry.

The "Note," an uncharacteristically short, and surprisingly carnivalesque, page of text, was not included in Perkins's large, scholarly edition; but was included by Adrian Mitchell in his slim, earlier selection (134).

The "Note" was perhaps unrevised by Harpur: as, according to Perkins, "Harpur invariably lengthened any poem he revised" (xxxiv). It is an assemblage that performs its own disassembly and acknowledges its breakdown with performative punctuation. It consists of three paragraphs and reads like a prose poem. The first paragraph is explanatory, in fitting with the work's title of a "Note." Apparently autobiographical, Harpur writes that he composed a drinking song following the memorable performance of another drinking song during a "carouse." The second paragraph consists of a reported anecdote, which quotes a policeman who wants racehorses (that are "acknowledged" to have "performed...splendaciously") to *"go faster"* [Harpur's italics]. The third paragraph compares Harpur's desire for alcohol to that of the policeman's desire; Harpur "cannot enjoy [it] at a moderate pace"—he "want[s] to see everything *go faster*": not at the sensible, hardworking pace of settlement, but at the wild pace of carnival. This tactic is not necessarily a defense against reader boredom. As Barthes writes in *The Pleasure of the Text*, the "modern text" requires an *"applied* reading." He further refers to—and resists in the modern case—the "belief that one need merely *go fast* in order not to be bored" (Barthes's italics; 12). It is at this moment in the text that Harpur moves from the past tense of the reported anecdote to the present tense of his dissatisfaction, thus fulfilling the modern as described by Sianne Ngai: "To be modern it seems, is to be addicted to surprise and speed, to jolts of adrenalin and temporal rupture: to be a shockaholic" (121). Harpur, then, is perhaps trying to outpace boredom, before all meaning is lost. In *A Philosophy of Boredom*, Lars Svendsen writes that "If boredom increases, it means that there is a serious fault in society or culture as a conveyor of meaning" (22). Svendsen figures an addiction to meaning, likening boredom to "meaning withdrawal" (30). Yet boredom itself has been blamed for destructive effects: Kierkegaard writes that "Since boredom advances and boredom is the root of all evil, no wonder, then, that the world goes backwards, that evil spreads" (Goodstein 18). In milder terms, Martin Waugh observes that "When we are bored...there seems to be only an endless present" (Spacks 19). A reverse notion is that if we know nothing of history the present will be boring: in other words, boredom as an effect of contemporary ignorance.

Not only is Harpur's third paragraph written in the present tense, it is deliberately slowed down. Harpur unsettles his own text, deliberately disrupting and fragmenting the syntax as if the words in his head *"go faster"* than he can put them down: "...Hence accrues my peculiar peril: Sot respectably, like a prudent profess...I cannot. To *dram it*, like a tinker...me...sleep over it, would bloat m...me." It mimics the slurring and wandering concentration of drunkenness. The paragraph and text conclude with a vow to stop drinking, the date "24th day of March, 1850" and a final phrase: "God Help me!" Perkins records that Harpur "for a time worked industriously to change the Singleton Temperance Society into a Total Abstinence Society," adding that "This conscientious extremism is typical of Harpur's life, for he had several bouts of intemperance, although he mastered the problem in a way that...other eminent men of the time could not" (xx). An earlier poem, "The Drunkard" from 1842, begins: "Disease was lurking in the cup!," the drunkard is "betray[ed]" by a "bacchanalian troop." It continues, "hellward":

> Yet, could he but forbear to raise
> The hellward-hastening draught again,
> Time yet might quench the lurid blaze,
> The fiery serpent in his brain! (761–762)

Harpur's text is "carnivalesque": his "'licensed' (authorised)" poet behavior has become that of "'licence' (excess)" (Stallybrass and White 34). Rather than his usual modes of letting off indignant steam, or aspiring to Romantic verse (Perkins 343, 347), it is the poetics of carnival and transgression that are foremost in the "Note." Perkins writes:

> Harpur believed he was innovative and original to the limits of poetic freedom, but his passionate respect for the tradition of the best English poetry circumscribed his creativity in form and technique. He would have shown a more truly creative genius had he produced poetry in which form and tone were more closely related to the milieu in which it was written, or to the ruggedness of his own mind. (xxix)

The "Note" fulfills Perkins's criteria of being "more closely related to his milieu" and "to the ruggedness of his own mind." Read in conjunction with the "Note," both these characterizations suggest an outdoors "milieu," such as the racetrack or the "rugged" mountains of the "pard": Harpur writes, following the mimetic ellipses of the "Note," "while to be as wild as I generally am when under its [strong drink's] influence—wild as a mountain pard, is nearly as low and brutal and far more perilous." "The Note" arguably fulfills Baudelaire's notion of "a poetic prose...rugged enough to adapt itself to the lyrical impulses of the soul" (Fredman 4). It enacts the "high and low" of carnival from one paragraph to the next, and in doing so as a literary conceit, proves itself not really low, nor really high (Stallybrass and White 3). If we take it that the "wild"ness is Harpur's, then it appears that the *not* "wild"—the slow, slurring drunkenness that the "Note" mimes—is not his, but a performance of how others' drunkenness manifests. The figure Harpur uses to illustrate wildness, "a mountain pard," is not a local reference, but a literary one. In Keats's "Ode To A Nightingale" pards are associated with revelry: they pull Bacchus's chariot (291). They are both trained and wild. It is also an archaic term for leopard (Concise 743).

When Harpur says he must settle himself and "give up...the liberty of drinking," he both denies and affirms the use of this literary, foreign simile. Harpur enacts the "catastrophe" of his life in speech; he "breaks his own dictation" (Agamben 83). Yet, paradoxically, language is the stay against this catastrophe. Giorgio Agamben writes in *The End of the Poem* that "poetry and life...are united...in a medium. This medium is language" (93). In similar terms, Stephen Fredman, in *Poet's Prose*, writes that "When the theoretical bases for both literature and philosophy are shaken, poets [and] philosophers...turn of necessity to the medium that remains...language" (6). In the "Note," Harpur represents his grapple with drinking and with writing, trying for the sake of his poetry and his life to bring them both under control. He is not "a profess[or]" or "a tinker" (that, punning on a "tinker's damn," "drams" it); he is "*like* the Policeman" and "wild *as* a mountain pard" [my italics]. He has no identity but the composing "I." But there is also identity in the ellipses of the "broken" "dictation": in the "...me..." and "m...me." It is at the point where he uses "me" and the second broken "m...me," that we lose the sense of these sentences. It is here that Harpur gives up the semantic. In *Punctuation: Art, Politics and Play*, Jennifer DeVere Brody argues for the ellipse to be "rethought as an active agent...the mark that hails the reader as a participant," suggesting that it is "ambivalent, enigmatic, paradoxical—the presence of absence" (71, 73). In these terms, then, Harpur performs self-obliteration in favor of punctuation and the reader, only to return, denying "liberty" and calling on "God." Harpur's use of the word "liberty" is ironic: his "Note" represents him as being under compulsion and lacking control when drinking. If "Life is what is made in speech and what remains indistinguishable from it and close to it" (Agamben 78), this is Harpur's "catastrophe" reduced to a "Note"; it is the "me" that is lost in elliptical speech, that mime: or "m...me."

The "Note" is far from "traditional English verse"; but not so far from the French tradition, being contemporary with the prose poems of Baudelaire who, according to David Lehman, "inaugurated the genre in France" in 1862 (13). According to Jonathan Monroe, the prose poem tends both to and from fragmentation, starting with precursors such as the German poet Friedrich Schlegel 50 years earlier: "the prose poem characteristically gestures toward both unity and sameness and toward fragmentation and difference" (269). As influenced as Harpur was by the English Romantics, he could also be critical of them: the prose poem represents "a reaction against the[ir] expressive effusiveness" (279). The "Note"'s relation to a drinking song also connects it with an earlier tradition of Greek lyric. Greek lyric poets were known for their drinking songs (Campbell 233). In its fragmentation, the "Note" resembles translations of Greek lyric fragments, such as "39" in David A. Campbell's versions of Alcaeus. In Campbell's English this consists of eight lines of words and phrases (12 in the original Greek), including the isolated word "wine" (255). Another comparable fragment is "255," reduced from eight lines to two in Campbell's version (327).

The "Note"'s prose form makes it a "fugitive piece" and an apparent exception within Harpur's oeuvre. Yet his poem "The Kangaroo Hunt" also employs prose: the verse is supplemented by a five-page prose introduction and an extensive prose commentary (453–510); Perkins admits to omitting further "prose attachments" (x). Monroe argues that the prose poem is a "dialogic genre." He writes that Baudelaire's prose poetry "appears...to be directed primarily against the inherited formal and thematic conventions of the verse lyric," adding that Rimbaud "stage[s] an even more explicit critique and projection of poetry-as-verse...as well as a critique of prose undreamed of by Baudelaire" (39). The prose poem is an unsettled, in-between genre: not just between prose and poetry, but "between the largest and smallest units of writing, the novel...and the epigram" (249). That the epigram is the smallest "unit of writing" is debatable, but Monroe's formula does suggest something of the abstraction and looseness of the prose poem that distinguishes it from contemporary genres like micro fiction.

The drama of prose against verse—and against itself—is played out by this short text. The text appears to critique its own prosaic introductory paragraph, and uses speech (the Policeman's) to dialogue with the narrator's own state, and, finally, expresses a further division between selves. With reference to Baudelaire, Monroe posits that the prose poem's dialogic nature is not only formal, but political, "allowing us to see that the problem of the individual's integration into a genuine collective society is none other than a *generic* problem, a problem fundamentally of gender and class struggle" (Monroe's italics; 27). There is a class aspect to alcoholism, but this is not explicit in Harpur. There does seem to be a gendered class-related inflection, however. He appeals to the Policeman's working-class camaraderie, referring to their dialogue as one between "comrades." Yet though the narrator is "like the Policeman" he is not one, and the Policeman's group of comrades only emphasizes Harpur's apparent loss of the "kindly and harmonious" gatherings of friends. He fails to insert himself into a lineup of other men and their occupations: "Sot respectably, like a prudent profess...I cannot." Harpur as poet represents an in-between profession. Spacks writes that boredom is associated with the middle-class (6); while Barthes denies that neither bliss nor "relish for language" are bourgeois: the "bourgeoisie" regarding language "merely as an instrument of decor" (Pleasure 38). Barthes adds: "the work is finally always written by a socially disappointed or powerless group...literature is the expression of this disappointment" (39). This description is difficult to argue with, especially with regard to Australian colonial literature, and fits Harpur in particular; despite his profile as a much-published writer, with poems dedicated to statesmen friends like Henry Parkes—impressive achievements by a son of convicts—he remains disappointed (Kane 51).

A "professor is someone who finishes his sentences" (Barthes 50). Harpur cannot "sot," nor write sentences, "respectably": he cannot even complete naming the professor's profession. He cannot descend to the less respectable "tinker" who "*dram*[s]" alcohol, either. His style of drinking enacts rather a stepping outside the human class, to be a leopard. This transformation is both romantic and aspirational, offering Harpur a self-image outside that of merely being a working man. Here Harpur demonstrates another aspect of the prose poem: that it "is both a utopian genre and a genre of ongoing utopian self-critique" (Monroe 31). Yet this moment is immediately dashed, expressing a despair that is yet another symptom of boredom (Spacks 11).

Horses were the topos of Australian colonial poetry, and we may readily substitute the horses in the "Note" for poetry. How can Harpur get his poetry to go faster? Through rhyming prose, and dashes: "'Yes,' he replied, 'they run well—capitally—first-rate!—I can't deny that, mate',", and through the fragmented ellipses quoted above. He cannot enjoy poetry "at a moderate pace." The lyric is not "wild" enough, yet his prose breaks down. In his introduction to *Great American Prose Poems*, Lehman writes that the prose poem offers a "feeling of escape or release from tradition or expectation" (23). But to Harpur this freedom soon appears to be "perilous" and must be given up, "God help" him. This is the "utopian death wish" of Harpur, and of the prose poem itself (Monroe 42). Harpur lacks proximity to a tradition of literature: the target of Baudelaire and Rimbaud. Monroe writes, "Fragmentation of form in [Rimbaud's] 'Mauvais sang' and *Une saison en enfer* generally corresponds to the...emphasis on the collapse of faith in the Old Christian order and the problem of constructing a new order" (129). Such disassembly and performed despair in Harpur are not that of a nation-building first poet, and yet, correspond to what Perkins calls his "conscientious extremism" (xx).

In a less desperate mode, Harpur composed a long poem on "The 'Nevers' of Poetry," including instructions relating to prose that imply its distinctness from poetry. The poem begins: "*Never* say aught in Verse, or grave or gay, / That you in Prose would hesitate to say." Toward the end, the poem proposes a variation: "And *never* let aught pass your bardic nose / As sweet in verse, that would smell vile in prose" (Harpur's italics; 143, 150). Harpur's "The "Nevers," resemble Pound's later "A Few Don'ts By an Imagiste," in particular, "Don't imagine that a thing will 'go' in verse just because it's too dull to go in prose" (205). Harpur suggests a double movement of poetry composition: that the sounds and smells of saying and thinking present first in prose. There are thoughts in the "Note" that Harpur "hesitates to say," but the hesitation is deliberate, performative; yet perhaps such hesitation is more fitting in prose. Harpur concludes the "Note" by vowing to give up drinking: "And so I *must* give up; and *have* given up henceforth for ever, the liberty of drinking any and every intoxicating beverage," and dates it, as if making a contract with God. We may become intoxicated through our noses as well as our mouths, and perhaps the very intoxication of poetry makes "aught" smell "sweet," that when in more sober, prosaic mood "would smell vile."

Unlike many of his poems, where it is the squatters, politicians, and journalists being skewered, in the "Note" Harpur's target is himself. Under this attack, the self crumbles, and the form of the text does also. The text performs the failing of meaning. As Elizabeth Goodstein writes in *Experience Without Qualities: Boredom and Modernity*, "Self and world collapse in a nihilistic affirmation that nothing means, nothing pleases, nothing matters" (1). While the "Note"'s semantic content points to the problem of drinking, the form of the text points to the problem of expressive prose: the genre trouble caused by a confrontation between desire and despair and the need to represent these feelings not just in words but in expressive form, when no form seems wild enough and only slows down. The very word "me" is strung out using an ellipse, and is perhaps about to go diabolically backward. This is an enactment of the "gesture toward a genreless genre" (Monroe 280). The "Note"'s conclusion is Harpur's tortured moment, where he calls on God to bring him back to the verse genre that is his forte. How sincere is Harpur's appeal? Baudelaire's view was that "modern life...is characterized by boredom or ennui," claiming that "Ennui is not so much sin as the state of sin" (Frye 51)—a state that Harpur appeals to God to escape. Yet appeals to God may also be interpreted as symptoms: "Boredom is part of the Logos too. You choose His word instead of someoneelse's [sic] because you are bored" (Spicer 304).

The "Note"'s attention to, and dramatization of, prose rhythm both constitute poetic prosody while avoiding metre. Deleuze states that "desire concerns speed and slownesses," going on to say "*desire only exists when assembled or machined*" (Deleuze's italics; Dialogues 95–96), while McCann writes specifically of colonial desire in terms of "commodity capitalism":

> ...the consumption of commodities implies the movement of desire through an otherwise prosaic and mundane world of utility and cyclical work-day patterns, the craving for more extreme experiences indexes the onslaught of a monotony... (331)

In other words, boredom was alternately fostered and catered to by capitalism, to make it "go." The spectacle of the races, drinking with friends, are normative entertainments that enable most people to bear their lives and keep working. Harpur is comparable to the novelist Clarke, McCann's example: "But if Clarke continually reminds his public how mundane their world is, he also bemoans the lack of truly stimulating spectacles, reproducing this economy of desire, consumption and spectatorship as the logic of his own prose" (332).

In the "Note" Harpur has narratively, rhetorically, and graphically "constructed" his desire. Yet his concluding invocation to God suggests another desire. Deleuze states that, "The process of desire is called 'joy,' not lack or demand. Everything is permitted, except what would come and break up the integral process of desire, the assemblage" (100). This corresponds to Monroe's claim regarding the prose poem's aspiration to "hybridization of 'fusion'," that yet "aspires also to a breakdown of generic, textual, and class barriers" (269). That which "would come and break up...desire, the assemblage" is what Harpur calls on, that is, "God." It is God that Harpur appears to lack and desire; however, the paradox here is that God has been incorporated into the assemblage. Again the "Note" is paradoxical: the plea for intervention is part of the contrivance of the "Note." Harpur transgresses through mimetic drunkenness, and by breaking the rules of normative grammar, yet by returning "to his senses" at the end of the text (by dating it, and calling on God), he demonstrates he has no need of God (or editor). In other words, the text performs Harpur's exclusion from both the human and textual (or genre) communities, yet it performs his/its redemption at its conclusion. Different kinds of rules, of breakings down and up, of self, of settlement, of assemblages, indicate different possibilities of disassembly and reassembly and demonstrate the provisionality of rules. But to return to the form of the prose poem: it is the poem that does not break, having no lines. The solidity of its prose structure is what allows for the representation of breaking within it, and why it was considered a revolutionary form, if no longer (Monroe 333). But perhaps it is the prose poem's reliance on the sentence and on content that produced its ultimate failure to become the "genreless genre," becoming rather what Fredman has called the "last genre" (3).

Harpur strives to put himself beyond criticism throughout the text: by blaming alcohol; by comparing himself to the law, the law's own desire being as his; by breaking down any substantive sign of writer or narrator (how to critique a "me"?—a two-letter word that has yet been fragmented further); and by taking on the role of the wild pard, thus putting himself out of reach of the human realm. In Nietzsche's terms, Harpur needs no "moral disguise": "It is not the ferocity of the beast of prey that needs a moral disguise, but the herd animal with its deep mediocrity, fear, and boredom with itself" (210). Harpur is opposed to the law and its herd of horses running in circles; he enacts rather a model for the law's desire as represented by the Policeman's desire for the spectacle to exceed itself. This enactment results in an excess of anxiety leading to breakdown. There is then a safety in boredom (the enclosure of the racetrack) that Harpur doesn't want to relinquish. Introducing the *Macquarie PEN* anthology, Nicholas Jose writes, in the context of "challenge[s to] convention and the status quo" within the history of Australian literature:

> Sometimes, combining terms that are unsettled and open to redefinition, Australian literature has a do-it-yourself quality...This may explain the open endedness and formal indeterminacy of many of the most intriguing works. Australian literature can even seem to be a fugitive phenomenon...(5, 6)

Jose points to literature that might be outside his anthology: in the "Note," Harpur abandons his verse models for a "do-it-yourself" approach. The performative aspects of the text contradict its ostensible status as merely an author's note on composition. Its exclusion from Perkins's edition emphasizes its fugitive status; further, it enacts Harpur being on the run from himself, though the success of his escape is ambiguous.

Almost a century later, Fullerton's literary quoting game "Bromide" also sought escape from the self: the awake self. "Bromide" was included in a letter to her sister Emily and Miles Franklin in Australia. Fullerton had been living in London since 1922. Though undated, the game and letter is placed with another letter from 1945, and has been ascribed that year by the State Library of Victoria, who keep part of Fullerton's archive. "Bromide," as a late text by Fullerton, is much later than most of the primary texts discussed in this book, and unsettles an easier notion of the colonial as pre–World War II. It is the only one not actually written in Australia, though it presumably relies on memories of reading in Australia, and it targets an

Australian audience: one perhaps made to appreciate the recontextualized or reterritorialized fragments of "Bromide." It therefore relies on a colonial reading relation. Fullerton is thought of as a colonial poet: she was born, coincidentally, in the year of Harpur's death, 1868, and is a contemporary of the canonical colonial generation of Banjo Paterson (1864–1941), Mary Gilmore (1865–1962), Henry Lawson (1867–1922), Christopher Brennan (1870–1932), and John Shaw Neilson (1872–1942). She was a generation older than Dorothea Mackellar and published her first book of poetry, *Moods and Melodies*, in 1908.

The game can be considered an example of the "little" referred to in the title of Fullerton's 1942 poetry volume, *Moles Do So Little with Their Privacy*, published under the pseudonym "E." In her chapter on Fullerton from *Stressing the Modern*, Vickery suggests that the title refers to "the actual boredom of an underground life" (114), further citing Fullerton's poem, "Biography":

Let us be glad we are not great.
But merely hedge folk, you and I
So no inquisitor shall come
To filch our privacy.

Vickery claims that "The sentiment here seems double-edged, at once glad for the privacy to be alone but also slightly regretful she was not offered the opportunity to be otherwise" (116). Again this is Barthes's idea of literature as an "expression of disappointment." The lines quoted also suggest a boring self, or boredom with the self. "Bromide" is an escape from self through quoting the lyrics of others, including the explicit fictional others that are Shakespeare's characters. Leonard Diepeveen argues, regarding such collaging, in *Changing Voices*, "The poet cannot avoid having a shaping intelligence show through. No quoting poem can therefore totally escape the lyric" (109).

The collage poem is prominent in American modernist poetry, and it has become a persistent, if under-acknowledged, feature of Australian contemporary poetry, but examples prior to Fullerton's 1945 text are scarce. One example is the "Notices" section of Brennan's *Musicopoematographoscope*, written in 1897, which consists of fragments from press "notices," or reviews, of his work and comments from his friend and addressee Dowell O'Reilly (see following chapter). The main text from this work, a pastiche of Mallarmé's "Un Coup de Dés," could also be said to participate in the genre of collage, as could Mallarmé's text: using, as it does, different typefaces, and disrupting linearity. The most notorious example of collage in Australian poetry history is the poetry of the fictional Ern Malley, produced just two years earlier than "Bromide" in 1943. Malley's hoaxing inventors, James McAuley and Harold Stewart collaged the poems from dictionaries, Shakespeare, and a report on mosquitoes (Mead 99–100). Although both the Brennan and Malley collages have social, extraliterary aspects, neither are games as such, despite Brennan's description of his text as a "NOVELTY" (9), and Michael Heyward's of the Malley hoax as a parlor game (109).

Collage itself has been referred to as a "game of meaning" (McBride 249). In *The Surrealist Collage in Text and Image*, which notes a number of poetry games practiced by the Surrealists (13, 50), Elza Adamowicz writes that "collage is a cosmogonic game...a playful activity and hence a liberating force, freeing collagist and addressee from perceptions blunted by clichés, codes and causality..." (25). Fullerton's intention, however, was not to free the reader from cliché, but rather, as a writer-player, to soothe oneself with, to indulge in the highbrow cliché of quotes from the classics. Her game stands in ironic contrast to the Malley parlor game, with its relatively more aggressive tactics, which resulted in court cases (Mead 87–185).

As Fullerton frames it, "Bromide" is a sleep-inducing game/text, a calming activity in a life that is far from boring: the accompanying letter is full of incident regarding the weather, herself and others (though we may well ironize the fact that the weather is the most interesting thing about wartime England). Spacks notes the traditional obligation of women to be entertaining in their letters. In a chapter on eighteenth-century middle-class women, "'Self is a Tiresome Subject'," she writes that "Their letters embody as well as narrate the escape from boredom" (92); and that they "accept[ed] the obligation of keeping their own letters from tedium" (98).

The archived text containing "Bromide" is an assemblage made of a letter, the rules to the game, and an example of the game itself. In Wittgenstein's terms, of course, all three parts are language-games, with descending levels of information giving and self-expression. These descents differ as I show here:

Highest level of information		*Lowest*
Rules	Letter	Game
Highest level of self-expression		*Lowest*
Letter	Rules	Game

The above interpretation is, however, open to revision. The letter provides information about the weather, and this is relatively objective, as Fullerton quotes from a weather report (though she records a rather poetical quote: "irregular hunks of ice as large as apples"). Yet what we consider useful information depends on framing. The diagram above assumes that "information" relates to the "world." But if we want information about Fullerton herself the problem becomes more difficult. The game gives us information about her reading, tastes, and memory (both content and accuracy). The letter tells us where she lives ("Sandbank"), about her leg ailment, her friends, how the weather affects her. Again, if we want information about English literature, the order shifts again: with the game being the most informative, followed by the rules, then the letter—which provides virtually none, if we exclude information about the author herself. The rules are not completely objective either. They "may," according to Fullerton, "be flexible"; they contain expressions such as "liberty" and "bad form"; the examples of words given are suggestive: "rose," "life," and "pleasure=dome" [sic]; and Fullerton both "bar[s] Script=ure [sic]" and emphasizes Shakespeare. She writes, "It should be bad form to quote overmuch from <u>one</u> author or <u>one</u> poem. I would except Shakespere [sic] from that—possibly make it a virtue to call greatly on him." (Fullerton's use of "=" recalls *The Case*; she uses them in place of hyphens or dashes, but not consistently.) It might be more useful to think of the three parts of letter, rules, and game as descending in levels of affect. The game seems to empty—or parody—the level of affect in the other two texts. For example, the underlining, which adds emphasis in both the letter and rules, becomes structural rather than emphatic in the game.

"Bromide" is played solo or in a "round." It is begun by quoting a line from literature, including nursery rhymes et cetera, according to the rules (Fullerton predominantly quotes from Shakespeare and other English poets such as Tennyson and Wordsworth). Recording the quote's author is part of the game. This is followed by another line that uses a word from the first. Fullerton appends a game she has played/composed of 100 lines. The game begins as follows:

1. Sumer is icumin <u>in</u>.	Unknown. about 1250
2. All <u>Summer in</u> the bag of a <u>bee</u>	Browning
3. <u>Where</u> the <u>Bee</u> sucks…in the cowslip bell I lie	Shakespere
4. Go <u>where Glory</u> waits thee	Moore
5. We left him alone in his <u>Glory</u>	Wolfe
6. Alone, <u>alone</u>, all all alone alone on a wide wide <u>sea</u>	Coleridge

The game continues for one hundred lines that create a collage, and suggest a self-portrait of the reader-composer's taste or reading history. Almost every line except the first and the last has two underlined words: the word that is replicated in the line above, and the word replicated in the line below. The exceptions are times when Fullerton quotes more than one word from one line to the next, or because of oversight underlines more or less than the rules demand. She appears to have misquoted both lines 2 and 3. The line from Robert Browning, from his poem "Summum Bonum," runs: "All the breath and the bloom of the year in the bag of one bee" (879): here Fullerton turns a year into a season; and in line 3 from Shakespeare's *The Tempest*, "a" becomes "the," and the possessive "s" from "cowslip's" is omitted (Shakespeare 18). As she writes, "Naturally no references, anthologies or other books used." Though technically line 2 still fits—as it contains the word "in," it is more likely that the misremembered word "Summer" prompted the use of line 2—the words Fullerton chooses as connectors are usually verbs or nouns, rather than prepositions like "in."

The game creates a form of internal repetition, making it a more elaborate version of a cento (a form of poem made up of quotes from other poets; traditionally, dead ones). The repetition gives the game-poem a sound structure, deemphasizing the semantics of both the lines and the underlined words. (There are traditional sound effects, however. As we see, Fullerton begins the game with several rhymes, perhaps automatically: "bee," "thee," "Glory," "sea"). Nevertheless, Fullerton points out in the rules that the example game she has completed concludes with references "welcoming <u>Night</u> and looking towards '<u>Tomorrow</u>.'" Further, perhaps unconsciously, as she doesn't refer to using it in the letter or rules, the game begins with the word "Summer," while the accompanying letter is full of descriptions of stormy summer weather. The game could be said, then, to start with an inclusion of the present and the season, a conventional beginning for any text, whether letter or haiku. Such a beginning is differently meaningful, however, when written for an audience in another hemisphere where the season will be opposite.

The first line "Sumer is icumin in" is contextually ironic, because Fullerton writes in her letter of the "Worst thunder storms & wind & heat for more than 20 years," recalling Pound's parody: "Winter is icumen in…Raineth drop and staineth slop / And how the wind doth ramm! / Sing: Goddamm" (Selected 38). Conceivably, a network could also be established between "Bromide" and Fullerton's verse through a study of allusion. The quotes in the game are lines she knows well, and are likely to appear to some degree in her verse. To give just one example, a line from an "untitled sonnet" quoted by biographer Sylvia Martin, "Better their fragrance float about your hair" (62), alludes to Coleridge and is misquoted by Fullerton as line 74 of "Bromide": "<u>Beware beware</u> his flashing, his floating hair." (She omits "eyes" which makes it ludicrously sexual.)

The form of the game performs a rejection of meter, as, though the quoted lines are metrical in their original context, out of context there is no scheme: the meter of one line is interrupted by that of the following. Fullerton interrupts meter further by using elision, for example, in line 3.

The underlining accents two words, creating an emphasis on word over syllable, while the words may or may not be emphasized in the line's original meter. The game, then, is a text in the Barthesian sense: "language without its image-reservoir" (Pleasure 33). "Bromide" empties out the English canon, remaking it as a sleeping draught for colonials resident in England and Australia. Conceptually, "Bromide" is as much a critical as it is a creative work. In *Structuralist Poetics*, Jonathan Culler, citing Barthes, assesses the role of boredom in relation to reading critically:

> A criticism which focuses on the adventures of meaning is perhaps better suited than any other to what ought to be the major task of criticism: that of making the text interesting, of combating the boredom which lurks behind every work, waiting to move in if reading goes astray or founders. "Il n'y a pas d'ennui *sincere*," says Barthes. One cannot, finally, be bored in good faith because boredom draws attention to certain aspects of the work (to particular modes of failure) and enables one to make the text interesting by inquiring how and why it bores. (262)

This negation of boredom resembles John Cage's much-quoted comment, "If something is boring after two minutes, try it for four. If still boring, then eight. Then sixteen. Then thirty-two. Eventually one discovers that it is not boring at all" (Goldsmith, "Being" 362).

Boredom, like the everyday, connotes settledness. In both Harpur and Fullerton, boredom relates directly to the notion that they are living/writing in an English or Western monoculture. In Fullerton's case, though she is literally living in England when she composes "Bromide," she presumes that "Bromide" is an apt text for her Australian audience. In the context of playing "Bromide," the composition itself becomes critical reading; yet it is not a criticism focused on semantics, but on lines and words themselves, and on their repetition in other lines from other works of literature: a network. Read as a list of well-known quotes, Fullerton"s example of "Bromide" may well seem boring, but the underlining, numbering, and citation (and error) emphasize other aspects of the text that create ongoing interest. I have only found one example of the "Bromide" form, but if a number were produced, after a while the repetition of the form itself would become boring, and the possibility of aesthetic interest might reemerge: that is, one game might seem more interesting than another. The poem-game of Bromide, with its combination of forms (numbers, lines, and author names), forms an assemblage within an assemblage. But unlike famous collage poems by Eliot, Pound, Williams, and Marianne Moore, there is no obscurity of phrasing, reference, or intent. Though the numbers and underlines etcetera might be obtrusive in a more semantically oriented text, in "Bromide" there is nothing to obtrude on. As a poetic collage, it enacts what Kenneth Goldsmith refers to as conceptual poetry's "strategies of copying and appropriation" ("Why" xviii). Considered visually, "Bromide" could, alternatively, be said to demonstrate what Ong terms "A typical visual ideal...clarity and distinctness, a taking apart" (72). Despite the chummy knowingness of "Bromide" being for "the right people," the text's errors are a counter to complacency. Though Martin writes that "one of her main concerns was her lack of education" (161), she also notes that Fullerton "embraced ambivalence and contradiction" (128); while Vickery quotes Fullerton from her "Memoirs": "the indefinite appeals to me much more than the cut and dried" (82). This conforms to Peter Quartermain's argument that, "we must keep our options open. The logical mode for the expression of such ideas, the form, is collage, for collage resists finality, resists categories and the notion of completeness" (Disjunctive 173). That Fullerton offers her completed game of "Bromide" as an example, points to it as an incomplete project.

Quartermain's version of an "assemblage" is drawn from the art context of Jean Dubuffet, and is apt in pointing to the conceptual openness of "Bromide":

> What is most striking about *assemblage*...is that its raw materials are often associationally powerful, almost always ready made, and *identifiable*...That is to say, they retain much of their previous history (their contextual residue); it is also to say, in the words of one critic that (compared to *collage*) "its ultimate configurations are so often less predetermined." (180)

"Bromide"'s "raw materials" are arguably "associationally powerful" in that they are memorable lines; further, it allows for associations (it has to start somewhere) with the present moment, or may act as a pointer toward completion, as Fullerton does with her references to "Night," for example. They are theoretically "always ready made," that is, the lines are intended to be direct quotes (unlike *The Waste Land* which deliberately mixes direct quotes with allusions, that is, indirect or altered quotes, Diepeveen 7–13). They are theoretically "identifiable," being memorable quotes, and are explicitly identified in the game's author column. Also, the "ultimate configurations" are "less predetermined" than a collage poem such as *The Waste Land*. There is no point, in fact, in editing a game-poem of "Bromide," unless for accuracy's sake.

How does this definition of assemblage fit the group of texts of letter, rules, game? It is perhaps too easy to ascribe the term to a group of texts found in a catalogue box in a library, to say that it is "associationally powerful," that it is "ready made" and "its ultimate configurations are...less predetermined": these criteria could be applied perhaps to any archived text. Continuing with Quartermain's definition, then, how "identifiable" is it? Of course it is identifiable in terms of being by Fullerton, and this possibility is already predetermined, that is, the game has already been identified. It is in an archive box with other materials by Fullerton; the contents are described in an attached note, as being the letter, the rules and the game; the enclosed texts are presumably in Fullerton's handwriting; the letter refers to the game and is signed by her. Yet there are other elements not quite as fixed. The exact date, though it has been assigned the year "1945," has not been identified, yet is presumably further "identifiable" through reference to other letters by Fullerton to Franklin, of which there are "about 800" (Martin 9), as well as through an eclipse mentioned by Fullerton, and of course, the storms. Then there is the handwriting itself: though I found most words identifiable (legible), other readers might have less—or more— trouble in reading Fullerton's writing in the letter. The writing is clearer in the rules, and the game itself. In the game, though, new issues arise. There is more support for identification of the lines as they are quotes from well-known poems (or Shakespeare's plays), and in all cases except one the author is "identified" by Fullerton (she omits the author for line 19: Omar Khayyam). Determining exactly the accuracy of Fullerton's quotation, however, requires a definite reading of Fullerton's writing. A thorough reading of the example of "Bromide" could be a fascinating exercise in textual criticism, where Fullerton's memory and supposition take on their own value.

"Bromide" demonstrates a unique method for unsettling the contents of the English canon, by literally rewriting what is most memorable in terms of the game's arbitrary requirements. It also introduces a different mode of quoting; whereas Diepeveen claims that modernists and postmodernists quote persons and texts, and L=A=N=G=U=A=G=E writers merely quote language (162–165), "Bromide"'s emphasis is on quoting memory. By quoting in a cento-like fashion, the writer-player of "Bromide" orchestrates collaboration between writers (Shakespeare et al.), but if the game is played in a round, the writer also collaborates with other players on a final collaged text. Here there may be, as well as competition, a form of seduction (or "cruising" as Barthes puts it, comparing reading to a game, Pleasure 4). Just two years after the Ern Malley scandal (itself a collaborative quoting project), Fullerton mildly lays down rules both for quotation and collaboration. The underlining (a form of punctuation) is the point as much as the quotation. The result is not intended to be aesthetic: "I favour making speed the chief aim." We see here that Fullerton also favors underlining.

Referring to the game in the accompanying letter, she writes, "extra marks for <u>author</u> & <u>poems</u> from which quotes come" and underlines her signature, "<u>Mary</u>."

Fullerton uses quotation in the letter also. Following a description of extreme weather, she writes of "'irregular hunks of ice as large as apples' (I quote report)." Later in the letter she writes, "You see we <u>have come through</u> though," presumably quoting DH Lawrence. The quotes themselves suggest another kind of game: a guessing game where naming the authors undoes the suspense. The framing of "Bromide"—its name, its game structure, its appeal to the canon, the naming of authors—smoothes out the disjunction of its collaging. The quotations' emphasis on lexical content rather than, for example, rhythm or theme, could be said to render the lines of poetry "prosaic," complicating the genre of the game-poem further, making it a prose poem composed in lines rather than in sentences. In her foregrounded use of sources, Fullerton is closer to *The Waste Land* than the antics of McAuley and Stewart. But while we can see that, if we type the game up, the numbered lines and columns give the poem a contemporary, "found" structure aspect—like a form borrowed from accounting—the poem also, being a collage from memory, resembles the oral poems of Homer, which, according to Ong, are a stitching together of clichés (22).

In "Bromide"'s rules it is curious that Fullerton offers not only as examples of words, "rose" and "life" and "pleasure=dome," but also, in admitting flexibility of grammatical form such as noun or verb, gives the example "I <u>strike</u>. a <u>strike</u>." The example enacts reversal in that she writes "noun/ or verb," yet its illustration—suggesting revolt—is in the order of verb followed by noun. Fullerton's reference to "speed" connects her text to Harpur's, and to the theories of Barthes in *The Pleasure of the Text*. She first refers to speed before she introduces the notion of "Bromide" as a round game; the designation of it as "an in-bed sedative exercise" comes between them. It is as if speed could itself speed her to sleep. Is what she is writing a "modern text," then, requiring, in Barthes's term, an "applied reading"? Not if read as a cento, an old form, but yes if read as a collage; and further, it requires an applied reading because not only does it require quoting from memory (reading the writer's own mind), it requires the "application" of underlining words. There is no slowing down if, as Fullerton suggests, "Bromide" is played as a round: there could be "prizes for speed." Fullerton, like Harpur, also refers to "liberty," but whereas he refers to the "liberty of drinking," words are Fullerton's (sedative, or pacifying) drug, "Liberty with words, tenses etc may be taken." Fullerton, in taking liberties with English, and with tenses, produces an anarchic stance toward both language and history: the past tense brought into the present, the present tense collaged with the past. Finally, there is also a liberty from audience if the game is played for oneself. The writer (as in the case of a diary) is the audience; and yet, even played as a round with others, the moment of reading coincides with that of writing.

Though clarity of language is not at issue in "Bromide" there is an ambiguity of form in it being an invented genre. Martin writes, considering Fullerton's sexuality and her love for women, that "Mary always recognised, and indeed, celebrated ambiguity in religion and in other areas of life. The appeal of the 'indefinite' was a crucial factor in her ability to forge a space for herself" (57). Later, she notes that Fullerton "maintained a public stance of asexuality" (60). That Fullerton first quotes the anonymous, and Old English "Sumer is icumen in" points to a time prior to the English canon, and to an earlier England, as if to say that England has a history too; it wasn't always an Empire. The quote also points to a time before that of the individual author: as the first quote, then, it adds a note of subversion to the notion of the author column. "Bromide" is not part of the Australian nationalist project; it doesn't even quote Australian writing, but casually uses the imported history of English poetry, re-exported by Fullerton in a letter as collage: it is a quick fix of language fun, that yet underlines sleepiness and boredom.

These two texts, or assemblages, by Harpur and Fullerton, two of Australia's better known colonial poets, are clearly distinguished from the rest of their respective oeuvres because of their form. Despite the ironic name of "Bromide" that Fullerton gives to her game, it appears to be a game of pleasure as much as boredom. The form is not one that appears to support "noble values," yet it is in a sense one of liberation. It is a game and, in contemporary terms, resembles a conceptual poem; it also participates in the genre of the list poem: taking pleasure in merely listing (and avoiding the self). While "Bromide" seems to honor the tradition of English verse, it also honors the Australian bush practice of improvisation (Ward 1), which Harpur also could be said to mime in the "Note," yet this is not the model of Australian literature we have been accustomed to. Perhaps the globalizing and technologizing of language gives us a new appreciation for the rougher qualities of Harpur (Mitchell xxix), and other early Australian writing, and perhaps also the uncorrected quotations of Fullerton's "Bromide," making the game both a diverting and a serious proposition, and "a beauty for the right people."

CHAPTER 6

Unsettling the Field

Ngarla Songs and Christopher Brennan's Musicopoematographoscope

Ngarla Songs. Written c.1920s; translated into English in preparation for publication, 2003, eds. Alexander Brown and Brian Geytenbeek.
Musicopoematographoscope. Written 1897; published in facsimile 1981, ed. Axel Clark.

Activities that have become metaphors or marginal activities in Europe are found to be present and central in a more literal sense in early Australia: this includes their representation in Australian writing. In the readings that follow I examine the literal use of the "field," more commonly termed "paddock" in Australia, before turning to the conceptual metaphor of the field that has become an influential model in contemporary poetics due to Olson's theories of the "open field" and "projective verse."

Ngarla Songs is a collaboration between an Indigenous and a non-Indigenous editor: Alexander Brown (1930–2010) and Brian Geytenbeek (1933–), and involves translation of Ngarla oral texts into English. The book was published in 2003, but includes compositions from the early twentieth century. The other work, the *Musicopoematographoscope*, by prominent colonial poet Christopher Brennan (1870–1932), was edited and published posthumously by his biographer, Axel Clark. It is clearly a composed creative work: an explicit assemblage of three parts, accompanied by a fourth text, the *Pocket Musicopoematographoscope*. The work is considered marginal to Brennan's oeuvre for reasons I shall discuss. Both *Ngarla Songs* and the

Musicopoematographoscope exist as book assemblages, and both have been explicitly edited: but this means something quite different in each case.

The *Ngarla Songs* were written by Indigenous stockmen about station life in northern Western Australia's Pilbara region. Earlier collections of Aboriginal song include *Taruru*, edited by C. G. von Brandenstein and A. P. Thomas (1974), and *Little Eva at Moonlight Creek*, edited by Martin Duwell and R. M. W. Dixon (1994). Both these collections are explicitly authored as white collaborations between a linguist (von Brandenstein, Dixon) and a literary editor (Thomas, Duwell), whereas *Ngarla Songs* is a collaborative project between a linguist (Geytenbeek) and an Indigenous stockman and singer (Brown). *Taruru* collects "tabi," individual songs (as opposed to communal songs) from 11 Pilbara languages (including one song from Ngarla). *Little Eva at Moonlight Creek* also features a range of songs, from four language groups, including "nurlu" (public songs) from Broome, in the Kimberley region of Western Australia (71).

While the "tabi" and "nurlu" and other nonsacred songs are comparable to the "yirraru" (anecdotal songs) of the *Ngarla Songs* in terms of both tone and theme, in *Ngarla Songs* there is a strong sense that all the songs come from one community: places, people, and situations repeat in different yirraru. Not only did Brown know the songs, "in most cases," Geytenbeek writes, he also "knew the composer personally," as well as the events behind the songs. This is significant because:

> He was thus able to explain to me the often vague and indirect allusions which are part of the style of the songs. If one is unaware of these indirect allusions, many of the songs are, in effect, a kind of indecipherable riddle. One has to be "in the know" as to what is being referred to, or else the subtlety of such songs will be completely inaccessible to the listener or reader. (10)

For non-Ngarla readers who don't have this song knowledge, Geytenbeek provides notations. The *Songs* are unique in this study in that they have literally contributed to an unsettling of Australia. According to anthropologist Nick Smith, who worked on the Ngarla people's land claim, the songs were presented in court as evidence of the Ngarla's long association with the land. (Smith remarked on this in a paper given at the University of Melbourne in September 2011). According to a news report of May 2007, "The Ngarla people of the East Pilbara have been handed down 11,331 square kilometres of land and water in the second native title claim to be decided in the region" (Hobbs n. pag.). This is an amazing example of songs (or poems as the published versions of these song texts appear to be) achieving a literal reterritorialization through the deployment of a textual assemblage of desire (presumably also including legal documents, witness statements etc.): to retake control of country. While the land in question was argued to be an Indigenous place all along, adapting Lefebvre (15), we might say that through the energy of the songs Indigenous space has been reproduced.

But what of the "field" of literature? If *Ngarla Songs* are to produce a significant space within Australian literature, that is an event still waiting to happen. The unsettling power (or energy) contained in this assemblage book in literary terms is of a different kind than that produced in court. Though its expression of attachment to the land is conceivably also powerful within a literary context, this attachment refers to a specific place, that of the East Pilbara in Western Australia. What interests me here are the unsettling literary facts of this work (which are also clearly political facts) and how they unsettle the Australian literature model generally.

The work is a collaborative production on more than the compositional level. As well as funding-related acknowledgements, Brown and Geytenbeek credit several people for artwork, in particular Jilalga Murray, who is also credited on the copyright page for "Illustrations" and "Internal Design Concept," and given biographical space. Murray's graphic elements punctuate the book, along with occasional photographs and notes by Geytenbeek. Albert Burgman is credited as a "Wangka Maya senior linguist [who] edited the work." It is, then, a more explicit collaboration than most anthologies: however, the roles played by Fremantle Arts Centre Press staff are not made explicit. (The copyright page says that FACP published the book in association with "Wangka Maya Pilbara Aboriginal Language Centre.")

The *Songs* are "yirraru": nonsacred, anecdotal songs of everyday life. The Ngarla stockmen who composed them were actively involved in the settlement of both land and sea: "Horse breaking and riding, mustering sheep, shearing, scouring wool," and working as "slave labour on pearling luggers" (16). The songs are not parts of a traditional Aboriginal "assemblage" in that they do not have a dance or painting "attached" (20). They are "composed and sung for pleasure" (23). The time of their original composition can only be determined by reference to historical incident and the lives of the composers; they were written in the early to mid-twentieth century. The songs were recalled by Brown and translated in collaboration with Geytenbeek. They are arranged in alphabetical sections according to the composer's name.

The first composer in *Ngarla Songs* is Miriny-Mirinymarra Jingkiri, "also known as Horse Boy Jimmy." His main occupation was mustering sheep, though he occasionally mustered cattle (25). The first song, on facing pages in Ngarla and English, is "Wirtiyamarra" / "The Unbeatable Bloke," a song of a card game, and a man, Wirtiyamarra, whose cards "always looked good ones." Nevertheless, he is beaten by a woman, Parrkuya (26–27). The song was written in the late 1930s, or perhaps earlier (the composer died in the late thirties), and provides an (humorous) example of feminist narrative unusual in writing by Australian men of that time. The following song ("Murrkamalu Jarnti Nyinuya" / "They Built It Right At Mirrkanya") involves a number of issues related to settlement. The title of the song refers to the building of The Lock Hospital in Port Hedland. According to Geytenbeek, within the hospital was "another locked compound in which venereal disease (VD) patients were kept." The hospital was built by A. O. Neville, Chief Protector of Aborigines. In the song about him, "Mr Nipurl," the narrator complains about Neville giving him the second-hand eating utensils of the dead (30–31). Jingkiri comments that the hospital was built "like it was made for cattle." He invokes the animal comparison made by whites against Aboriginal people, but also distances himself from the comparison. Wire is used to prevent the patients climbing to the trees. Jingkiri notes, "he knows we're fond of witchetty grubs" (28–29). Here traditional life is juxtaposed against the new strictures of settlement. The hospital is more like a zoo than a hospital. The pretext for the hospital is the other diseases that whites brought with them to Australia, diseases that had a devastating effect on Aboriginal populations. Hundreds of Ngarla people died from measles, as well as smallpox and respiratory diseases (16, 19). The song concludes in lines that are emblematic of the unsettling of the colonial assemblage, of living a parallel or secret Indigenous life:

> In spite of all that and the parallel wires
> we'll still find a way
> of continually exchanging little things
> through the gaps and the cracks.

The patient–prisoners exchange secrets within a secret enclosure. Neville presumably wants to contain venereal disease, but also hide the cause of it: sex between Indigenous people and settlers. The everyday represented in *Ngarla Songs* is not the Western everyday of representing the individual experience as universal; and it admits to sexual disease without prurience. Another poem, "Murrkanyakarni" / "Going To The Lock Hospital" has a light attitude toward the possible death that their destination implies ("'Will we go home better, or / will we go home to die?'"); it also refers to the truck's "humming a tune." The anthropomorphizing, agency-ascribing description of the truck here is unsettling and resistant, despite the mildly jaunty tone: it serves to void white people and their tyranny from the (world of the) song (32–33).

In "Wariyarranya Nyurranga Ngurra Pungkarriya" / "Wariyarranya Is Not Your Country Any Longer," Jingkiri has a similar theme of travelling to death, and of being locked up in "well-prepared pens." Here Jingkiri reverses the human animal relation, through using the colonially representative animal of the sheep. The title refers to sheep being taken by ship to Port Hedland to be slaughtered: "You are headed for your graveyard" (44–45). Unlike the ship in another song described as being homesick and blowing his whistle, this ship is merely a vehicle (40–41). The poem "Wariyarranya..." is remarkable in bringing the sheep into an Indigenous relation with the country, and in opposing them to "Fleming" (the stock and station agent who gives the order), rather than the more expected notion of sheep representing—and belonging—to the settler, and complicit with settlers in destroying the land. Jingkiri presents a mutual sympathy between that of the Indigenous stockman and the animals they spend their days with: the "poorfella sheep" that Paddy Roe describes in *Reading the Country*, that are the first to die in a drought (Benterrak 83).

One feature of the Ngarla yirraru is the avoidance of thematic or perspective subordination. The songs ascribe subjectivity to, and express empathy with, machines and animals as much as humans. "Piyuwiki" / "Buick" by Wirrkaru Jingkiri (a younger man than the composer above, presumably related), is composed of two stanzas. The first stanza praises the car for its "smooth" ride, while the second praises the driver for his "relaxed" driving style. There is a further level of meaning here in that the Buick, because of its "excellent suspension" (Geytenbeek's note), has a smooth relation with the road and the ground, whereas the driver has a similar nondominating relation to the car: "he let it go free" (50–51). It is not necessary for non-Indigenous poets to appropriate the yirraru as a form in order to learn something from the Ngarla songmakers' democratic representation of the everyday. I do not mean to idealize the Ngarla in terms of their relations with other entities in the world. The songs are constructed works rather than slices of reality. Yet they do contribute something distinct to Australian poetics in terms of their construction, their characteristically generous attitude toward the everyday, and their humorous tone. Humor is present even when, as in the younger Jingkiri's "Mirtanya" / "The Old Rooster," violence is being threatened: "How does it feel when I hit you on the head?" (54–55). Another yirraru by Wirrkaru Jingkiri implicates the sheep in the workers' protest: "We're going to that yard to holler and yell!... You're all fenced in in that yard" (59).

In these representations of stock animals in relation to Ngarla stockmen, the relation is not static, but rather tactical, depending on the situation described: building a hospital, sheep being rounded up, stockmen being treated like sheep that need to be penned, a humorous altercation with a rooster, or shooting a kangaroo (79). The yirraru suggest that, rather than struggling with the modern, the Ngarla had a relaxed attitude toward it. It was not modernity as such that the Ngarla resisted, but rather the living conditions that accompanied it. If we pay attention to the settlement texts of Indigenous writers then the assemblage of the Indigenous is also unsettled; the yirraru also unsettle the assemblages that are (or contain) animals and machines, and the hierarchy of relations between animals and humans, and machines and humans.

"Wupuri" by Miriny-Mirinymarra Jingkiri and "Marrpawarna" / "The Overland" by Yintilypirna Kaalyamarra, tell of the same man, a famous horse breaker known as "Wupuri" (his clan name is "Marrpawarna"). The first, by Jingkiri, describes a "mob gathered in the house" talking and joking about Wupuri. They then go down to the yards to watch him break a horse. The song ends, "Wupurilu parrpangka jan" / "Wupuri will make him sweat" (42–43). The second song, by Kaalyamarra, describes the same man driving fast in the Overland (a model of car): "swooping round the bends / with a whining roar" (62–63). Read together (and it is possible that Kaalyamarra knew, and was parodying, Jingkiri's song: Brown, after all, remembered both), there is the implication that, just as Wupuri has control of the horse, he also has control of the Overland. For the Ngarla, the horse and the car are both modern. The skills required to ride and drive are both new to them. The horse, then (as well as other introduced animals, such as the sheep), is a different, more modern kind of topos in Indigenous literature to the revival or colonial difference that it is in settler poetry.

The biographical note for Wirrkaru Jingkiri says that "When there was no mustering he'd do fencing. In 1946 he joined the strike for pay and better conditions for Aboriginal workers on stations" (47). The poor work conditions and lack of pay emphasizes the similarity of the living conditions of the Indigenous workers with that of the stock animals (but the sheep didn't have to build their own fences). In *The Landscape of Australian Poetry*, Brian Elliott refers to fences in distinguishing between a field and a paddock (in the Australian idiom). He writes that "If the area is fenced it is more precisely called a paddock than a field" (244). Yet fences also enclose smaller spaces such as yards and pens. Bill Ashcroft, in an essay, "Reading Post-Colonial Australia," notes Patrick White's questioning the role of fences in *The Tree of Man*. White's character, Stan Parker, wonders if, rather than mark property boundaries and establish ownership, fences in fact self-enclose, self-imprison (Ashcroft 25). Ashcroft further notes that in David Malouf's novel *Remembering Babylon*, "The fence...symbolizes not only the separation of the 'civilized' from the 'primitive' world but also a border between two incommensurate discourses" (26). The fence defines the agricultural and the settled practice of the farmer, and distinguishes the farmer from the hunter and the nomad.

The incommensurateness of the discourses relating to land is the primary division between the Indigenous and the settler. In *Reading the Country: Introduction to Nomadology* (1984), a book collaboratively authored by Krim Benterrak, Stephen Muecke, and Paddy Roe, in a section titled "The Key to the Country," a photograph shows two figures on either side of a gate with a sign that says "NO ENTRY / TRESPASSERS PROSECUTED / ROEBUCK PLAINS STATION." Above the photograph, Muecke writes:

> If one wants to drive through the country one comes up against the barrier of the boundary fences which have gates with locks. These cut across the tracks Paddy Roe's people used to follow. Short of destroying these fences, the only way to gain access to the country is to drive to the homestead to ask the manager or owner for a key. We did this on several occasions, Paddy Roe bringing a diplomatic boomerang: a metaphorical key perhaps, one that would "unlock" any opposition from the station people. (Benterrak 75)

The use of a boomerang—a weapon—in peaceful diplomacy is a postcolonial twist, although Roe could be said to be "hunting" agreement, access and country. As the photograph demonstrates, fences can be climbed over: it is the desire to drive through the country that is blocked by the fences. Fences also appear in Benterrak's paintings of Roebuck Plains. Muecke refers to the fences as "ugly," adding, "Krim cannot ignore them because they are the visible violation of the space he is reading, a reading which is also articulated with Paddy Roe's statements about fences which politely conceal the frustration of his nomadism." Muecke notes that Benterrak gives the fence a positive, "imaginary function: the protection of the springs" from cattle (103, 105). Fences violate—or punctuate—the space of country, yet like the car or ship may be turned to creative advantage, as in Benterrak's painting.

So far I have discussed aspects of the semantic content of the *Ngarla Songs*. But there is more to the unsettling text than semantics: punctuation and the visual, for example. Punctuation (as part of the assemblage of a chirographic culture) is a non-Indigenous import. When read in terms of sounded meaning, punctuation is read as affecting time. When read visually, however, as part of a page's composition, its role is a spatial one. In transferring and translating song to the written, published page, decisions regarding spatial (textual) distribution must be made. Ngarla yirraru are represented as two languages—Ngarla and English—on facing pages, and on both sides the editors display a conventional and similar use of punctuation (commas, full-stops, exclamation marks); there is an apparent difference in the use of hyphens, however.

Brown and Geytenbeek consistently use hyphens in presenting a characteristic feature in the *Ngarla Songs*: that of word repetition. Sometimes the repetition is exact, such as "nyirnti-nyirnti" or "wurta-wurta" (28), at others it is a repetition with extension, suggesting an extension of the meaning expressed: for example, "ngartaly-ngartalyala" and "pukaly-pukalykartaya" (30), or, finally, a repetition with truncation, such as "malukurru-kurru" (32). Presumably the hyphens represent a speeding up of normal word delivery, just as in representations of spoken English. Linguist Leendert Plug describes this effect in *Where Prosody Meets Pragmatics*: "Hyphens are used to present a 'cut-off': an abrupt, premature end to the articulation of a word, often accompanied by a glottal constriction" (256). A hyphen is used in translation from the Ngarla in the English words "worn-out" (31), yet we can see that this literally tired phrase involves slower vowel sounds than the Ngarla "wurta-wurta," and of Ngarla sounds generally (as far as I can tell). There is a difference, though, in representing two hyphenated words depending whether the words are the same, similar or different. If the hyphenated words are the same there is no semantic progress: rather there is emphasis, insistence, a sense of time stopping and, in terms of sound, an articulation that is completed. In terms of semantics, the hyphen momentarily blocks the flow of meaning. In words that are similar, that momentarily appear to be the same but change, like "ngartaly-ngartalyala," the hyphen is more like a pause that begins the flow again. A similar pause effect occurs when there is a repetition of the latter part of the word only, as in "malukurru-kurru," where there is presumably an emphasis on part of the meaning in the first word. In words that are completely distinct, like the English "worn-out," there is a blurring of semantics in the joining of the two words, with a corresponding speeding of rhythm. In Ngarla, to adapt a concept from Nicholas Birns, the hyphens present what might be termed "homosemantic" moments where same is joined to same, suggesting further the joinedness and sameness of all things. According to Birns, who derives his argument from Foucault, Quixote is "homosemantic," that he is "awaiting," in Foucault's terms, 'the great, unbroken plain of words and things' of the previous era" (58). The use of hyphenation in English, is then, heterosemantic, requiring differentiation. This points to the constant differentiation of English sounds. Yet this very differentiation suggests the possibility of change, and it is the dynamism of the hyphen (or of the Ngarla repetition) that seems to affect the representation of English in a yirraru about a dance. The composer is Wapirrku Kanturrpamarra, who worked at a slaughter yard and died in the 1920s. The yirraru is titled "Wilangku" / "Kimberley People," and the last couplet as published contains two sets of hyphenated words in Ngarla: "ngurtu-ngurtu" and "pikunkurla-pikunkurla," and one in English: "rapid-stamp":

> Jurrka ngani manpiya pananya ngurtu-ngurtu
> pikunkurla-pikunkurla Jangarrimarranya!
> Look at them dance, a rapid-stamp dance,
> Look at Jangari in action, zigzagging! (92–93)

Without knowing what the individual Ngarla terms refer to, it is apparent from the translation that, apart from identifying Jangarrimarranya through his name (though I can't be sure if an equivalent of the English deictic of "Look" exists in Ngarla), the words describe the action of the dance. The hyphenated words seem to attempt a mimesis of the dance, and it is this hyphenated phrasing that comes across in the term "rapid-stamp," which is unconventional English phrasing. That is, the English apparently mimics the Ngarla, whereas the Ngarla, it is implied, mimics the dance. Without the hyphen the English "rapid stamp" would just seem descriptive, and slower (nonmimetic in two ways). It is, then, the hyphen that is being repeated, untranslated: it hyphenates the languages. The hyphen doesn't actually exist in Ngarla, but is rather deployed by Brown and Geytenbeek when representing words in repetition. The hyphen travels from English to Ngarla and back again, implicating the languages in each other, using punctuation to unsettle not just the assemblages of language and mimesis but also colonial notions of translation.

Translation is, in a sense, a parodic exercise, where texts are repeated with a difference (Hutcheon 65). In terms of semantics a translation that was a parody would be an ideal: that is, if a repetition of semantic meaning were attainable where the "only" difference was in language. However, if we read the translation in terms of visual form, and through punctuation, then we can see that translation is parodic without the need for idealization. In fact the representation of the Ngarla songs with facing translation enacts parody's Greek etymology of "beside" and "song" (Concise 745, 741, 704). The term "hyphen" is also Greek-derived and its etymology provides a lesson in language and ideology. The *Concise Oxford* states that "hyphen" comes from the Greek "huphen," meaning "together." However, the entry is further elaborated in breaking "huphen" down further into "hupo," meaning "under" and "hen," meaning "one" (491). The hyphen then stands for a version of the colonial project, where ostensible "together"-ness, is, at its root, rather, "together under one." The different uses of the hyphen by Brown and Geytenbeek, in the Ngarla and the English, enact this in their respectively "homo" and "hetero" combinations: joining the same together in the Ngarla, and the different in the English. Yet as in the example of "rapid-stamp," with the two words' similar sounds (a short "a" and a "p"), this difference is not settled.

This reading of Ngarla songs has been concerned with composers who literally worked in the fields: in an Australian context, also a modern invention. The songs tell of the everyday lives as stockmen. The songs' belated publication in a translated, bilingual edition brings a new form of song (or poem) into the Australian repertoire: the "yirraru." Although the songs are composed individually, their collective representation by 11 songmakers unsettles the local white image of the pastoralist poet, extending the range of treatment, and in a sense (considering the negative framing of killing sheep, and the inclusion of songs about going to hospital with a disease) providing an Indigenous example of anti-pastoral. Yet the yirraru unsettle even this contemporary, critical term, in that the Ngarla stockmen are not writing in an antigenre; their tone is accepting and sympathetic, and not a reporting of what Kinsella terms "pastoral wrongs." Though they are pastoral workers and use their own language, it cannot be said to be a "working class" or "rural" language. What the yirraru do, arguably, is define the "anti-pastoral" as a settlement genre.

The yirraru provides an alternative model of worker poetry outside urban working class diction (and outside English), as well as outside urban production. The Ngarla songmakers are literally assemblers of fences, yards, and fields: in other words, settlement. Their songs are therefore significant in discerning the possibilities of unsettlement, of disassemblage. This means reading them through the editing assemblage work of Brown and Geytenbeek. As their translations make clear, the songs' expressions of irony, pragmatism, humor, and empathy are other than supportive of the white settlement project, even when ostensibly assisting it. I turn now to a work that investigates the field of the page: a deliberately parodic work, Brennan's *Musicopoematographoscope*.

Brennan is a much-anthologized (or canonized) poet who wrote through the 1890s into post-Federation Australia. He was a classics scholar, and lectured at Sydney University. Although he has never been popular, interest in Brennan's life and work has persisted. He was the subject of a biography by Axel Clark (1980); his *Poems (1913)* were reprinted with a new introduction by Robert Adamson (1992); and a fictionalized account of a year of his life has also been published by John Stephenson as *The Optimist* (1996).

The *Musicopoematographoscope*, however (with accompanying "Pocket" version), is far from canonical. It was written in 1897 but not published until 1981, and has never been anthologized. It has received scant critical attention. Apart from reviews, the only exceptions are Katherine Barnes's 2007 article in the French journal *XIX: Dix-Neuf,* and Kate Fagan's 2012 paper on contemporary Sydney poet Chris Edwards (also a "Mallarméist"), which suggests that "for Australian poetry the twentieth century arguably began" with the first reading of Brennan's work (1). There are several reasons for the work's lack of status. It was originally produced as a private entertainment for one person (Brennan's poet-friend Dowell O'Reilly); it is difficult to typeset (it was published as a large format facsimile of the handwritten original); it is (partly) a pastiche on "Un Coup de Dés"; and its tone is jocular and therefore a departure from the seriousness and decorousness of Brennan's other published work. Unlike the hoax poetry of McAuley and Stewart's Ern Malley, it seems that the creator of the *Musicopoematographoscope* has been taken at his word: because Brennan appears not to take it seriously, neither have its critics, largely ignoring the *Musicopoematographoscope* in favor of his normative verse oeuvre (though admittedly this verse was considered "highly unorthodox" at the time, and it was the negative reaction to these poems that generated the poem under discussion, Clark 3–4). Even now, when pastiche is a more acknowledged practice, Brennan studies (see, for example, the 2008 special issue of *Southerly,* "Double Exposures") is preoccupied with his formal verse.

Brennan's critical reputation is, though generally conceded, unstable: swinging through deep ambivalence from positive to negative extremes. Hodge and Mishra comment that: "In histories of Australian literature Christopher Brennan's work is treated as an anomaly, a sport" (182). The following are late twentieth-century critical reactions: "Brennan led Australian poetry in disastrously wrong directions," and influenced the "'Poetic' rhetoric [that] has been the curse of Australian poetry" (Dutton 3); "His example was one to be envied and shunned" (Buckley xvii); "Although Brennan was almost immediately recognised as an important poet, many found his poetry obscure and un-Australian" (Perkins, Literary 58); "The history of both poetry and scholarship in this country has been remarkably indebted to Brennan," with his "lofty, pure aesthetic" (Wallace-Crabbe, 220, 230); and "[Brennan] will not go away, and he cannot be tamed into perfection" (Vivian Smith, qtd. Kirkpatrick 210). Geoffrey Dutton was writing in 1976, before the *Musicopoematographoscope*'s publication, but none of the others, writing after, mention it.

Perhaps attitudes are changing, however. In a 2007 article, "With a smile barely wrinkling the surface," Barnes writes of the diversity of what she terms the Mallarméan "spoof" that is the central work of the assemblage, writing of "the quite remarkable variety of calligraphic styles that Brennan employed to imitate the typographical variety of the *Coup de dés*" (44): adding that the work "can be thought of as a handmade book" (53). With the poster-poem of the title page we have an explicit contradiction of the image of Brennan's work: Brian Elliott has written of Brennan's poetry that it contains "no poster art of any kind." Elliott's use of the term "poster art" is metaphorical: he refers to the kitsch nationalism of those with a penchant for "wattle blossom" and "kangaroos" (265). Yet referring to "poster art" in metaphoric terms only is typical of the conventions of formalist criticism. Brennan's poster poem deserves further examination.

The innovation of the *Musicopoematographoscope* goes beyond that of a pastiche or parody of Mallarmé, though this is how it has largely been seen, even by Clark and Barnes, who despite asserting its significance, primarily read it in relation to "Un Coup de Dés," and read the work's paratexts of title page and "Press Notices" only in terms of their relation to Brennan's main text. The *Musicopoematographoscope* is an assemblage of three works, with an attendant mini-work titled *Pocket Musicopoematographoscope*. The former three works comprise a parodic poster poem; the ostensible pastiche; and a collage of critics' quotes of Brennan's work. The *Musicopoematographoscope*s (plural, if we include the "Pocket" version) unsettle Brennan's own canon (as well as the critical canon that has constructed the creative one), changing our picture of him as a poet, of his poetry, and of the history and possibilities of practice and range in Australian poetry generally.

As Perloff notes, Mallarmé was himself influenced by the "posters and proof sheets" of newspapers, as were the later dadaists and surrealists (Dance 180; Bohn, Reading 82). Poster poems are also a reference point for Brazilian concrete poets (Drucker 41). Critics conventionally assign the beginnings of collage to the examples of Picasso and Braque in France, and Marinetti in Italy (Perloff, Dance 35, 60); though Drucker cites the example of other futurists, Carlo Carra and Ardengo Soffici, and alludes to collages within Russian, German, French, and other contexts (41). Yet this perception of collage is changing, as I will explain below.

Brennan's *Musicopoematographoscope* consists of a title page in an over-the-top poster style; followed by instructions for performance of the following poem; followed by the poem itself, which clearly mimics (though handwritten) the spacing and varied typography of "Un Coup de Dés" (16 numbered pages, including a final blank page), representing a riposte to Brennan's friend, O'Reilly, who had "attacked Brennan for obscurity" (Clark 4); followed by a collage of extracts titled "Press Notices of [Brennan's] XXI Poems," which has at the foot of the page a similar list of quotes titled "Private Notices"; followed by a fourth work, the shorter "Pocket Musicopoematographoscope" (four pages). The published version includes an "Introduction" by editor Clark, a photograph frontispiece of the heavily foxed first page of the "Pocket" poem, as well as typeset title pages. Though the announcing of the *Musicopoematographoscope* refers also to Mallarmé's poem, I consider the constitution of the poster, and the collage page, as discrete poems in themselves. Therefore, my use of *Musicopoematographoscope* refers to the work as a whole, and I will distinguish between the several forms as necessary.

Brennan's work is not only diverse in form, but takes on the diverse institutions of typography, the page, the audience, and poetry reviewing, in explicit, indecorous, and avant-garde fashion. It is, in other words, an assemblage. In his introduction to Brennan's work, Clark uses the terms "synthesis" and "fusion" in relation to Mallarmé's, and his follower Brennan's, aesthetic aspirations of synthesizing different art forms. But he refers also to Brennan's biography, writing that "After losing his Catholic faith in 1890, he [Brennan] had tried various ways...of restoring unity to life," and that "in 1893 he came across the poetry of Mallarmé, which encouraged him to believe he might find, through poetic symbol...a sense of organic wholeness—of "Eden," as he now called it, after Mallarmé" (3). As well as a symbol for wholeness, "Eden" might well, from a Christian perspective at least, function as a symbol for a garden, and from a twenty-first century ecological perspective, for a biodiverse ecosystem.

The problems relating to anthologizing the *Musicopoematographoscope* point to its importance as a work of Australian poetry: it is a model assemblage of different forms. It resists fusion and synthesis. Though the work is to an extent reliant on European literary history, like Fullerton's "Bromide" it also appropriates and ironizes that history. It is a grand, unsettling statement, one that opens up poetic space, one that ironically "DAMN"s (Brennan 19) those who would close it down. It is a model for different kinds of poetry coexisting, rather than merely different styles of the same thing: the differences create a "whole thing."

Stephen Fredman theorizes the importance of "wholeness" in his book *Poet's Prose*. He opposes the term "wholeness" to "completeness," writing that "...*wholeness* will represent organic, implicit, or generative forms of the sentence (often employing parataxis), and completeness will represent normative, explicit, or preconceived forms of the sentence (often exhibiting hypotaxis)" (30). The *Musicopoematographoscope*, then, tends to wholeness rather than completeness, as it not only tends to parataxis but also challenges normative conceptions of, and relations between, para- and hypotaxis through its use of the page, script size, and style. For example, a line that is broken and staggered down a page suggests subordination that may not exist syntactically, and is distinct from more regular, stanzaic forms. Lines, or sentences, that are in large script might be said to subordinate those in smaller, regardless of narrative or syntactic relation. Further, spacing creates a sense of disjunction that interrupts hypotaxis, making the line sound paratactic to an extent that wouldn't occur in prose, while at other times, as Clark notes, subordination has a harmonic effect (5).

The problem with terms like "synthesis" and "fusion" is that they suggest the work has already been resolved: elements have already been fused, synthesized, the differences dissolved, assimilated. In reading Brennan's *Musicopoematographoscope*, I favor the term "assemblage," as adapted from Deleuze and Guattari, while also taking into consideration the more literal definition that both Perloff and Quartermain have borrowed from art criticism. Even without the French connotation of agency, an assemblage (though it may be said to be already assembled) lacks the stability of synthesis or fusion: there is still the possibility of disassembly and reassembly. An assemblage also suggests different kinds of elements: elements that are perhaps not so easy to synthesize or fuse. As Deleuze explains in *Dialogues II*: "What we call an assemblage is, precisely, a multiplicity" (132).

The *Musicopoematographoscope*'s multiple forms constitute an extended open form (or megaform) that fulfills the criteria of Quartermain's definition of assemblage. It is "associationally powerful" (Barnes refers to the "Notices" collage as a "metaphorical landscape", 46), and to an extent "ready made": the poster-poem and the pastiche refer explicitly to Mallarmé, as well as to the extended list of possible forms encapsulated by Brennan's full title, while the collage of quotations that conclude the main work (there is still the coda of the "Pocket" version to come) lists their sources: "The Freeman's Journal," "The Bulletin," et cetera.

That Brennan in 1897 produces an explicit collage is an unsettling of accepted history, which, until recently, emphasized collage's beginnings in Europe in the early twentieth century (Perloff, *Dance* 35; Drucker 41; Kotz 103; Zavatsky and Rogow 167; Bohn, *Aesthetics* 9; de Campos 365), following the practice of the Cubist painters. The earlier "Un Coup de Dés" could itself be read as collage considering its layout of type, while John Lynen in his 1969 book *The Design of the Present*, has argued that "Whitman uses collage" (Cameron 222, 271). More recently, however, Perloff has noted in *Unoriginal Genius* the 1877 precedent of Brazilian poet Joaquim de Sousa Andrade's collage poem, "Wall Street Inferno" (68). The poem was published in English translation in Jerome Rothenberg and Jeffrey C. Robinson's 2009 *Poems for the Millennium Vol. 3* (655). This discovery unsettles the Northern Hemisphere's narrative of modernism, suggesting a more diverse, fluid, or networked history, one that suggests a textual history of collage that may intersect with, rather than follow, that of the visual.

Avoiding the concept of collage for the most part, Leonard Diepeveen also emphasizes the early twentieth century as the starting point for the subject of his study of the modern "quoting poem." He distinguishes between "collage artists" like Braque and Picasso and "quoting poets" such as Eliot, Pound, Moore, and cummings. Diepeveen assumes that quotes are inserted into a somehow preexisting poem (rather than being part of the poem's production) and that "quotation increases a textural disruption that complicates reading" (13). He argues that "Quotations inevitably distort the subject matter of the new poem" (43), and that "to quote a text is to deny it its original status, and to turn its language into an image" (45). The quotes that make up Brennan's collaged page of "Press" and "Private Notices" are themselves distorted, but there are no words of Brennan's to represent "subject matter of [a] new poem" other than the headings. The "Notices" page has some of the visual power of the other texts, yet here the effect is subtler in that the handwriting is small and cursive. Many of the extracts selected by Brennan are negative, such as "jar of many voices," "occasional obscurities," and "should not so often use the same adjective"; yet one critic notes "The fine lucidity of Rossetti": the quote emphasizing contradiction in the writer's stance. The quote, "jar of many voices," mocks the critics, as in this new context their remarks become obscure and jar with each other. As well as selecting, arranging, and writing the quotes out by hand, Brennan adds punctuation. He inserts ellipses that vary from two to six stops between the quotes, as well as providing them with quote marks. This is in contrast to the preceding pastiche poem, where punctuation is minimal; the "Notices" return rather to the style of the poster page with its many exclamation marks and hyphens. According to Diepeveen, "All quoting exploits an alien texture" (15), adding, "When a work of art quotes, the emphasis on a 'paraphrasable,' nontextural world fades" (16): Brennan quotes his "alien[ated]" reviewers in a spirit of satire, re-quoting them against themselves. He follows the "Public Notices" with a mocking addition:

Private Notices

D. O'Reilly, Esq., M.L.A., Patron of Parramatta Shaconian Society: "Wants translating....Public....desperate effort to escape commonplace....Public....should make money....Public....obscure....Pub-

Brennan turns his friend's remarks into babble, insulting him further by cutting him off mid-word, with perhaps a suggestion that the words are a drunk ramble by turning "Public" into "Pub-." There is an uncanny correspondence here to Harpur's elliptic "Note." Brennan's intimate sarcasm seems to override Diepeveen's notion of "alien texture"; however, he has made O'Reilly's remarks into something "different" and arguably "better," like Eliot's "good poet" (Diepeveen 64).

Diepeveen's quoting poem tends to resemble collage. In an argument derived from both Eliot and Sergei Eisenstein, he refers to the concept of heterogeneity and the production of new meaning through sounds of different origin (71–72). This describes the consistently quoting collaged works of Diepeveen's study. Brennan's work is more aptly called an assemblage. It assembles entire homogenous works into a new heterogeneous whole; in other words, it is a book. In the *Musicopoematographoscope*, Brennan begins with the exaggerated generic voice of the spruiker; the following poem mixes elusive and allusive fragments with a capitalized curse ("DAMN," 19). Arguably there is more alien texture in the first two works: in the poster poem's use of voice, and in the pastiche's borrowing of cadence and diction, than there is in the explicit quotation of the "Notices." In the "Notices," Brennan neutralizes the reviewers' comments through quoting, fragmenting, and punctuating, ultimately mocking the meaninglessness of expert opinion. Although critics can make nothing of his poems, he can make a poem from their reviews. Rather than the collage poems of the twentieth-century modernists, the "Notices" resemble conceptual poetry's "strategies of copying and appropriation" (Goldsmith "Why" xviii). Goldsmith terms such writing "uncreative writing" (xxi), which suggests the postorganic, the lifeless, the endgame of poetry. Yet, in Brennan's work at least, through its openness to possibilities of network and assemblage, it rather suggests life: combining stasis and active expression like an ecosystem. For the colonial text to upset, to unsettle its own coloniality, it cannot be merely a resettling of an inert, settled text. I conclude my reading of Brennan's *Musicopoematogrpahoscope* with a consideration of how we might read its diversity in terms of an ecocritical viability: that is, as a biodiverse text.

Biodiversity is a key term for Jonathan Bate in *Song of the Earth*, one of the earliest texts to explicitly name "ecopoetics." Bate describes the John Keats of "To Autumn" as a poet aware of biodiversity, which, he writes, "depends on a principle [of] *illusory excess*" [Bate's italics] (106). The example he gives is the "wild flowers" in Keats's poem. In this reading, Bate has already constructed the field as a place of produce, where "wild flowers" fit his definition of biodiversity as dependent upon "illusory excess": rather than considering the poem itself as a potentially biodiverse language construct, or as a distinct organism within Keats's oeuvre. For instance, Keats's poem "To Autumn" is in three stanzas; in Random House's Modern Library edition the stanzas are numbered (though not in Bate's version), and the poem both follows and precedes poems of one stanza. Go a poem further back and there is the unfinished "Hyperion" in one long canto and a truncated second; go one forward and there is the "fragment" of the verse tragedy "King Stephen" (370–390). Bate's argument therefore is limited by its semantic, what we might call "monopoetic," interpretive reading. The notion of "illusory excess" is itself a weak definition: requiring an interpretation of excess outside the system of the poem—that is then corrected as illusory—whether by the same reading consciousness or a more enlightened one is not clear. To be fair, Bate's reading goes beyond this: for example, he points out that, unlike other poems by Keats, in "To Autumn," "the self is dissolved into the ecosystem." The poem is therefore a decentered network (107) and a Romantic alternative to Olson's later theory of the open field, with the poet as object within the field.

Bate's choice of "wild flowers" as "illusory excess" is a curious one. There are other contenders, the "small gnats" or the "hedge-crickets" in stanza three, for example. The poem itself points explicitly to an excess of produce in both stanza one (the "o'erbrimmed" honey), and stanza two, with its reference to a "gleaner," whose very existence depends on a (nonillusory) excess. Bate's reading, in other words, displaces the notion of excess as an ordinary effect of agriculture (or other production, such as *poiesis*) with the more abstract one of excess as something illusory. In this way he avoids the notion of the poem itself being in any way excessive or vulnerable to deconstruction, eliding in a sense the act of his own criticism by showing the perfect match of poem and ecosystem. Such an exemplary reading creates the possibility of other poems being read in similar fashion, but the complete reliance on semantic content makes for limited possibilities of the biodiverse poem; moreover, Bate's failure to make anything of the explicit excess described by Keats suggests that an even closer reading of the semantic may be apt.

That the published version of Brennan's title page is preceded by Clark's typographical version—of title only, without Brennan's embellishments—suggests that Clark also thought of Brennan's title page as a work in its own right. It is here that we are introduced to Brennan's "remarkable variety of calligraphic styles," getting a sense of the page as a poem, and as a visual work that refers back to the ornate title pages of earlier centuries, while proclaiming "THE ART OF THE FUTURE!!!" The title page seems to embody a portrait-in-words of Mallarmé, Brennan's *"Hieratico-byzantaegyptic-Obscurantist"*: complete with party hat, moustaches and his own converted name ("MALAHRRMAY") as teeth. The phrases "THE PERFECTION OF THE PAST!" and "THE ART OF THE FUTURE!!!" float to the left and right like doves, or rough balloons. It is an advertisement for what follows, the invention from "Paree": the "PROSE-VERSE-POSTER-ALGEBRAIC-SYMBOLICO-RIDDLE-MUSICOPOEMATOGRAPHOSCOPE." What follows is not exactly Mallarmé's invention, however: "With," as Brennan adds, "many improvements / freer use of counterpoint / &c. &c. &c. &c." Posters, of course, don't evoke fields other than as vertical, static, metaphoric reductions, such as a playing field, which may be scored, but is limited dimensionally. Yet the rhetoric and tone of a poster's announcement, and the dynamic of its page design, can leave horizontal forms looking literally flat. Perloff writes in the context of postmodern poetry's multiplicity that "a new poetry is emerging that wants to open the field so as to make contact with the *world* as well as the *word*." Perloff explicitly refers to the openness of "posters and newspapers" (Dance 181). It is here that we can say that Brennan, like the later futurists and surrealists, diverges from Mallarmé, by explicitly incorporating a poster into the *Musicopoematographoscope*, and parodying Mallarmé in the process.

The conceptual verticality of Brennan's title page is enhanced by his use of exclamation marks: "THE PERFECTION OF THE PAST! [one exclamation mark] THE RAGE OF THE PRESENT!! [two] THE ART OF THE FUTURE!!! [three]." Here Brennan opposes the future against "PERFECTION," which is consigned to the "PAST," and admits the wildness of the "PRESENT" moment (in "THE RAGE"), while combining them in temporal assemblage with the "ART OF THE FUTURE!!!" (The reference to the three temporal categories eerily echoes Kelly). Each "time" is symbolized by its respective number of exclamation marks. Brennan then mocks his own formulation by consigning it to the "LATEST NOVELTY." The novelty is both imported and local, incorporating "MANY IMPROVEMENTS...&c. &c. &c. &c." The repetition of the "&c" implies a differentiated abundance: "MANY IMPROVEMENTS" can't be measured purely in numerousness, they must be different improvements, and it is here that we find a use for Bate's "illusory excess," perfectly conveyed by the "&c."'s. The "&c."'s are excessive only in semantic terms: they can be justified prosodically in both visual and sound terms, and as an evocation of the carnivalesque tone of voice appropriate to that of advertisement. Brennan composes a poster that both announces and enacts a field of literature, but also recalls the carnivalesque field of tents offering various marvels.

In contemporary poetics after Olson, "field" as a term has another, less settled, and more dynamic connotation than that of the page as paddock, deriving from Olson's theory of "composition by field," and his concept of "projective verse." Olson refigures the act of writing poetry as a field of operations where the poet becomes an object within the field, speaking. According to Olson scholar, Eniko Bollobas, this conception brings physical and "processural" elements into writing poetry, rejecting systemic approaches (58, 62), and is proposed as a practice of ethical awareness and attention (65), and as poetry both unsettled and unsettling, alive, and breathing: when the field is "opened" (Robert Duncan's suggestion), "chaos is the opening" (Rasula, This 43).

A recent critical anthology, *Towards the Open Field*, edited by Melissa Kwasny, attempts to construct a history of Western poetry (largely North American but beginning with Wordsworth) in terms of Olson's schema. To do so requires some broadening of terms. Kwasny proposes to use the field:

> as a general term for a range of modern poetic forms that, from the romantic period on, have been variously designated as organic form, free verse, open form, the prose poem, and the scored page...a kind of patterning (at the level of line, syntax, rhythm, diction, even punctuation) shaped not by inherited conventions but rather by the specific demands of the individual poem, or poet, or subject. (xi)

She adds that the intention of the anthology is "to trace a movement *from conventional form to exploratory field*" (Kwasny's italics, xi). The anthology culminates with Olson's "Projective Verse" essay, and by doing so recasts the history of poetry in English as retrospectively (or progressively) Olsonian. As provocative as this is, Kwasny's redefinition of "open field" despecifies Olson's project to the extent that it becomes an uncritical one, a generalization: "anything goes." Brennan's poem fits into Kwasny's reconceptualization easily. But to say so is not that meaningful: at best a form of cataloguing. It does, however, reemphasize the *Musicopoematographoscope*'s "meta" quality, in it being combinations of different varieties of what Kwasny would call "open field" poems: we can call the poster "open form," the Mallarméan central text is explicitly "scored," while the final section of the *Musicopoematographoscope* proper is a prose collage. What Kwasny does, despite her claims for the individual poet, is to shift the concept of open field from its relation to the individual poem, or model of practice, to the field of poetry itself.

In the 1950 essay, Olson speaks of the poem as energy. Poets themselves are "in the open," hunter and hunted. This image more readily recalls Kelly than Brennan, yet Heriberto Yépez sees Olson as more of an imperialist force than a rebellious one: "Projective verse and the projective are," he writes, "an aesthetics of military speed, of the enthusiasm of the soldier and the cameraman of the battlefield. It is the poetics of a triumphalist culture of the postwar period. Projective is *take over, enemy seizure*" (216). Yepez is protesting against Olson's perception of the world as property: as if the field is his. In the earlier *Call Me Ishmael* (1947), which Yepez cites, Olson, with apparent arrogance, refers to the "Americanization of the world," comparing this conquest to that of the Roman empire (76). Yet by 1950, Olson was apparently rethinking this phrase, apparently seeing American energy waning: "where do you see it expressed?" (von Hallberg 15).

Olson's notion of America as energy (DuPlessis 89) leads us to another concept that Olson incorporates in his theory of "Projective verse": that of the force field. Yet although his influential essay provides an escape route from formalist verse, the theory's abstraction from the material, means it is unable to consider the limit of the page and the relation of the form of the poem to this limit: as if the two kinds of field assembled together (energy and page) were ignorant of each other. Further, Olson's theory, by emphasizing speech, ultimately emphasizes linearity. If we consider Brennan's poem we see the energy: we also see the potential for reading a diverse, decentered poem that has no issuing locatable ego. A poem that is able to move, that is untied to unit of the line, can further be read "radially" rather than progressively (McGann, Textual 120).

While Olson attempts to combine a conceptual poetics with one of the body, specifically the breath, a poetics of the breath could not create a poem like Brennan's. While following Mallarmé in terms of using the field of the page, it is heavily reliant on pastiche, and, in the "Notices," on appropriation. Its potential as a field constructed by hand (as opposed to a field composed via a mimesis of breath or of the conceptually whole body in the field) is one that has been underutilized in Australian poetry (though the work of Edwards in *People of Earth*, that includes his own version of "Un Coup de Dés," is one contemporary example).

According to Anne Day Dewey, Olson's associates Robert Creeley and Duncan were more materially oriented, and went on to a poetic practice more concerned with the page itself (81–87). She writes that Creeley and Duncan "developed a sort of Romanticism without nature that renders the blank page rather than the natural landscape the ground against which the poet articulates ideas" (81). The page is compared to a canvas (87); both page and canvas are therefore conflated with the ground or field: "topographic space is coextensive with a typographic dimension" (Rasula, This 60). To think of the field in terms of ground is to think of changed or cultivated ground. A field, like a page, is manufactured, defined, bordered; the production of either is rarely the work of one person, but rather that of a collaboration or community (or industry). Yet the fact can't be allayed that a field is cleared ground—cleared of its original plants, animals, and people: "everything is removed" (Serres 177). The settled field is predominantly the agricultural field; Keats's and Bate's Romantic visions notwithstanding, it is not biodiverse. Perloff, in fact, characterizes the move toward a more diverse poetry as a move away from the Romantic, framed in terms of the postmodern:

> Postmodernism in poetry...begins in the urge to return the material so rigidly excluded—political, ethical, historical, philosophical—to the

domain of poetry, which is to say that the Romantic lyric, the poem as expression of a moment of absolute insight, of emotion crystallized into timeless patterns, gives way to a poetry that can, once again, accommodate narrative and didacticism, the serious and the comic, verse *and* prose...a new poetry is emerging that wants to open the field so as to make contact with the *world* as well as the *word*. (Dance 181)

The poetics contexts of Keats, Olson, and Brennan are, of course, different. Reading Brennan in the early twenty-first century is not to read in the same Australia in which it was written. Current ecological trauma resonates with the effects of Indigenous dispossession. The notion of a settled Romantic agriculture has, arguably, never settled, nor is the clearing of the land a distant memory. In a poem that is generally considered—if considered at all—to be a "side project," Brennan's poem paradoxically fulfills Perloff's criteria for emerging new poetry. The "political, ethical, historical, philosophical" elements are also there: manifest in formal as much as semantic terms. In the central section of Brennan's poem, the use of handwriting styles that parody typographic fonts suggests a practice of intimacy: a care for the field of the page. Brennan's care doesn't extend to the reader, however. He disdains the claims the "press" or the "public" have on "the poet" (11–25). The agency of the text (its dispersal, or fragmenting, of lines throughout the work, its assemblage of different styles, genres etc.) resists, and could be said to field (to use the term as a verb), the poem's addressee's—O'Reilly's—claims for the public's reading requirements: "I DON'T GIVE A TINKER'S DAMN FOR THE PUBLIC AND THEY RETURN THE COMPLIMENT." This exclamation, distributed throughout the document in small phrases and singular words, follows the poem's performance instruction that calls "for eight Voices... & no Audience" (10). It suggests instead a field cleared for the work: preparing us for the stark negation of page nine (see below).

A tinker (in Mallarmé a *thinker*, Barnes 50) is a mender—but what is broken? O'Reilly might say the patience of the public. Brennan doesn't give a (tinker's) damn. It is not his job to mend the (illusory?) gap between public discourse and poetry, or poetry and money; his is rather that of the artist, the punctuator, mending the arts into a whole assemblage: PROSE-VERSE-POSTER-ALGEBRAIC-SYMBOLICO-RIDDLE-MUSICOPOEMATOGRAPHOSCOPE. The title enacts its journey to wholeness, in that the hyphens fall away at "MUSICO..." As tinker, then, Brennan can be seen to care for a wholeness of culture.

Page nine of Brennan's poem (Clark's page 19) features the single word in large capitals: "DAMN." Read as a pun, it becomes a "DAM"—the "N" its own negation. A dam is a constructed waterhole, and as presented by Brennan it supports no life: no "hawklike" critics (17) or foxing (ii, 5) or "streams of text" (Barnes 52). It is an ironic, caustic representation of ecosystem: a damned field. It follows the French symbolists in equating the inorganic with the Satanic (Payne 63). Page nine, despite its "waste" of space, is clearly not blank nor empty; and clearly more could be made of this page as an image of colonial Australia with this word-figure "refusing to come to the party...enunciating the space of disappearance, where things refuse to quieten or settle down" (Carter 6). Quotes from the central poem readily adapt themselves to ironic anticolonialist interpretation, to the extent that the (negated "no") audience becomes identified with settlers: that is, no settlers ("immemorial / inexistent / desert isle"; "eternal nothingness / had more prestige"; "the phantom treasure"; "that by which they think they're something / their nothing", 20, 24, 25). The switch from identity to possession, in using "they're" to "their," recalls the word effects of Harris. The ambiguous page nine, unlike pages eight and ten, has been left unnumbered by Brennan. Nine is negated by its anagram and punning German homophone of "Nein." (Brennan had lived in Germany and married a German. Barnes refers to the significance of punning in Brennan's work, following Mallarméan practice, 47–49.) This page is the cursed alternative space, the place of quietude opposed to the activity and multiform life of the rest of the poem: "the Voice / that must / for aye / be / silent" (25). Yet again—and ironies seem always to multiply in Brennan—there is the whiteness, or quietness of a page surrounding the largest, blackest, loudest swearing: perhaps paradoxically embodying the silent response of the "no audience."

The notion of a biodiverse nineteenth-century Australian poetry is a provocative one, one that is not easily discerned from anthologies, or from literary histories. Although they may contain varieties of tone, rhythm, and diction, the constraint of left-justified stanzas means that convict ballads can end up looking very similar to formal lyrics. It is as if the original poems, however lively and varied once, are now buried in the same coffin-shaped plot. While Bate appears to open up English poetry to ecological approaches, in doing so he also uses the concept of ecopoetics to further solidify a narrow canon of, as he says, the "chief 'Romantics'," and a "small but powerfully representative selection" of the "geographically widespread" poets of the twentieth century (vii). This is Bate's assemblage: but of course it requires no assembling at all. Bate writes that "The poet of biodiversity will also celebrate cultural diversity" (233). What of the critics of biodiversity? A biodiverse system requires "constituting that which has fallen outside the realms of discourse" and "making present that which has become absent from the history of the recent past" (Harrison, Historical 102). The Australian case must be different to the English: our "recent past" is implicated in theirs, but theirs is not ours. Australian culture includes convict and Chinese culture; it includes different kinds of farming culture; most significantly, it includes Indigenous cultures. Bate attempts to acknowledge this difference by referring to the "representative" Australian sources of Bruce Chatwin and Les Murray. There are no references to Aboriginal writers themselves, and although he warns against idealizing "Australian Aboriginals" (74), they are separated from the "we" of the book: "Where did we begin to go wrong?" (24). He imagines an Aboriginal reading of John Clare, and is confident in speaking that reading himself; he refers to "songlines," but doesn't refer to a single contemporary Aboriginal poet (165–166). For Bate the representative Australian is Murray, termed by Bate an (small "a") "aboriginal" (241). To what extent white Englishman Chatwin and white Australian Murray can be considered representative of Australia (and they cannot be of Aboriginal Australia) is besides the point. The representational model is itself opposed to that of the biodiverse. Arguably, then, despite the use of the term "ecopoetics" ("a making (Greek *poiesis*) of the dwelling-place—the prefix eco is derived from Greek *oikos*, 'the home or place of dwelling,'" Bate 75), Bate's book is a continuing of what *ecopoetics* journal editor Jonathan Skinner refers to as an:

> "Environmentalist" culture [that] has ignored most developments in poetics since Ezra Pound. The literature...largely Anglo-American...may be "eco"...but it certainly comes up short in "poetics"—demonstrating overall, for a movement whose scientific mantra is "biodiversity," an astonishing lack of diversity in approaches to culture, to the written and spoken word. (7)

Bate has also been criticized by Harriet Tarlo. She writes in *How2* that *Song of the Earth* is "a critical work which uses the term [ecopoetics] to describe a rather exclusive club of neo-romantic, male poets (with one or two modernists among them, but no contemporary innovative poets)" (n. pag.). This criticism, made in gendered and aesthetic terms, avoids those of race, and the particular form of racism that elides the Indigenous—which is alluded to in the Skinner quote above, "approaches to culture." Perhaps the term "ecopoetics," and its ready adoption, is part of the problem: assuming a Western origin in the Greek it constructs the earth in terms of (human) home, rather than allowing the diverse existence of creatures and things. (As represented, for example, in the Ngarla yirraru.)

Brennan is also a white canonical poet. However, I suggest that Brennan is a starting point—that may go in any direction—rather than an arrival; and one that can be read alongside Indigenous Australian literature such as the *Ngarla Songs*. Brennan's *Musicopoematographoscope* goes further than Bate's notion of celebration. Rather, it attempts to enact cultural diversity. Brennan does not have a "pure aesthetic" after all. His work is an assemblage that desires further assemblage, creative and critical. Recovering the diversity and energy of the field of Australian poetry requires a critical openness to form and a willingness to read texts beyond their immediate contexts: to not just take poets at their word.

CHAPTER 7

Writing to Order

Gladys Gilligan's "The Settlement"

"The Settlement." Written 1930 (or late 1929); published in Maushart 1993.

As alluded to in the chapter on Harris, settlement was not just about the establishment of white British culture, with anomalous European and Chinese additions. It was also intent on the forced resettlement of Indigenous people, particularly children, and especially lighter-skinned children: with a view to assimilation. What follows is something of an ironic gift: a reading of a meta-text I would rather did not exist, or at least that the conditions that produced it had not. It is a text called "The Settlement," referring to a particular place on Moore River in Western Australia where Indigenous people were resettled (the Australian version of reserves). Gladys Gilligan (1915–c. 1944), a removed (or "stolen") child resident of Moore River Native Settlement, wrote "The Settlement" under direction from A. O. Neville, the Chief Protector of Aborigines, at the age of 14.

When "The Settlement" was published, it was as part of a greater assemblage: the oral and document history *Sort of a Place Like Home: Remembering Moore River Native Settlement* (1993) edited by Susan Maushart. The book includes a representative assemblage within it. What Maushart refers to as the "unsettling" "inspiration" of "The Moore River Scrapbook" (10, 207–269), is a self-conscious gesture that could be said to be her guiding aesthetic: breaking up Gilligan's text through the insertion of photographs. "The Settlement," constituting the book's first chapter, "Introduction One: The Place" also represents a kind of scrapbook (13–21).

Before focusing on "The Settlement" in terms of its poetics, there are implications that relate to reading it as an instance of life writing. In an article on Indigenous life writing, Michele Grossman records that Jackie Huggins, in writing about coauthoring *Auntie Rita* (1994) with her mother, Rita (1921–1996), uses the dual terms "liberated" and "literated." While the latter term "literated" evokes the forced schooling and Anglicization of Rita Huggins's generation of Aboriginal people, and the consequent loss of their own culture, the term "liberated" is also, as Grossman notes, "complex": adding that for the younger Huggins, as a member of a different generation, and as an academic, "writing is not only a tool or technology of oppression and dispossession that was historically used against Aboriginal people; she also deploys it self-consciously as a weapon of cultural resistance, a medium of self-expressiveness and an instrument of political change" (Xen 295). Grossman argues that *Auntie Rita* "is an instance of...the vernacular text...[a] strategy [of writing that] hollows the majority text from within, minoritizing and unsettling both Standard English and conventional writing and reading practices in the process," adding that it "tenants an interstitial zone between the polarities of 'black orality' and 'white writing'" (296–297).

In what follows I draw on several articles by Grossman on Indigenous life writing: though only one, "When They Write What We Read: Unsettling Indigenous Australian Life-writing," addresses Gilligan's text specifically. "The Settlement" can be read as a vernacular text. According to the *Concise Oxford*, "vernacular" is "native, indigenous, not of foreign origin," and ultimately derived from the Latin *verna*: "home-born slave" (1193). By this definition, the concept of vernacular English in an Australian context is oxymoronic. As adapted by Grossman above, it becomes the English practised by the "native," and in Gilligan's case, the "slavishness" or otherwise of her composition is a matter for debate. In Grossman's terms, it is a matter of reading for agency or resistance toward the project of settlement.

"The Settlement" is a "literated" commentary on Moore River Native Settlement: which, however unintentionally, functions as a meta-commentary on the settlement of Australia. Is Gilligan's text settled, or unsettled, by the editing practices of Maushart? In one sense, "The Settlement" is an exemplary "literated" text: written by Gilligan upon the request of the Protector, Neville. It serves doubly as propaganda: as both a description of the Settlement and as a product of it. It purports to show what the Settlement can do with and for Aboriginal children taken from their parents and brought up under a white regime (later known as the Stolen Generation). As edited by Maushart it is also a collaborative text, as Maushart supplements Gilligan's words with 14 photographs of the Settlement: apparently "rhetorical" landscapes in Barthes's terms (4). The photographs extend the text's length appreciably, and add another level of discourse. They break up the text, and quantify the text as a largely visual one.

The text begins with a note to Neville (13):

3 January 1930
Mr A O Neville
Chief Protector of Aborigines

Dear Sir:
   I am forwarding the composition about the Settlement that you asked me to do when you were here. I hope you will like it as I did my very best to have every word complete.

Yours respectfully,
Gilligan

Here we have the author's commentary on her own text, clearly stating the reason for the text being written: it is not a voluntary expression, but a "composition," an exercise. There is a nice ambiguity in the line as broken: "I hope you will like it as I did / my very best to have every word complete." The complete sentence emphasizes the technical nature of the assignment, while the word "do" in the previous sentence, rather than "write," emphasizes that the writing is an uncreative task. "Complete" functions as both adjective and verb, suggesting that the words have been perfectly and correctly written: but also that the words complete a description. The use of the surname only as her signature suggests that, rather than Neville's student, Gilligan is his employee (or prisoner). Other documents relating to Gilligan show that she had been known by that name since she first came to Neville's attention (276–281).

The cover note suggests Gilligan's textual authority, but her texts are framed and undermined by Maushart's editing practice. The cover note introduces Maushart's book: it is the first page of the book proper (following title, copyright, acknowledgments and contents pages); it has a header with the word "Introduction," followed by the words "One: The Place," and a thumbnail black-and-white photograph of a young boy looking off-camera to his left, his left hand to his mouth. This format is repeated for every chapter, using the same photograph. (The format is dropped in the 2003 reprint.) The boy is a detail from an uncaptioned black-and-white group photograph of an Aboriginal woman (kneeling, facing the camera), behind ten small children, boys and girls, arranged for the shot, some standing, some sitting in the dirt, more or less distracted (31). This photo also serves as the book's main cover image (another group photo, less focused, and sepia-toned, is used for the reprint). The group photo accompanies a text by former resident Ralph Dalgety. Dalgety refers to his "Mum" and his being one of a lot of kids, but he cannot be referring to this photo because the children are clearly too close in age to be biological siblings. The boy becomes an icon or, in Zizek's terms, a site of nostalgia. Jennifer Friedlander, in a reading of Barthes' *Camera Lucida*, cites Zizek's argument that "Nostalgia... involves fascination with the 'gaze of the naïve "other" absorbed, enchanted...'" (12). The boy's gaze and gesture are ambiguous: he could be watching something happen just outside the frame, or he could be looking beyond the frame of the Settlement itself. As a marker of the text, though, the boy functions like an arrow: we keep reading to find out what he sees. We can only see his gaze, however, so our reading is destined (designed) to be nostalgic.

Below the note is another photograph, of a dirt road. The perspective is in the direction of the road. This perspective is ambiguous: are we heading somewhere or leaving somewhere? We see the road thinning off to our right, over a rise; the land is relatively flat, the vegetation low. There are no buildings, people, or animals discernible in the shot. The point of the photo is the memory of travelling that road (13). There are three more photos inserted before Gilligan's text begins: the first is of a road approaching Moore River, with a few trees and buildings suggestive of a farming community—except the land doesn't look like farmland; the second of a broad street with houses obscured by trees and about ten people, including children; the third, on a new page, frames Gilligan's title of "The Settlement" and its first sentence with a fourth photo. The third is a close-up of a rough building of wood and corrugated iron and no apparent windows, and in the foreground a cropped, upturned bathtub, some lengths of wood, and possibly a tin container or two; the fourth is a more distanced shot of a row of shacks and a couple of diminutive human figures, with more elaborate buildings further off (14–15).

In "When They Write What We Read," Grossman describes the genre of life writing as "a particularly attractive genre for Indigenous Australians wishing to revision and rewrite historical accounts of invasion, settlement and cross-cultural relationships." She adds that:

> the range of texts that may be defined under the banner of "life writing" is instructively diverse... including both conventional and experimental auto/biography, oral history, testimonial writing, ficto-memoir, biography, essays, and auto-ethnography. [Further], its expansion of and at times resistance to conventional strategies of textual organisation and

conventional codes of textual valency has proved hospitable to authors, and sometimes editors, who wish to allow modalities of oral and written composition to co-exist within the text. (n. pag.)

Grossman describes Gilligan's text as "anodyne," but finds a trace of resistance in its first sentence, which runs: "The Settlement lies on the bank of a river which is called the Moore River, the hills surrounding it making it look quite a pleasant little home" (15). Grossman hones in on the phrase "making it look," writing that "it is possible to read this as a subtle but defiant subterfuge" (n. pag.). We might also see such slippage in "a river which is *called* the Moore River" (called that is, in English), rather than which is the Moore River. It is the word "home," however, that is of most interest to me here. What else does "settlement" mean but making a home somewhere? A home that is "sort of," to refer to Maushart's book title, that is "like" home, that "look[s]" as if it is home, recalls Freud's theory of the uncanny. Freud analyzes the relation between the German translation of uncanny, "*unheimlich*" (unhomely) and its opposite "*heimilich*" (homely): though ostensibly opposites, the two meanings at times coincide. He cites the expression, "we call it '*unheimlich*'; you call it '*heimlich*'" (345–347).

Gilligan's conventional phrase "a pleasant little home" is, to use Grossman's term, "anodyne," but such a phrase would conventionally be used to describe a single house, not a place like the Settlement, which resembles a village with a main street or an estate with servants' quarters. Gilligan gestures toward the "home" as a space that extends beyond a building. Her next sentence emphasizes this, as she shifts the description from "home" to "houses": "The houses are opposite each other..." (17). The active life of the Settlement that Gilligan describes mimics that of settlement on a larger scale. This metonymic aspect is "anodyne" but also perverse, as if the "protected" Aboriginal people were the white people's dolls, living in an extended (and strict) dolls' camp. Grossman points to Gilligan's "lingering over the regimentation of the bells" (the bells are also emphasized by Maushart 45), as well as "the slippage [relating to "subject position"] between 'they' and 'our,'" as in "they catch a fish" and "our colour" (20, 21), which puts Gilligan at a remove from the text. This slippage is echoed in Grossman's title: "When they write what we read."

Despite the settled life of bells, classes, sewing and prayers (18–19), there is also a semblance of continuity with Aboriginal life: fishing (with reeds), hunting (of kangaroos and rabbits with dogs), and gathering (mushrooms in barks) (20). However, hunting now takes place "on the weekend," shifting it from Indigenous everyday life to colonialized pastime. The forced residents are no longer self-sufficient, though self-sufficiency was apparently the

Settlement's aim (85). Former residents recall that sheep were kept and crops grown (100, 113), but there is no reference to farming by Gilligan. She perhaps hints at the failure of this enterprise when she writes, "Everybody here appreciates the goodness of the Government and Chief Protector in providing food and clothing" (21). With this statement from the third-last paragraph, Gilligan shifts her commentary from description to summary. She refers to "the teacher who has taught them to read and write which is the most important thing to know." The ambiguity here is between the practices of reading and writing being "the most important thing to know" and an inexplicit content to absorb or express. This statement leads directly onto the second-last paragraph: "As Mr. Schenk of Mt. Margaret Mission said a little while back, some of our colour who are still uncivilised are being cruelly treated by some of the bad white people" (21). The implication here is that this is "the most important thing to know": what goes on outside the Settlement, the cruelty of "bad white people"; cruel because they are "bad," not because they are "white" or "civilised," and that it is important to make distinctions between people and places. In other words, the Settlement is a safe place, where "our colour" are (being) civilized, and the "white people" are good. There is a promise with an underlying threat here also: that learning to read and write might be an escape, through becoming "civilised," from "cruel treatment." Yet such "civilization" can bring its own problems: as Frederick Douglass, the African American writer who escaped slavery, wrote, "I would at times feel that learning to read had been a curse rather than a blessing. It had given me a view of my wretched condition, without the remedy" (Goodwin 55).

Gilligan presents, rather than expresses, the sentiment that the Settlement is a separate, superior civilization to that of outside, settlement Australia. Her writing style is formal, if not always grammatical: she quotes Schenk as if reporting the statement of an eminent colleague. Gilligan's final sentence runs: "The people here are very thankful for all they have got and they are trying hard to help one another" (21). There is no explicit division made here between the people "of our colour" or the whites. The emphasis on "very thankful" suggests that "all they have got" is "not a lot"; "trying hard to help one another" also belies the image of the Settlement as a haven. It is perhaps, in the words of Lefebvre, a "reduced model...of space...and of so-called culture" (107). Tellingly, Gilligan removes herself from "The Settlement" through the cover note, and, in the text of "The Settlement" itself, through the use of tone, phrasing and third person. If we return to the phrase, "making it look quite a pleasant little home," we see that the word "look" emphasizes Moore River as an image of a home; while "little" bespeaks constriction, of there not being room for Gilligan herself. The Settlement mimics English settlement, but fails to provide a home for its residents; Maushart provides plenty of evidence of this in the following chapters. Yet, as she also records, the experience for many was mixed, particularly because they spent time out of the Settlement in the bush (167–178).

Maushart's book, with its doubly qualified title, *Sort of a Place Like Home*, is a commentary on and an explication, critique, and contradiction of Gilligan's "The Settlement," containing adult testimony, fictionalized narrative, official documents, letters, newspaper reports, and many more photographs. The creation of Moore River Settlement unsettled Aboriginal people from their homes (Maushart 22–41), but the mixed success of this unsettling—mixed even in the colonizer's own terms—was arguably due to the providing of what was not an alternative home life, but an institutional life. In terms of diet, its (in)adequacy was based on a comparison with prisons; Maushart records that Neville considered a prison diet "extravagant" (84). Etymologically, the roots of "institution" and "settlement" are phonically and thematically related. "Institution" derives from the Latin *statuere* = "set up" (Concise 520). If the residents were not "set up" for food and drink, another colloquial version of "set up" is all too pertinent: they were "set up," tricked, or framed, for a crime that wasn't committed. If we set "set up" against the root of "settlement," the Old English *setl*, "place to sit" (964), we think then of the command that children "sit up," while wondering if the residents got many chances to sit, to "sit down, relax, be at home," rather than "sit and work" or "get up" at the latest bell. If we read the Settlement as a prison, it appeared to be lax in some respects, if not liberal, allowing residents to go into the bush to hunt and mix with nonresident Aboriginals (20, 168). This example makes for a perverse history, as the children were themselves originally hunted by police and brought to Moore River, one resident reporting the threat of being shot (24).

How religious was this order, then? In his book, *Religion and Cultural Memory*, Jan Assmann draws on Ancient Egyptian texts, as well as contemporary sociological and cultural theory, in order to discuss the relationship expressed in the book's title. The crucial moment in his thesis is the West's rediscovery of the break made by Akhenaten from traditional religion to monotheism (48). He writes that "The Western horizon of memory is gradually beginning to expand to include its Oriental [Egyptian] roots" (189). Assmann defines religion as "order as such," noting further that, "order is sacred...in contrast to disorder" (34). Perhaps settlement, in general, then, and Moore River Native Settlement, in particular, can be likened to a new religion: one that largely displaces the old, but incorporates some traditional elements to keep the people happy and ensure its own survival. Assmann refers to this larger order as "invisible religion" (Thomas Luckmann's term) and "primary religion," "visible" and "secondary religion" being that of "faith, confession, parish, church" (35–36). This is comparable to the primary, invisible order of British settlement, and to the secondary visible order of school, assimilation, and places like Moore River. The order of Indigenous life was invisible to the colonizers, or at least ignored, thus allowing them to think of projects like Moore River as "bringing order."

Freud's essay "Moses and Monotheism," an important text for Assmann, hypothesizes Moses as a follower of Akhenaten (48). "For Freud," Assmann writes, "the history of religion is a psychodynamic process of repressing and remembering" (46): an apt enough description of the history of settlement, and of Maushart's book. According to Assmann, the moment of Moses's speech to the Jews just before they cross the river Jordan to the "Promised Land" "marks a changed way of life, from the nomadic life in the wilderness to a settled existence in the Promised Land" (16–17). The role of memory is crucial, as:

> The people are expected to master the trick of remembering privation in the midst of abundance, and to recollect their nomadic lifestyle while living a settled existence in towns or in the fields. In short, they must recollect a way of life that is not confirmed by any "framework" of their present reality. That is the exceptional situation of a counterfactual memory. It keeps present to the mind a yesterday that conflicts with every today. (53)

Assman's summary of the Jews' situation corresponds to that of Moore River's residents. They were "chosen people": chosen for their "colour," as one resident remembers, the not-dark, not-white of the half-caste (24). There is a corresponding threat to the loss of culture, despite the differences in context: the Jews were made nomads by exile while the Aboriginals became exiled in settlement, in what was called a "Settlement." Thus the "privation in the midst of abundance" formula has very different implications. There is in fact a double cultural memory to acknowledge for those who lived at Moore River, the first being that of life before the Settlement, the second of life in the Settlement. Elaborating further, Assmann writes:

> counterfactual memory... ensures that people live in this world without feeling at home in it, a memory that far from making you feel at home, denies you a home. This explains why, because of this extraterritoriality, this memory is so greatly at risk, so threatened by forgetfulness, so much in need of every memory technique to help it survive. "Thou shalt not forget" means "thou shalt not become assimilated," not even in the Promised Land. (54)

The "home" or unhome of Moore River Settlement no longer exists. In *Sort of a Place Like Home*, residents remember this home, and the one they had before Moore River. To remember means to resist settlement: in Assmann's unsettling words, "'Thou shalt not forget' means 'thou shalt not become assimilated.'" The not-forgetting and the not-assimilating conflicts when such memories are published in book form often with the involvement of a non-Indigenous editor or coauthor. Maushart's subtitle, *Remembering Moore River Native Settlement*, is designed to function on more than one level. The act of remembering and of making a public record of that memory is the primary one. In terms of Australian cultural memory, remembering Moore River is also important:

> No one is alone with his memories; each man is always part of a whole. The more monstrous the memory, the greater the inevitability with which it finds its way into symbols and into the public sphere. The history of the memory of Auschwitz is only just beginning...the events of Auschwitz do not concern just Germans and Jews, but the whole of mankind, and because of their enormity they create a memory for the whole of mankind. Auschwitz has become part of a normative past from which future generations will derive values and guiding principles. Later still, the history of this memory will some day be written. And it will shed light on the society in which we have lived and which we were. (Assmann 178–179)

The events of colonialism and the destruction visited on Indigenous peoples also "concern the whole of mankind." Moore River has become emblematic of this destruction in Australian cultural memory, primarily through Jack Davis's play *No Sugar* (1985), and Doris Pilkington Garimara's biographical *Follow the Rabbit-Proof Fence* (1996), made into a film by Phillip Noyce (2002). These well-known texts by former residents demonstrate their experience of the Settlement's mistreatment, though inevitably in more dramatic terms than Maushart's book. Assmann's terms the "history of memory," and "every memory technique," suggest the significance of how we remember and what we do with cultural memories. One "memory technique" practiced by Maushart is that of the visual, as it pertains to Gilligan's text in particular; another is that of assemblage: both are techniques that structure Maushart's book as a whole. There is a relation between the two strategies, but they have different implications. Grossman, however, considers them part of the same "surveying" editing perspective.

In her 2001 article "Bad Aboriginal Writing: Editing, Aboriginality, Textuality," Grossman refers to the use of visual materials and paratexts ("introductions [Maushart's book has two], appendices, charts, maps" etc.) in Indigenous life writing as "visualism," a term borrowed from anthropology studies. She argues that the effect of such practices is that:

> One's attention is continually drawn, as a result to the *craft* of text-making, and to the centralising role of the editor in that process. This makes it difficult to "read" these texts in any conventional sense: rather, one surveys them, and it is this mode of surveillance that I want to posit as a key feature in the management of the textual economy of Aboriginal writing. (157)

Jennifer Jones's book on the same topic, *Black Writer White Editors*, provides a different perspective. Jones focuses on the editing of recent Indigenous women's life writing: works, that is, written for publication. Gilligan's text, then, is outside her purview. Nevertheless, Jones provides a counterexample to Grossman's negatively characterized "visualism," as well as demonstrating how editing has a depoliticizing effect on the texts in her study by removing Aboriginal perspectives of spirituality and racism (see, for example, "Editing Oodgeroo," 4–47). As Jones shows, both the manuscripts of Oodgeroo Noonuccal's *Stradbroke Dreamtime* (1972) and Margaret Tucker's *If Everyone Cared* (1977) contain visual elements that were discarded in the editing process (24–30, 85–88). In Oodgeroo's case the erasure of the visual aspect of her legends (such as the story "Burr-nong" ("Bora Ring"), that Oodgeroo presented in shaped form to evoke the Bora ring) was displaced by other visual emphases: the illustrations of non-Indigenous artists, and issues over the cover (40–47). The fact of this displacement, where the visual is as aligned with the writer as much as the editor, contests the negative cast that Grossman attributes to the visual as such, and suggests, rather, issues of control: whose visuality is presented?

Grossman contrasts what she calls the "inferred trace" of the role of book editor, in most cases of editing non-Indigenous authors, to the "editor-as-overseer," in the production of Aboriginal life writing texts (157–158), and questions the effects of their authority. The "editor-as-overseer" is a role comparable to that of Chief Aboriginal Protector Neville. Neville is the dominant figure in "One Half Caste Girl," Maushart's biographical chapter on Gilligan: he checks on her chaperonage (287), gives permission for her to go for a walk (290), and both supports and challenges Gilligan's story of her child's paternity (305, 313). Almost six years after writing "The Settlement," Gilligan would write in a letter to Neville, "I don't want to bore you with my life story" (314). Maushart's book, though not mentioned in Grossman's article, fits the description of so-called visualism, and, therefore, according to Grossman requires "surveying" rather than "'read[ing]'...in any conventional sense." This (earlier) position is contradicted by the quote from Grossman above where she argues for the "vernacular text"'s potential in "unsettling both Standard English and conventional writing and reading practices." This may indicate a move away from "conventional" reading by Grossman (the article on the "vernacular text" is from 2005): perhaps she is now happy to have her reading practice unsettled?

An unsettled reading and a reading that has withdrawn into "surveillance" are not the same thing. Yet if such editing practices have themselves become conventional, why are they then so difficult to read? Should they ("difficult" stories after all) be easily available for the purposes of what Carter and T. G. H. Strehlow have described (in the context of Aranda song-making) respectively as "European-style...enlightenment," and the "vice" of "easy comprehension" (Lie 40). Such difficulty participates, paradoxically, in the everyday: "The quotidian has no center, no inner meanings, no deep structure...And this is what makes it so difficult for interpretation to define it, or authority to control it" (Shaviro 112). Different power relations reside in the difficult: Indigenous authority may be preserved by the difficult; difficulty may resist a ruling authority. Alison Ravenscroft, in a book-length work on the problems of White readings of Indigenous texts, *The Postcolonial Eye*, writes of protective silences (17), aporias (2), and the "achievement" of the "necessarily impossible" text (47). In a translation context, Muecke cites an instance from Andreas Lommel's 1938 fieldwork where "for rhythm and sentimental reasons [the Kimberley songmaker] changed the language so that some of his songs could not be translated"; such deliberate obscurity creating what translator Stuart Cooke has called a "haze" (Preface 9). Difficulty might then resist "surveillance." Grossman's "difficulty," however, appears to of a different order, and related "to the difficulty of talking about visual prosody" (Dworkin 32). Dworkin's uses Perloff's term "visual prosody" in relation to the work of American poet Susan Howe, who borrows historical life writing documents in order to create new work (see, for example, *Singularities*). Howe frames these works as poetry, however, rather than history, and they are accepted as such by poetry's institutions. (As Maushart's work is similarly accepted by the institutions of non-fiction: *Sort of a Place Like Home* won the Adelaide Festival Prize for non-fiction in 1994.) Dworkin writes: "The unconventional look of Howe's pages...is one aspect of her work which critics have consistently noted but failed to seriously address...we lack a sophisticated critical tradition and ready vocabulary" (32).

As Grossman's term "surveillance" suggests, she is concerned with the replication of the colonial in editing practice, specifically with regard to

Aboriginal life writing. This is yet another instance of Aboriginal lives being managed and controlled by white authority: life writing is seen; Indigenous life writing is overseen. In other words, it is co-opted for settlement. Grossman claims that in such texts, the "role of the editor" is "centralis[ed]." In *Sort of a Place Like Home*, Maushart identifies as the author of the work, and refers to her editor in the acknowledgments. She writes of "'The Moore River Scrapbook' [that it] was a last-minute inspiration of my editor Bryce Moore, whose ability to understand what I was getting at even better than I did was sometimes unsettling" (10). Maushart appears to use the term "unsettling" obliviously, without any notion of what "settling" might mean in terms of the book's production. She describes writing the book as both a "quest" and "the adventure of a lifetime," adding that the material had been "dug" from "a goldmine of Aboriginal Australia" (viii). Such are the metaphors of colonialism.

Grossman's desire for both a conventionally readable text and a text that resists the latest convention in editing practices is contradictory. A tentative reading of Gilligan's work in terms of its visual prosody, that is, in terms of the poetics of contemporary poetry (where such editing practices are not conventional), may appreciably unsettle "The Settlement." In order to do this we must read it in terms of its pages, rather than its sentences. It is the page as poetic unit, as Perloff argues, that is "behind...the alteration and juxtaposition of 'verse to 'prose'" (Dance 110), adding that such alterations result in a "change in prosody," and "in perspective, tone and mood" (112–113). The page becomes a "ground" where "shifting" (unsettling) occurs. Like Grossman, Perloff also writes of "seeing" the page, but her terms are those of the avant-garde: "The page is to be seen, its contrasting juxtaposed elements recalling the bits of newspaper or photographs pasted into Cubist or Dada collage" (113). Such notions of the page rely, of course, on a Western, Gutenbergian conception of writing, whereas "in the case of Aboriginal Australia this [writing] would include sand paintings and drawings...body markings, paintings as well as engravings on bark or stone" (Davis et al. 306). Yet Perloff's visual reading also gestures outside the page, towards Cubist painting, for example.

In Perloff's critique, "assemblage" is merely a broader term for "collage" and therefore a practice that can be subsumed under (visual) reading (34). The differences in the critiques of Grossman and Jones can also be defined in terms of reading the assemblage. While Grossman seems to object to the construction of an assemblage that interferes with reading, Jones decries the dismantling of a preexisting Indigenous assemblage of both form and thought. In Deleuze's assemblage, "The difficult part is making all the elements of a non-homogenous set converge, making them function together.

Structures are linked to conditions of homogeneity, assemblages are not. The assemblage is sympathy, symbiosis" (Dialogues 52), adding that "an assemblage...is a multiplicity" (69). We can see that, in Deleuze's terms, Moore River was conceived as a structure designed to homogenize and assimilate; but it is more interesting to read for the ways in which it was an assemblage. In opposing two kinds of order, that of assemblage and structure, Deleuze provides a way to move beyond the religious reading derived from Assmann above. If we consider Grossman's professed inability to produce a "conventional reading," we could say that she makes the mistake of reading for structure rather than assemblage; whereas Jones's critique could be said to describe the displacement of assemblage for structure, for homogeneity: literally, through Oodgeroo's and Tucker's editors' (typographical) justifications. I am not claiming that the deep sympathy of the presettlement Indigenous assemblage allows it to be read as a Deleuzian structure; but in the context of settlement, of texts produced by the Indigenous appropriation of English, and of these texts' consequent reappropriation by non-Indigenous publishers and editors, we are in assemblage "country." The multiple is everywhere: multiple literacies, multiple writing and editing practices, multiple perspectives, and multiple outcomes.

The issue for both Grossman and Jones is the control of the text, and how or to what extent it becomes a text that supports settlement. In Jones's studies, it is crucial to remember the oral history of Indigenous writing and what could be called the poetic assemblage of dance, painting, and song. This is not to primitivize or to deny the innovation required to produce written English texts, but to note the connection demonstrated (at least between the visual and writing) in Jones's examples of Oodgeroo and Tucker. In Gilligan such a connection is not manifest, but the issue of control is still pertinent: how Gilligan's two texts (the cover note and "The Settlement") are reassembled in the company of anonymous photographs under Maushart's authorship. The complexities of Gilligan's "anodyne" text are a result of the complex conditions that produced it. "The Settlement" as published, which has as its appendage a book length history of Moore River, is further complicated by its publishing context. Maushart, as Grossman notes, "offers no verbal commentary [on] or contextualisation" of "The Settlement" directly; Grossman refers to this strategy as "now familiar": this "not wanting to speak for, over-write or otherwise occlude Indigenous voices" (When n.pag.). She adds that the inclusion of photographs of the Settlement "give the lie, visually speaking, to the bucolic scenes sketched out in the opening lines of the composition." As these photographs lack "commentary," it is difficult to read them as "giving the lie" without making the assumption that this is Maushart's intention. They are illustrative, but not simply so. There are photos of the sewing work-room, the Settlement's "avenue," and of children lining up for school; there is also one of a washroom and another of what appears to be an improvised humpy, but might also be a shed. Grossman argues that the insertion of photographs "participates in a specific cultural history of representational strategies in which writing is rendered suspect by image and the witness of the image-recording "eye" of the photographer is juxtaposed to the witness of the textually encoding "I" of the scribe" (n.pag.). Grossman objects to this practice as it "positions Gladys Gilligan as a suspect narrator"; yet following the same logic, the image and the (uncredited) photographer's "eye" are also rendered suspect. Further, Grossmann presumes that all images work in the same way.

In his essay "The Uses of Photography," John Berger argues that "photographs which already exist" (as opposed to news photographs, for example) are "Normally used...to illustrate an argument...they are used tautologically, so that the photograph merely repeats what is being said in words" (60). Though this seems somewhat simplistic, avoiding the effect that the words have on producing the meaning of the image, what Berger suggests as an alternative has the potential to construct a word-image complex of greater dimension. Berger argues for creating a "Now" by using photographs in a "radial" and "associati[ve]" manner, miming the working of memory (60). Alternatively, Geoffrey Batchen proposes that "the more banal the photograph, the greater its capacity to induce us to exercise our imagination" (88). Any photo of the everyday can be termed banal: and the banal has particular resonance in the context of Moore River, if we know that it derives from "compulsory" (Concise 67). How much inducement is there for readers to "exercise our imagination" if we take our cues from the text? We might imagine life at Moore River from the photos in Maushart's book, but to reverse Grossman's complaint about writing being visualized, at every step we find the photographs textualized. While this approach may not necessarily make Gilligan's narrative suspect, an imaginative response to the photos necessitates disregard for the written text. Grossman appears not to consider the possibility of a more integrated, Indigenous-authored representation of word and image, a possibility that Jones reveals in her publication of extracts from Oodgeroo's and Tucker's manuscripts; Grossman's attitude is perhaps produced by the history of visual erasure that Jones reveals.

The text of Gilligan's cover note appears on one page, uninterrupted by photos, but, nevertheless, framed by the thumbnail of the boy described above, and by the photo of the road. The boy could be said to represent the obedient child that Gilligan was then, hand to mouth, seeing and not saying; while the road represents the one that Gilligan would disappear down (13). If we apply a prosodical reading to the photo itself we might imagine a "whoosh" or a "zip" as the real Gilligan evades being caught in the composition. What, referring back to Perloff, is the change "in perspective, tone and mood"? The child in the photo is inattentive to the composition of the photo, he is looking to his left, his hand to his mouth. If "Photography transform[s] subject into object" (Barthes 13): is the boy an object? This not-yet-repeated image of the boy-as-symbol was an insightful choice by Maushart, for it is this boy among the group whose gaze is ambivalent: not resigned, obedient, skeptical, or even distracted exactly, though he is distracted; it could almost be said, deliberately distracted. This ambivalence, emphasized further in the book by the photo's "unanalyzable" repetition (Pepper 76), gives the boy a level of (admittedly ambivalent) subjecthood: marking as he does Maushart's editing "thumb." For the boy is not merely a photographer's portrait, but an editor's cropped detail. As an icon, he "expresses" Maushart's editorial object, rather than "represents" or "symbol[izes]" anything (Freeland 55). He becomes in effect Maushart's signature. Maushart enacts the removal of the boy from community and makes him do work: to punctuate and "mind the gate" at each chapter. Being subject means being subject to the Settlement, another form of objecthood, objecthood beginning also to repeat. Yet as Freeland argues, citing art historian Charles Barber, an "icon...is not a site of identification...but a site of desire" (56). Within a religious context, an icon is believed to "protect" and to "conduct miracles" (57). It is sacred: in other words, produced by "sacrifice" (Bataille 119). If the icon of the boy expresses seeing or memory, the reader's desire may be multiple: to see and remember, to absolve, to protect against recurrence, to enact change, or to make the story fictional.

The photo is a fact, reinforced by the date and the addressee's name that follow in the note: "3 January 1930" and "Mr A O Neville"; his role: "Chief Protector of Aborigines"; and the conventional address: "Dear Sir." The perspective has changed from that of the anonymous photographer to that of Gilligan; the object is no longer the photo of the (gaze of the) boy, but the fulfillment of an exercise for Neville. The note itself is two sentences. The first ("I am forwarding the composition that you asked me to do when you were here") contains an even lyrical exchange of pronouns: "I...you...me...you." The second ("I hope you will like it as I did my very best to have every word complete") shifts the ratio in Gilligan's favor: "I...you...I...my." The emphasis on the excessive "my" is directed toward her own self-estimation: "my very best." Once we have noticed this, the conventional signature, "Yours respectfully, / Gilligan," suggests a giving up of Gilligan's "my" to Neville's "yours": or irony. Then there is the photo of the road. By including it on the page with the first introduction's title of "The Place," Maushart suggests that the Settlement is a place to arrive at or leave, but not a place to be. Yet the road could also be read as an image of openness. Whether the photograph can be read as one of Indigenous perspective is not clear from Maushart's book. Anthropologist Eric Michaels has argued that too easy readings of Indigenous landscape images are a mistake, noting in a video-making context that

> attention to landscape is so persistent... that it seems unlikely that it can be analysed as naïve or unintentional [but]... derive from the ways that this nomadic culture looks at the landscape, recalling details of topography, outline, vegetation, associating all this with stories which serve mnemonic locational and historical functions. (63)

We might then consider the photo of the road as being as iconic as that of the portrait: an icon "depicts the spiritual, not the physical" (Freeland 57); yet from Michaels' description this is not an easy distinction to make. Rather it suggests that from an Indigenous perspective, the physical and the spiritual are one.

An Indigenous person's perspective of landscape—that of Paddy Roe—is demonstrated in the photographs included in *Reading the Country*: another Western Australian book project, albeit one more explicitly collaborative. Muecke writes that "Paddy Roe constructed the country as we walked along" (40). Photos accompany the text, one of which shows "Nyigina man" Roe facing the country that is being written of (Roebuck Plains, near Broome, northwest Western Australia), with his back to the camera; another, also taken from behind, shows Roe with arm outstretched, indicating the country described in the text (15; 40–42). The photos frame the land and Roe's perspective of it. The collaborative nature of the project resists any perception that it is a white, or otherwise homogenous, framework: "with three authors one cannot imagine that the book is guided by any poetic unity or harmony" (15). I provide this example, and the Michaels quote, not only to emphasize that Indigenous texts, visual or otherwise, may resist Western paradigms of reading (despite the utilization of non-Indigenous forms such as video-making and composition exercises), but also to point out that other models of combining text and photography and authorship, in the context of Indigenous and non-Indigenous collaboration, existed prior to Maushart's book.

Both *Reading the Country* and *Sort of a Place Like* Home were published by Fremantle Arts Centre Press. Both books were designed by the same person (John Douglass). Maushart's book is historical and relies on archival materials, whereas that of Benterrak et al. is a contemporary reading, though informed by Roe's historical—or traditional—knowledge. The authorizing function of *Reading the Country* is exemplary in its democracy, sharing credit equally with the painter of the book's images (Benterrak), scribe, essayist, and photographer (Muecke) and elder-narrator (Roe). There is no "centralising" editing function. Perhaps the risk of displacing the editor's "centralising role" with that of the critic is what Grossman resists in her tentative use of "unsettling" as a term. I don't disagree with her implication that there is room for ethical improvement in the publication of Aboriginal life writing texts. However, it is the necessity of developing a reading practice of such "visualised" texts that I am arguing for here. When we pay attention to the visual prosody of such a short text as Gilligan's cover note, we notice the alternation between short lines that function similarly (in terms of contrast if not scale), to two kinds of poetic line. What appears to happen, when semantics and rhythmic prosody are deemphasized in favor of line length and visual prosody, is that the short factual statements, "3 January 1930" and "Mr A O Neville / Chief Protector of Aborigines," the address, "Dear Sir," and the signature, "Yours respectfully, / Gilligan," seem to perform the poetic, while the "lyrical," personal, informational sentences perform the prosaic. The effect of prosody is in the contrast. If we recognize this, then we allow a reading of the rhythm, rather than an emphasis on the semantic.

Photographs, like texts, can of course be edited. This fact is easily lost in the blur of what editing entails: it may mean selection and organization; it may mean alteration. Turning from Gilligan's cover note, the next facing pages consist of four landscape photos and the first sentence of "The Settlement." On the left are two photos (14); on the right the other two photos sandwich the text (15). The margins for both pages are the same, indicating that the photos on the right have been cropped to make room for the text. If we read the first photo, with a road in the foreground, as following the road photo from the previous page, then it seems the road was designed to lead us to the Settlement, which can be seen in the background. The photo follows this by taking us into the Settlement itself. As the cover note is presented as text between two photos, the narrow band of white between the two photos on the following page (that is, without text) suggests silence. But a silence of what nature? Is it representative—the falling silent of the new resident as they approach their new "sort of" home—or is it a dramatic pause before Gilligan's narrative proper commences? This gives a sense of eeriness, as there are several children, one apparently skipping, in the bottom photo. Without "verbal commentary or contextualisation," the introduction of these uncaptioned photos has the unintended consequence of "occlud[ing] Indigenous voices." Gilligan's text becomes secondary, as if it is written to accompany the photos, a pretext to empty out and silence the Settlement. The photos at the top of the next facing pages are out of focus as if blurred by time, making the figures of the people (and dog) in them into ghosts (16–17; see also the cover of reprint).

Unlike the facsimiles of Gilligan's handwritten letters later in Maushart's book (302–303, 311–312, 314–315), "The Settlement" is typeset. The typography gives Gilligan's text a more contemporary effect than that of the blurred photographs (in the reprint the letters are set in a font that suggests handwriting). Rereading "The Settlement" after reading her letters, what becomes noticeable is Gilligan's direct, firm style: "There is also the patch of young pines of one year's growth, which are all growing rapidly. They were grown by Mr. Neal the Superintendent of Moore River" (17). In a 1935 letter, objecting to Neville's claim that her child was too dark to have a white father (313), she writes, "I know very well that Frank is Grady's father and I'll stick to that as I've said before colour doesn't count by any means" (315). Gilligan adds, "What matters? Why recall the past? It is the future I'm looking forward to" (315). I don't agree that Gilligan's narration is rendered "suspect"; but I agree with Grossman that Gilligan's texts are *de*centralized by Maushart's use of photographs, that is, by her editing (authoring) role. Consequently the photographs and Maushart's use of them are rendered suspect, in that they tend to divert us from Gilligan's writing about the Settlement, representing it as empty and silent; and by using de- or re-authored (appropriated) photographs. Reading "The Settlement" in terms of its visual prosody enables us to be critical of the effect of "the *craft* of text-making" [Grossman's italics], and of "centralising [the] role of the editor." But as one critic of concrete poetry argues, to see and read are now the same (Espinosa 80); while another argues for "simultaneity" of reading, where the visual and semantic meanings are appreciated at once (Bohn, *Aesthetics* 66–67). These theories may seem inappropriately aesthetic in the context of Gilligan's "The Settlement," however, on a more politicized note, another Italian visual poet, Eugenio Miccini, argues that it is a feature of contemporary civilization that the image is already colonized (Espinosa 80).

The problematic task of reading Maushart's appropriation of Gilligan's "The Settlement" can be rethought—reread—through Barthes's theory of the "punctum." Barthes describes the punctum as "this element which rises from the scene, shoots out of it like an arrow, and pierces me." The punctum is a "wound," a "prick" (26). Like the colons in Bennelong's "Letter," the photos in "The Settlement" can be read as wounds within the text of "The Settlement." If we think of the detail of the boy used throughout as a punctum of its original photograph for Maushart, this makes sense, as his image punctuates the book. Punctuation marks, like texts, also form a collectivity, a community: "they can never appear 'alone'," but are in "necessarily unstable and taut equilibrium." These quotes, from Jennifer DeVere Brody (56) and Jean-Luc Nancy (xxxvii), recall Mead's networks of language. Sontag, too, can be said to allude to a need for punctuation in *On Photography*; she argues that photographs "are a grammar, and even more importantly, an ethics of seeing" (3). Sontag enlarges on her theme of ethics, writing that "To photograph is to appropriate the thing photographed. It means putting oneself into a certain relation to the world that feels like knowledge—and, therefore, like power" (4).

Maushart did not take the photographs in *Sort of a Place Like Home*, but she did edit them, order them: constructing a knowledge, or knowledgeable affect, of Moore River. It is as if the memory now belongs to the reader: "Memory freeze-frames; its basic unit is the single image" (Sontag, *Regarding* 22). This aphorism is parodied by retrospective claiming of photographs as memory. Such an image is itself an assemblage, according to Deleuze and Claire Parnet, "The minimum real unit is not the word, the idea, the concept or the signifier, but the *assemblage*. It is always an assemblage which produces utterances" (51). Their argument corresponds with Perloff's for the page as an uttering assemblage. Bataille describes the process of appropriation as a cyclical one of consumption and excretion: Maushart consumes photos and texts (memories), and produces/excretes an assemblage we in turn consume. Bataille introduces the image of communion here, Christian communion being both consumption and memorial (94–95). We might think, then, of Maushart as a priest who approaches the conceptual disorder of a state of memory and institutes a new memory-structuring religion.

Maushart's book can be read, then, as rather a hallowing, or enforcing of settlement, rather than an unsettlement, an ordering of a multiplicity of experience. That the photographs are not literally memories for its audience suggests that they represent memory in general: memory—or "remembering"—displacing history. Yet if, as Sontag suggests, "the photograph is like a quotation," then its claim to objective testimony is already suspect. Sontag refers to print as "less treacherous" than photographic images: the written being "frankly an interpretation" (*Photography* 22), whereas taking photographs "is essentially an act of non-intervention" and of "refusing" "experience" (11, 9). In adding such images in the "editing" of "The Settlement," Maushart diverts us from Gilligan's interpretation: from, as Sontag puts it, her "statements about the world," toward "pieces of it, miniatures of reality that anyone can make or require" (4). Sontag returns to this theme in the later *Regarding the Pain of Others*, when she states that photographs from a war "create the illusion of consensus," adding "No 'we' should be taken for granted when the subject is looking at other people's pain" (6, 7). Further, as Berger writes, "The picture becomes evidence of the general human condition. It accuses nobody and everybody": in other words it is "depoliticized" (40).

It is such "illusion[s]" and "evidence" that drive and mask the wielding of power. The complications, contradictions, and ironies within—and without—Gilligan's text are muted in favor of an assumed, undifferentiated perception; a perception that remains implicit. The ethics of reading "The Settlement" visually requires a non-seeing, and a refusal of the editorial. The photographs, then, might be seen to function as large, nonverbal, textual marks. This is not to replicate the emptying of *terra nullius*, for photographs are not country. They are not even memory for most readers (not even, necessarily, for former residents). If we consider the content of these photos compared to the others in the book, they appear to be leftovers, uncaptionable: and therefore, unreadable: Mary Price claims that "Describing is necessary for photographs... It is the act of describing that enables the act of seeing" (6). Though several include human figures, none are quite portraits (excepting the thumbnail boy). Their placing, their nonrepresenting of the no-place of the Settlement, is uncanny; and Freud's concept has similarities to Barthes's punctum, as Friedlander notes: "the *punctum* exists not at the level of content, but rather at the level of form. The *punctum* thus functions similarly to the Freudian notion of a dream detail" (25). As form, then, its wounding action is not aggressive but defensive (Iser 44).

To let each photograph that accompanies the "Settlement" become a punctuation mark, a punctum, is to memorialize the wounds of Moore River. Barthes writes: "I now know that there exists another *punctum*... [other] than the 'detail.' This new *punctum*, which is no longer of form but of intensity, is Time, the lacerating emphasis of the *noeme* ('*that-has-been*'), its pure representation." Although the example Barthes gives is a photograph of a condemned man, he extrapolates a truth that applies to all photos, "I read at the same time: *This will be* and *this has been*; I observe with horror an anterior future of which death is the stake" (96). A reading of the photographs as punctuation need not preclude other readings, but rather proffers a potentially conventional textual reading practice among multiple, possibly simultaneous practices, including that of reading the visual prosody of the photos themselves. As Barthes indicates, a reading of the punctum "brings the Photograph (certain photographs) close to the Haiku" (49). His comparison suggests the formalized nature of the punctum.

"The hunt for more dramatic images... drives the photographic enterprise" (Regarding 23). Sontag's context for this remark is that of news reportage; yet in the "photography of atrocity," she writes, the hunt is for "authenticity," adding that "people want the weight of witnessing without the taint of artistry, which is equated with insincerity or mere contrivance" (26).

Such "amateur" (27) images serve Maushart in authenticating *Sort of a Place Like Home*, while diverting attention from (yet ultimately back to) her own editing "artistry." A reading of Gilligan's text as a text punctuated by photos in maximal addition to conventional punctuation, constructs a visual poetics, adding a new element of diversity to the field of the page.

Grossman suggests that Gilligan's agency is a parodic one, ironically playing the Protector's puppet:

> it is possible to read "The Settlement" not for whether it is able to speak "authentically" or "truthfully" as an instance of Indigenous articulation about colonial structures, but for how mimicry and ventriloquism may be deployed to call attention to the arguable stratagems and duplicities of the text's constitution. (When n.pag.)

Following this shift from writer to text, Grossman argues that "'The Settlement' unsettles a range of critical and theoretical constructs that have been mobilized in thinking about and evaluating Indigenous life writing and raises questions about genre, valency and—pre-eminently—'voice.'" She further speaks of the problematic "distinctions...between 'expression' and 'representation'...[and the] oral and literate." To exclude a text like "The Settlement" from the Indigenous life writing genre would, Grossman argues, be "valorising this [genre] as a mode of uncomplicated self-*expression* rather than conscious self-*representation*" [Grossman's italics]. Further, she is critical of "Arguments that seek to establish 'orality' as the constitutive feature of 'authentic' or 'inherent' Aboriginal identity." Grossman finds that such arguments "homogenise and unify a construct of 'Aboriginal culture,' past and present, in ways that do not accurately reflect...uneven histories [and]...fail to attribute to Indigenous Australian people...the agency that governs their ability to invent and manage their own identities, stories, representation and destinies" (n.pag.).

Grossman ascribes agency to "The Settlement" through the use of "unsettles" as a critical term. What has been unsettled, she asserts, is critical constructions of "Indigenous life writing." The term's relationship to settlement as such, however, appears to be thematic rather than (anti-)structural. The evidence of Jones's book is that recent examples of editorial control replicate earlier settlement structures; that is, such control is of a settling determination. Grossman's use of the term "unsettling" resonates in both the anti-colonial and the affective senses if we compare the fates of Indigenous life writing texts to the lives of the writers themselves, writers such as Gilligan. The micromanagement of her life (Maushart 272) becomes displaced by constructions of her story. "The Settlement" introduces the notion of ironic life writing: it is the deliberately depersonalized story Gilligan is allowed to tell of her "home," while the story of her original home, and of being taken from it to be brought to Moore River (271), remains largely unwritten (though there are potent glimpses in Maushart's book). Moreover, "The Settlement" comes with its own brief commentary: the ironically personal cover note.

Gilligan's description indicates that Moore River Native Settlement didn't quite mimic English settlement in Australia, nor did the English definition of "home" prevail. In relation to the broader settlement of Australia, then, as well as in relation to Aboriginal people in the area, the Settlement at Moore River functioned rather as an "*un*settlement." Gilligan's "The Settlement" functions, consequently, as a representative unsettling text.

CHAPTER 8

Homelessness

Ann Williams's and Sarah Davenport's Travelling Diaries; Drover Bush Texts; Wiradjuri Club Drawings; Charlie Flannigan's Baroque Drawings 1893

Williams's and Davenport's diaries written 1882 and 1840s; published Frost 1984

Drover boab texts published Lewis 2008

Wiradjuri clubs published van Toorn 2006

Flannigan's drawings published van Toorn 2006

In the *Networked Language* chapter (also called "Homelessness") on twentieth-century poet Judith Wright, Mead quotes her poem "Habitat" (1973): "Inside the books were read and the words were scribbled" (326). Much of the writing we have considered so far was done outside. In this chapter I go beyond the limits of the literal field in order to read the texts of travellers and drovers: the diaries of Ann Williams and Sarah Davenport as they accompany their husbands in a new country, looking for grass, never themselves settled; the carved (and sometimes painted) road texts of drovers; the carved letters that appear on Wiradjuri clubs following settlement; and the text included in the drawings of an Indigenous stockman, Charlie Flannigan. These texts demonstrate unsettlement—materially, structurally, and grammatically—and thereby contest the settled model of Australian writing, which represents a settled nation.

Settlement was based on two kinds of displacement: of the settlers themselves, who came to find a new home in Australia, and that of the Indigenous people who were dispossessed by this process. Inevitably, then, the advent of settlement produced new forms of homelessness. While Indigenous people were forced to move around, in furtive or rigid parody of their previous nomadic existence, non-Indigenous settlers became pastoral nomads as they searched for an Australian home. The word "nomad" derives from the Greek "nemo," meaning pasture (Concise 688), and refers to seeking new pastures for herds. Nomadism derives from preagricultural farming culture ("agri" being "field" in Latin, 19). In the context of colonization in German Southwest Africa, John K. Noyes writes that:

> Nomadism has become an integral part of our understanding not only of other cultures, but of our own. Still, it remains a misleading concept. The conceptual location of nomadism at the intersection of pastoralism and spatial mobility is not accidental. (198)

The literally unsettled writers of this chapter are not the first of this study; many of the writers already considered (Kelly, Bennelong, Jong, Fullerton, Miriny-Mirinymarra Jingkiri, Gilligan) were unsettled, unhoused, displaced, and their texts were directly produced from those circumstances.

Jennifer Rutherford, in a chapter of *Halfway House: The Poetics of Australian Spaces*, offers thoughts on the colonial concepts of home and house. The book's title alludes to Bachelard's *The Poetics of Space*; the "Australian" qualifier and the pluralizing of "Spaces" indicating a desire to modify and extend Bachelard's framework. From Rutherford's "Undwelling; or Reading Bachelard in Australia":

> ...in the Australian context, space and its poetics cannot assume the innocence with which Bachelard imbues the house. From the first moment of cultural contact, Australian settler spatial poetics rides on a complex raft of intersubjective and intercultural dialogue and conflict. The house never simply contains, nor is it simply present in the world of things. Its materiality is brought into question and its existence hinges on both exile and displacement. The production of space for white settler culture occurs always in a space of pre-existing spatial memory, imagination and invention, in which every act of housing is coterminously an act of unhousing. Since its first theoretical articulations, the poetics of Australian space has emerged as a response to this specific politics of place. (114–115)

In using the term "unhousing" here, Rutherford not only suggests Indigenous displacement ("intercultural...conflict") but also the negative ground that cannot find the harmony that Bachelard proposes; this is, as Rutherford insists, politics as much as poetics. Rutherford notes further that:

> Unhousing is not anathema to Bachelard. In fact, he identifies it as the proper domain of psychoanalysis in contrast to the healthy and happy psyche of the well-housed subject. Bachelard's unconscious is the font of poetic genesis and its house the site of felicitous memory. The psychoanalytic unconscious by contrast is all that cannot be housed in the ego; the repressed, the unsaid, and the unimagined. It is this unhoused detritus of the subject—the radical other of Bachelard's subject of felicitous space—that I suggest we find appearing again and again in tropes of unhousing throughout the white Australian literary tradition. (115–116)

There is an implied critique or contrast between the settled nation (Bachelard's France) and the nation in the process of being settled: that is, Australia. The notion of "the well-housed subject" implies a bourgeois exemplar that could not be taken for granted in colonial, convict, Aboriginal Australia. Rutherford goes on to list literary "unhoused" examples, mainly from fiction, but alluding also to Harpur's poem "The Creek of the Four Graves" (120). Yet though these works provide a reading of the unhoused, such a reading relies on the thematic and semantic, rather than unorthodox or unhoused forms of literacy, grammar, punctuation, lettering, and—in the case of tree and club carvings—sites of textual production (or enunciation). While settlers brought with them the notion or invention of the house, they also learned about Australian outdoor living. In his study *With the White People*, Henry Reynolds cites a humorous example:

> an early West Australian settler on an expedition with Aboriginal guides: "Where shall we make a house, I said to my assistants?" "What for house make?" said she, pointing laughingly to the clear blue sky and bright moon. I felt ashamed of my effeminacy, so followed their example in laying myself down upon the ground, with my feet to the fire. (38)

A contrasting situation is presented ironically in a scene from Katherine Susannah Prichard's story "Marlene": "The half-caste held herself with some dignity: her faded eyes, ringed like agates, looked up at the pleasantly smiling, healthy, fresh-complexioned woman on the big horse. 'I'm not used to living out of doors'" (382). In Rutherford's "construction," Bachelard's reduced assemblage (rid of its detritus) of house and memory is one that fails to hold in an Australian context. She points to Carter's essay, "The Forest in the Clearing" (from the same volume): "Carter...argues that the limits of Bachelard's poetics lie not simply in its universalizing of a local imaginary but in its failure to understand how a poetic-spatial imaginary itself is produced from complex history" (115). Carter himself cites Lefebvre:

> Bachelard cannot explain how the spaces of dwelling are *produced*: his conception of production as "a causing-to-appear, a process of emergence which brings a thing forth as if a thing now present amidst other already-present things" is "restricted and restrictive." (136)

As Lefebvre points out, the "solidity of the house" is imaginary: it is rather a "complex of mobilities" consisting of "streams of energy which run in and out of it by every imaginable route: water, gas, electricity, telephone lines, radio and television signals, and so on" (93).

"The very nature of their [nomads'] existence is the negation of building, which is the basis of civilization," writes Thomas J. Barfield in *The Nomad Alternative*, citing "fourteenth century Arab social historian Ibn Khaldun" (3). Noyes echoes this sentiment when he asserts that "the social order of the nomad has been discussed as the barbaric negative of the *polis*" (199). He further cites nineteenth-century French philosopher Auguste Comte, to the effect that "the 'prime human revolution' is the 'passage from nomadic life to the sedentary state'" (201), and nineteenth-century German psychologist Richard von Krafft-Ebing, who considered that "civilisation 'is hastened whenever nomadic habits yield to the spirit of colonisation, where man establishes a household. He feels the necessity for a companion in life, a housewife in a settled home'" (202). This is all very conventional. More interestingly, Noyes cites an "Ancient Greek tripartite classification of human society," adopted by both Rousseau and Adam Smith, "of hunters, nomads and agriculturalists" (213). This classification suggests that all three types can exist at once, examples of which can be found in both Indigenous and colonial non-Indigenous cultures.

If a house cannot be a home, can a home exist outside a house? (Reynolds's anecdote above suggests so.) In Rutherford's terms, where "unhousing" and "undwelling" are synonymous, what of "unhoming"? New settlers, Ann Williams and Sarah Davenport, describe their struggles to hold onto a sense of civilization, without having a building to call home. Lucy Frost finds Williams's diary (which she included in her anthology of writings by settler women, *No Place for a Nervous Lady*) "almost childishly naïve," adding that:

> Spelling follows sound as often as it does the dictionary. The unheard "e" in "homely" remains unseen as well. Sentences, too, are shaped by sound rather than rules. They neither begin with capital letters nor come to an end with a fullstop, and yet the prose is seldom difficult to read because she has a much better ear for the language than textbooks alone can hear. (212)

Frost notes that "Education does not always aid expression," and that Williams's 1882 text "seems familiar to a modern ear" (214). Frost's reference to the word "homely," or as Williams writes, "homly," cites a description by Williams of people she liked: "they seemed like very nice homly people." Frost hones in on this uncanny word use, as if the word "homely" could not be maintained on the road: the "spell" of the home has broken down, exposing Williams's longing.

Williams' diary extracts are included, aptly enough, in a section of Frost's book titled "Travelling through a Strange Land." For instance, Williams writes, "I don't know the place that we stopped for dinner but it was not very far out of Braidwood"; "we will soon be in the wild country   a little further on is the Araluen Mountain   I thought that we was at it last Night for I thought that we was in a pretty wild country but it is 4 miles further on"; "we have been following a River since last Tuesday   they call it the Dooey River   I never heard the name before"; and "I saw the big sea but I would not have noticed it if Tom had not told me that it was it" (217, 222, 225). Williams travelled with her husband and young son Albert (and their animals: bullock team, horses, cat), to find work (the Sam referred to is a friend who is with them for the first few days):

> Ist Day   Started on Friday 6th Oct 1882   beautifull day …   came by a lot of men working on the hill   when we got to the camp we had to load some wood for night   got to the camp   had tea fixed our tent   Sam and Tom took the Bullocks away to the river   I made the bed and put Albert to bed   he went to bed early   it is a miserable camp to night so windy and no grass much   we let the cat out of her box when we stopped and I have not seen her since so I suppose she has cleared out. (my ellipse, 215)

In its lack of punctuation, the form of the entry resembles contemporary prose poetry. Williams uses spacing to punctuate the text, enacting the spaces where the group would stop, but not for long. In conventional terms it seems that Williams didn't know how to write a sentence. Yet, as Frost asserts, Williams's text remains readable over a century later. Williams makes reference to grass for the bullocks and horses: this is the literal, if temporary, pasture that the nomads seek. On the second day there are several references to grass: "heard very bad accounts of grass along the road…asked about the grass   he said there was very good grass at Bungendore … found not a bit of grass" (215). Knowing where to find the good grass is the crucial knowledge about the country that the travellers do not know, and need to know. After three weeks they arrive in Moruya but Williams is not so keen on the home she will have: "it is a Weatherboard house that I have to live in" (224) and "I wish I had a fireplace" (227). They have lost much of what would have constituted their home in an "Accident" that destroyed their chairs, the "Preambulator," and cradle. (221). Williams's pretext for writing is over:

> My travels are done now   I dont think that I have anything els to tell
> you must excuse this writing, for sometime I had not much light and no table and after the Accident I had not even the grubbox to write on for it got all smashed up   I dont expect that you will be able to make it all out but I will send it for I promised to. (227)

Even when she attains a home she is unhoused, without a table to write on. In a critique of "groundedness" in a postcolonial context, titled "Turning the Tables—or, Grounding Post-colonialism," Carter notes the significance of the table itself:

> In more ways than one the off-the-ground table inscribes, shapes and writes the other history of colonialism—that shadow narrative of domestic spaces where the colonized world was being dreamed, theorized, modelled and re-enacted. (32)

Williams writes a different "shadow narrative" from the other side of the "domestic space." She has even lost the de facto table of the grubbox and lacks the confidence that her writing can be read completely: unlike those "dream[ing and] theoriz[ing]" "the colonized world," in the quote from Carter. It is curious that it is at this point on the last day that she writes her only comma (in the text provided by Frost). Williams is apparently apologizing for the writing's legibility rather than grammar or style; but she is at this moment attending to the writing itself rather than her travels, and places a comma as a signifier of manners or correctness. In Williams's text, which is shorter and less prone to spelling error than Kelly's, there are less notable poetic effects of illiteracy; yet as the text concludes the missing "e" of "homly" (or of "els") comes home to roost in "fowels": "I am going to try tonight to get some fowels it is a job to get any here." The misspelled word seems to pun on "vowels" and the uncouth speech of the small town: "they call it a town but it is not much of a town." Williams suggests the disturbance of the text when she says she intended to send it earlier "but it was not quiet ready." Finally, the mosquitoes—a favorite image of Kelly's—are stealthier in Williams: "we are nearly eat alive with Mosquietoes and fleas" (227). The humans are pasture to the insects.

The second text I consider from Frost is a diary from the 1840s by Sarah Davenport, which begins in England with Davenport leaving Manchester for Liverpool and finally sailing to Australia. Davenport's text is titled "Sceth of an emigrants Life in austrailia from Leiving England in the year of our Lord 1841." The distortion of Davenport's misspelling in the first half of the title, compared to its correct and pious second, suggests the unholy journey ahead; though it may also indicate that Davenport has written the latter phrase before earlier diaries. Unlike the Williamses, the Davenports (Sarah, husband and children) "sould" their "house hold furniture" before their journey. The "sould" makes the "hold" seem like a pun on holy. But the tone of the "Sceth" (sketch) is not one of regret. The Davenport's in-laws in Australia were "making money fast," so the Davenports headed for Australia too. As Davenport writes, "we was coming to beeter our selves" (239); Frost borrows the quote as a title for this section, but corrects "beeter" to "better" (238). Like the Williamses, the Davenports too have an accident—their ship runs aground and they lose most of their belongings: "we had broke up our home and lost all in the wrek" (241). It is as if both families had to undergo a ritual unhousing in order to find a new home.

Due to the number of arrivals in Sydney, housing was scarce and expensive: "thair was not a house or roome under ten shillings per week but the government Provided tents for the Poor Pepol" (243). It is striking that Davenport can spell "government" but not "people," and that she capitalizes the latter. She spells phonetically; and the consistency of capitalization is also sound-based: words starting with "p": "Plow," "Pasangers," "Pounds," "Paid," "Police" and "Praktice" (244). Davenport's misspelling of mosquitoes—unlike Williams's "Mosquietoes"—doesn't refer to sound, but rather to color, intoxication or the sweetness of blood: "the muscatos did play up with my face" (243). The Davenports take a house together with the family of "a neighbour from home," but soon afterward move into another house that they rent out part of, and where, Davenport writes, "we could count the [stars as] we lay in bed and when it rained we could keep nothing dry" (Frost's insertion; 244). Davenport gets involved when a neighbor's son hides a "parchment" needed for a property dispute, and refuses to give it up. Davenport threatens him—"i will give you to the blaks"—and begins to blacken him with a brush: the boy screams and returns the parchment (246). It is curious how the "blaks" become implicated here in a story of a property dispute between whites in Sydney. The Davenports move to the bush, "as things was getting worse in sydney...we onse more broke up our home" (246–247). They are metaphorical as well as literal nomads in their search for somewhere to live, showing how easy it is to unhouse themselves, to disassemble their home. The distinction between themselves and stock is not a strong one: "we onely went a few miles to what they caled the accomdation paddocks...our beds was on the ground." The Davenports are also travelling with bullocks, but Sarah's husband, being "a bad bush man," loses one (247). The Davenports camp outside "Yas" (Yass) for a couple of nights before going into the township where, Davenport writes, "with some difficulty we got a room from 'jemey the flogger' as he was caled." Then Davenport leaves again with her two sons for their in-laws' place, her husband and daughter to follow them (248). They camp along the road, presumably in tents, though several times they manage to get a room. Davenport displays the same ignorance of the country as Williams: they meet up with the brother-in-law and travel to "the Ovens and got thaire in three days" but somehow they have been mistaken in their destination: "i had not been more [than] 3 weeks before i found i [was] in the wrong place and i [sent] a letter to my husband not to come" (Frost's insertions, 250–252). Eventually they find a house in "Aulbury" (Albury), but one morning while her husband is away Davenport wakes to find the house threatened by a flood (255). They have to leave, and her neighbors construct "a bark gunia" for her and the children (256). The family itself is regularly unsettled; even when they have a place, members of the family are sometimes elsewhere: most often the father, either working or looking for work, and the sons as they grow older go with him (258). Another time Davenport leaves the two youngest in the care of her eldest daughter in Melbourne to join her husband on the goldfields (259–263). There her husband buys a house with their gold earnings, but the man who sells it to him defers signing the deed and later "boasted he wold never sign them" (263). Soon after, the diary breaks off: it ends with Davenport living in a tent in "castlemain" (Castlemaine) just as her husband and sons return from Bendigo where they "whent...a prospecting," her other children still presumably in Melbourne (264).

Davenport's diary is similar to Williams's in being unpunctuated and in using spaces and paragraphs to structure her text. The text poetically enacts its narrative in not allowing for stops. The diary breaks off without an explicit stop or settled ending. Perhaps the ending and the elisions enact exhaustion, as they travel almost 900 kilometers from Sydney in New South Wales to various destinations in Victoria.

Employed drovers are more than directed Williamses and Davenports were with their small mobs of livestock, yet their texts are perhaps the most unsettled of all. They are written on the road, carved anonymously into trees. They are usually anonymous (though sometimes naming others) and of indeterminable race or gender. Although the texts are sometimes dated, at other times the date of the writing is questionable. These are works that come directly out of the practice of settlement (of droving cattle and sheep): the writer-drovers, while simultaneously assisting settlement, were themselves unsettled. As writers, they were, in a sense, looking for fresh spaces to colonize (such as a blank boab tree); and although their texts tend to practicality, they are also expressive, as we will see. The texts potentially unsettle the literary, in being unauthored, written in capitals, of no established form, heavily enjambed and barely punctuated. They are unique texts: unless and until they are reproduced by historians like Darrell Lewis as an image in a book; there are no versions or drafts; or, they are all first drafts (although it is possible that drovers may have worked out their text beforehand on paper). They are outside, unhoused texts.

"Nomadic poetics" as theorized by Pierre Joris, draws explicitly on Deleuze and Guattari's notion of the "rhizome" (Joris ix–x). Joris's theory is a conceptual one that addresses the problematic of global mobilities, and, like his predecessors, valorizes the rhizome over the rooted tree (9). The rhizome is "always on the move" (26). His book *A Nomad Poetics* is itself a suggestively discontinuous assemblage of quotes, notes and poems. In this chapter I consider the texts that are literally the closest thing we have to nomad texts, in that they are written by those seeking pasture. While the texts of Williams and Davenport are, in a sense, rhizomic, being "on the move" both in terms of narrative and as physical diary, the drover texts oppose the theory of the rhizome, as they are literally written on trees. The drovers' journeys, and therefore the "textual sites" of the trees and water tanks, could well be described as rhizomic, however: suggesting the possibility of a mixed model that combines the arboreal with the rhizomatic. After all, to disregard the tree is to disregard the material: of the drover texts and of Joris's book, as well as a range of Indigenous practice of writing on tree and wood.

The model that Deleuze uses for an assemblage is that of a horse-rider: "MAN-HORSE-STIRRUP" (Dialogues 69). Yet in the case of the scribing drover, we see that this is also the assemblage of the writer; the assemblage extended through the addition of a knife (or paintbrush): as well as a tree, water tank, or even cattle skull (Lewis 282) as a "page." Ward, in *The Australian Legend*, records visiting English novelist Anthony Trollope's description of the "nomad tribe of pastoral labourer—of men who profess to be shepherds, boundary-riders, sheep-washers, shearers and the like..." (9). His use of nomad here is largely metaphorical: it is the workers who are seeking fresh pastures, rather than the stock they are working with. This "tribe" accomplished much of the initial labor of settlement. One of the "like" referred to by Trollope is the drover, also known as an "overlander." Ward cites a bush song called "The Overlander" in which the same unhoused freedom of the drover is ascribed to sheep and cattle:

> No bounds have we to our estates
> From Normanton to Bass's Straits:
> We're not fenced in with walls or gates—
> No monarch's realms are grander.
> Our sheep and cattle eat their fill,
> And wander blithely at their will
> O'er forest, valley, plain or hill,
> Free as an Overlander. (7)

The fluidity of occupation suggested by Trollope is supported by Lewis: "many men frequently shifted from one occupation to another, so that someone who was a drover today could be a stockman tomorrow, or a prospector, or yard builder, or any of many outback occupations," to which we might add that of writer (279). The indeterminacy of occupation of the bush worker is arguably an aspect of the freedom in the song above. According to Lewis, the drovers were not necessarily restricted in terms of race or gender. While "stereotypical[ly]"

> a white Anglo-Saxon or Anglo-Celtic male...many drovers were Aborigines, usually paid in clothes, food and tobacco. There were also drovers of European-Aboriginal descent, and a few of Chinese-Aboriginal and European-Chinese descent. (279)

Lewis adds that there were also women drovers. A drover text may, then, be read as a white male production, but it cannot be read so with certainty— and uncertainty is unsettling. Their literal historical provenance is also unsettled: Lewis writes that "the surviving messages were created in the period 1940–1960...but some messages are undateable and some were created in earlier times" (282). In their public, quasi-anonymous enunciation and in their form (being generally brief and written in capitals), the drover messages are comparable to the more contemporary practice of graffiti. Yet they also resemble posters. One "signpost boab" message recorded by Lewis was "almost certainly" written in 1897:

> 9 7
> **JU NC T I ON**
> **C ATT LE CK.**
> AND
> BAINES

This is only an approximation. Type cannot do justice to the 3D effect of words cut into a tree that have aged and grown with the tree, the tilt and rise and spread of certain characters. The "97" without an apostrophe may refer to the year or something else. If the year, the writer assumes the century will be understood as the eighteenth. The words refer to the meeting of Cattle Creek and the Baines River, both stock routes (283).

In this small text we have something quite poetic, where clearly decisions were made: the assonance of the "n" sounds of "ninety," "seven," and "junction," and the near rhyme of "seven" and "junction," combine to form a trochaic pentameter line with an extra (eleventh) syllable, that might be managed verbally by deemphasizing the "AND," which is what the writer has done in writing it smaller. Of course, the line as such does not exist: it has been chopped into much smaller units, but the rhythm is still there. The enjambment creates other effects. The word "JUNCTION," for example, would normally be read as having an accent on the first syllable. But when it is one line on its own, this slows down reading and tends toward the spondaic, so that we read it with an accent on both syllables. "97," written as a number rather than words, quickens and lightens the rhythm, avoiding the slowing of the long "i" vowel of "Ninety," so we move onto the quick, short vowels of the "U" of "JUNCTION" and the "A" of "CATTLE." Yet it is not quite that simple; we can't help but slow at "JUNCTION": it is designed as a stopping place. It is the largest and longest word, and fits the exact amount of space as the two words "CATTLE CK" below. The abbreviating full stop that follows lies further right. The text suggests that Cattle Creek is both larger and of greater significance than the Baines River; yet it is "CATTLE" itself as a word that is emphasized, the word that signifies the grass-eating stock: the need for the route (and the drover's job) in the first place. The stop provides another reading stop on the third line, a stop between the creek and the following "AND," rather than slowing in the long elided "e"s of "C[REE]K." The punctuation mark is as expressive as the words. It represents the stopping that the sign conveys, as well as the stopping required to write the message. It allows for an emphasis of stock over place, yet insists on place. The full stop and the word "JUNCTION" unsettle each other's role. The sign punctuates the drovers' journey; and by puncturing the tree it suggests the punctuating quality of all text, of words as well as punctuation marks. The words are punctums: literal wounds. Despite the text's brevity, it assembles a plurality of meanings: date/time/number; place/travel/rest/joining; animal/agriculture/farmer; water/geography; settling/naming.

The textual assemblage is supplemented by the tool necessary to incise the tree; and by the tree itself, which provides an indigenous element. To read the tree as indigenous is not a superficial reading. The carving of letters on wood connects this drover writing practice with a postcontact Indigenous writing practice, recorded by Penny van Toorn, of carving Roman alphabetical letters on wooden clubs (74–79). Van Toorn quotes Lancelot Threlkeld, a missionary: "…we had about a dozen youths learning to read and write the Roman Alphabet which they frequently cut with their hatchets in the bark of the trees, showing the march of the intellect in the very bush" (41). Threlkeld's note is ambiguous: is the learning of the youths the "march of the intellect"? Is it their learning of the Roman alphabet in particular, or does the presence or agency of the alphabet itself produce this march? Van Toorn notes, moreover, that (analphabetical) Aboriginal writing on trees existed presettlement (20; see also Sayers 98–99).

In *Forests: The Shadow of Civilization*, Robert Pogue Harrison makes explicit the connections between the "material" and trees. He writes:

> As for matter, we cannot speak about it in any logical fashion. There are neither words, images, or categories for undifferentiated matter, since form is the condition of our logical access to reality…Aristotle…is the first to give the word ["*hyle*"] its philosophical meaning of "matter". But *hyle* in Greek does not originally mean matter, it means forest. (28)

Harrison notes that the Romans translated *hyle* into *materia* despite the cognate being *sylva*, adding: "But even the word *materia* did not stray very far from the forests. *Materia* means wood—the usable wood of a tree as opposed to its bark, fruit, sap, etc." (28). Drover texts on trees and carved clubs return us to the root (the pun is unavoidable; Harrison also makes it) of the material: both in terms of the word's Latin/Greek etymology and of the origin of the materiality of the paper page, and the clubs, both derived from trees. We have left the enclosures of house, of field (where a tree can mark a boundary, or provide the material for fences), and of (enforced) settlement, for the bush; the secrets of the code and the enclosed letter, and books, for the sign in the open. Yet such apparently open texts are also coded: we cannot be certain that "97" is a year; and once reproduced and decontextualized, who would know that the sign refers to stock routes? The space provided by any one tree is also limited, requiring the severe enjambment and condensed expression of a road sign: they are, like posters or road-signs, conceptual one-page texts.

In his *Study of Modern Manuscripts*, Donald H. Reiman defines manuscripts as:

> handwritten memoranda or communications on paper and other flexible surfaces of animal or vegetable matter (such as parchment or linen) that have been used to *transmit* written records across distances—but not on stone, bronze, or materials traditionally used to *record* written messages at particular spots. (1)

The tree-carvings are the only texts in this study that are neither manuscripts nor derived from manuscripts (though the *Ngarla Songs* have an oral provenance, the book is presumably derived from Brown and Geytenbeek's manuscript, or typescript). They are written to "record," but not to be "transmit[ted]...across distances." Nonetheless, Reiman's further classification of manuscripts "as either *public, confidential* (or *corporate*), or *private* (or *personal*)" suggests a way of thinking about the audience of the drover messages. He defines the different types as follows:

> Public manuscripts record texts that their authors expect or hope will be made accessible to a multiplicity of readers whom the authors do not know and who, at least initially, might have little or no interest in the writers themselves... *Private*, or *personal*, manuscripts...are addressed to specific people, selected in advance, whom the writers know—or hope—will take personal interest in them. Some documents may be intended only for the eyes of the writer (e.g., a private diary or aide-mémoire) or for the eyes of one other person (e.g., a love letter)...Of wider circulation than the strictly private document are *confidential*, or *corporate*, manuscripts, not intended for the eyes of a wide and diverse readership, but addressed to a specific group of individuals all of whom either are personally known to the writer or belong to some predefined group that the writer has reason to believe share communal values with him or her: an audience that will receive the communication in the spirit that corresponds to the purpose of its composition. Such confidential communications may be friendly and sympathetic or angry and accusatory. (38–39)

This definition might also be thought of as describing a "community" manuscript. The drover messages, though not fitting the classification of a manuscript, and despite their apparent public aspect, aptly fit Reiman's "confidential, or corporate" classification (though the messages quoted in Lewis are also now public). While the "97 / Junction" text above is neutral in tone (or perhaps in the context of letting drovers know where they are, "friendly"; another boab message has "EASE UP MATE / THATS THE / BAINES"), many of the drover messages are "angry and accusatory," such as this one left on a water tank in "red paint and very large letters" (as if even the writing on tanks must present wounding):

>   **NOTICE**
>   **THE CUNTS**
>   **THAT LET**
>   **THERE CATTLE**
>   *I*NTO MUGELTONS
>   WATTEHOLE ,
>   **O**UGHT TO BE
>   FUC **KE** D.
>   **SUDD**EN
>   15/8 / 41
>   (289)

Again, this is an approximation. The harshness of the sentiment is emphasized by the style of the writing; it is written on flat metal, and the text is flatter and more angular than those written on the boab trees. Lewis suggests that "SUDDEN" is the writer's name. But it is easy to read the word "SUDDEN" into the message. The title of "NOTICE" readily becomes a verb. The misspelling of "THERE" (reversing Harris's spelling noted previously) deictically dispossesses the cattle. The misspelling of "WATTEHOLE" means that it is not "whole," nor wholesome; it also suggests wattle (tree and cattle body part). Where "Sudden" pauses for emphasis, the grammatically redundant comma creates a cattle trace of manure or hoof; the musical message is that the "CUNTS" "CATTLE" "FUCKED" "MUGELTONS / WATTEHOLE" and that they deserve to be "FUCKED" in return. There is suggested release in the "uh" sound, and an emphasis on "t" and "l" sounds that rhyme with the flat metal of the material. The full stop after (the slowed because broken up into three parts) "FUC KE D" gives extra weight to the following "SUDDEN." Sudden's anger and frustration at not knowing who the "CUNTS" are produces the text; the not knowing is also represented by illiteracy: by Sudden's not knowing the spelling of "waterhole."

The punctuation stands in for Sudden's knowing: they know that there are protocols to writing, which is why punctuation is used. The word "protocol" derives from the Greek *kola*, meaning glue: it keeps everything together (Concise 828). This text suggests that the assemblage of community is easily disassembled: that the bush has protocols (in this case, regarding the use of waterholes) to follow.

The explicit nature of these texts expands the limits of what American critic Brian Kim Stefans perceives as the "decorum" of Australian poetry. Stefans writes:

> In thinking about [Martin] Johnston and his contemporaries in *Modern Australian Poetry*, I am most struck by the apparent valorization of "good taste" and refined style in the poems...one notices a highly-developed sense of decorum and style, and even formality, in their writing...[in contrast to] Ginsberg, Baraka, Corso, Olson. (n.pag.)

The Latin term "decorum" is a weaker one than the Greek-derived "protocol," meaning only "seemly" (Concise 248). Stefans admits that he is no expert on Australian poetry; perhaps if he had been familiar with Kate Jennings's *Mother, I'm Rooted* anthology of women's poetry, or the poems of Lionel Fogarty or ΠO, he may have reached a different conclusion. Stefans refers back to the situation in Australian poetry following the Ern Malley scandal, "wonder[ing] if...[Max] Harris's humiliation...has dissuaded poets from ever being so frank, suggestive, or humorous about the matter [of sex] since" (Harris faced obscenity charges as a result of publishing the Malley poems.) Arguably, the decorous is what dominates Australian literary anthologies; though, yet again, the *Macquarie PEN* anthologies are exceptional. Future editions may include writers like Sudden.

Drover messages are beyond the fences, far from the paddocks; the routes themselves traverse state borders (limits). In other words, they fulfill certain conditions of the baroque—or rather the neobaroque. The neobaroque, also known as the colonial or counter-baroque, is posed in Latin American literature as a counterconquest mode, and is distinguished from the baroque by Cuban critic, Severo Sarduy thus: "Baroque space is superabundant and wasteful. In contrast to language that is communicative, economic, austere, and reduced to function as a vehicle for information, Baroque language delights in surplus, in excess, and in the partial loss of its object" (287). Yet, he adds, all this can still add up to harmony, whereas the neobaroque "reflects structurally the disharmony, the rupture of homogeneity" (289). The act of writing them disrupts the writer's journey, while the texts themselves disrupt the harmony of the bush, the tree (or tank), and, in the "Sudden" message, the idea of settlement as harmony.

In *Ideas of Space in Contemporary Poetry*, British critic Ian Davidson adapts Australian film critic Angela Ndalianis's framing of the opposition of the classical and the baroque to a poetry context. Davidson writes:

> According to Ndalianis, the "classical" concerns itself with "closure," a closure which comes about via a perception of space as "ordered" and which has a sense of a "centre," both of which give the work a particular perspective. Baroque, on the other hand, "suggest(s) worlds of infinity that lose the sense of a centre"...the "baroque's difference to classical systems lies in its refusal to respect the limits of the frame." The work will spill over established borders and boundaries. (146)

The material context of the drover messages enforces a minimal style; and yet, when they go beyond the merely informative, they are, nevertheless, excessive, extravagant, traversing the "borders and boundaries" of the road, the property, and the state. Ndalianis's definition also recalls Gertrude Stein's "act as if there was no use in a center," which Steve McCaffery characterizes as "cannily prophetic of contemporary cultural desires" (100). The Australian center has been unsettled from the beginning of settlement: the imperial center of London could be said to have directed Australia as satellite; Sydney (and later Canberra) both have claims to the position; as does the mythical inland sea; Uluru; and the desert generally. While "ordered space" suggests fences, Ndalianis's conception suggests the experience of the nomad. The colonial frame, in the literal form of a fence, is a tool or imposition of the colonizer. In the context of writing we can see a page or book as a frame. The frame as a metaphor borrowed from visual art is emphasized in Davidson, when he writes (in an argument derived from Certeau): "With the book and the individualized practice of silent reading, the experience of the text becomes visual." He further quotes Certeau to the effect that "reading frees itself from the soil that determined it" (169). The drover messages are contradictory in these terms in that they are very much visual texts, but they are not books, and they are not "free...from the soil that determine[s]" them (Certeau's statement becomes true, though, in Lewis's reproduction).

In the Australian context, the baroque itself can be read in anticolonial terms. Ernesto Livon-Grosman refers to characteristics of the baroque in an introductory essay on Cuban poet José Lezama Lima: for instance "the way in which nature seems to extend or multiply itself in cultural products" (xxii). In the drover texts we have a more literal example: "nature" (the tree) is the "cultural product" of the text. Another critic of the baroque, Gregg Lambert, quotes Gérard Genette:

> The Baroque, *if it exists*, is not an island (much less a private hunting-ground), but a crossroads... Its genius is syncretism, its order is its very openness, its signature is its very anonymity and pushes to an absurd degree its characteristic traits which are, erratically, found in all places and in all times. It hardly matters to us what belongs exclusively to this name, but rather what is "typical" of it—that is to say, *exemplary*. (Lambert 9)

Rereading the quoted drovers' texts above through Genette's definition, the "Junction" text can be seen as "exemplary": representing, marking, a crossroads. More generally, the texts' "anonymity" (the name of "Sudden" is ambiguous, and we know nothing else of them) is their signature. As actions, rather than as visual texts, the drovers paradoxically produce "syncretism" through reconciling writing (and settlement) with the bush, literally. An Australian literature that was not expressive of settlement could be called "syncretic" in its attempts to "reconcile differing schools of thought" (Indigenous schools and non-Indigenous; prose and poetry; visual and written) and hence, "baroque" or "neobaroque" (Concise 1084). Lambert, in *The Return of the Baroque in Modern Culture*, derives a theory of the "baroque eon" from early twentieth-century Spanish literary critic Eugenio d'Ors:

> D'Ors' "baroque eon"... does not provide the logic of a history or of reason in perpetual progress, but rather the "logic of culture"... that is open and in perpetual revolt: a culture, or cultivation, of either new forms that... represent the excavation of the "states of exception" that have been elided from any official history. (8)

The drover texts have become part of history in that they have been published in a history book, but are not included in literary history. Lambert's discussion continues with a notion of "baroque history" that "will constantly invert the experience of Culture founded by the principles of education, accumulation and progress" (9). This describes the "state" of unsettlement: an inversion of the "experience of Culture," in other words, a history of writing that is not merely critical, but that provides an "invert[ed]... experience": such as a literature written directly onto trees. This textual practice has the added effect of unsettling the tree from its role in the picturesque (White, Inventing 30, 85), while the book is displaced by its origin the tree. Writing becomes part of the land: wounding the tree to the extent that it goes beyond the surface of the conventional page. The tree, therefore (as well as the symbolically wounded water tank), represents a textual field.

An Indigenous variant on writing on wood returns us to the theme of hunting. Van Toorn records the example of "two Wiradjuri clubs made near Wagga Wagga [in southern New South Wales] in the 1860s" (75). The clubs are unsettling artifacts on a number of levels. First, they are weapons and point to the use of the English language as a weapon against Aboriginal people (in Aboriginal legislative "Acts," for example); they point to armed Aboriginal resistance, using weapons such as clubs: both wounded (in the sense of scarred with markings, including alphabetical letters) and wounding. But they also point to the use of English as a means of defense (in petitions etc.).

The Wiradjuri use of letters shows the appropriative ability of Aboriginal cultures. An unsettling fact, though, is what van Toorn calls the "non-phonographic" use of the letters (74). The characters are used as letters only, not as elements in a word; they are not apparently representative of anything other than their image. They are like concrete poetry in their abstract, material use of letters, as well as being appropriative examples of exophonic writing. Like Jong's reproduction of letters, the Wiradjuri club-makers also use serifs: these are not just representations of Roman characters, but typographical appropriations, assembled along with other pictorial or decorative elements such as traditional crosshatch designs and human and animal drawings, as well as actual nails (van Toorn 76–78). Such writing assemblages are outside the frame of Australian literary history, yet they have an obvious resemblance to visual poetry, despite their unusual use of design and the fact of being produced on a weapon. The use of nails is also an appropriation from non-Indigenous culture, pointing to the metal of type. The nails enhance the wounding ability of the club: they are not used to hold anything together. They are the club's punctuation (but also potentially punctuating).

The image of the clubs reproduced by van Toorn are not photographs, but are "sketched by the author" (77). The sketch of club "B" is striking in terms of its relation to definitions of the baroque. The effect of book production (including its conceptual framing), as well as that of editorial intervention, tends to the settling of a text's power. Despite a particular text's frame-breaking capacities, publishing is itself a form of framing. Here, however, in van Toorn's "quoting" of a club in the form of a small drawing, the effect is to enhance the agency represented by the club: its letters, geometric designs, people (one wearing a hat), and animals. Instead of flattening, obscuring, or showing separate front and back views of club "B," van Toorn chooses to show elements of the club design outside the frame of the line drawing of the club. A dog, a human figure, some markings and the letters "H A—" (including the dash; the letters appear to be sans serif, though all other letters shown are serifed) have all travelled into the blank space to the right of the drawing. Here is an example of editing in order to unsettle writing (already unsettled on the club in terms of its relation to drawing and its nonphonographic, non-semantic representation). The club as a text is outside the field, frame, limit of settlement literature, and, as a bush weapon, literally outside (though potentially threatening) agricultural settlement. Although on one level the club is contained within van Toorn's book, it is unsettlingly outside the assemblage of its origin. This innovation is an effect of van Toorn's material involvement with the original text: she redrew or rewrote it herself by hand, rather than have it photographed or using a typographical approximation.

In a further example of the decorative use of the Roman alphabet, van Toorn reproduces two drawings made by Aboriginal stockman Charlie Flannigan in 1893. Flannigan made these drawings while awaiting trial for murder in Darwin's Fanny Bay Gaol. Both can be read as visual poems. One shows a sign over a depiction of Wave Hill Station where he had worked, with the words "Song Fellow" in the sky above, while the other depicts whimsical characters climbing over letters and riding emus, above another scene of a tree and someone riding a bucking horse. Both contain a double horizontal line—a kind of bar—across the center of the picture. In the "Wave Hill" drawing it appears to hold up the station name above the buildings like a sign; in the other it holds the figures and the letters above the tree, the horse and its rider. Yet in this latter case there is no clear division between the two planes: both the top of the tree and the rider's torso are above the bar. Both pictures contain letters drawn as outlines, like cartoon snakes or skinny balloons. The letters "E" and "T" in the "Wave Hill Station" drawing are like lengths of wood joined together, and have a 3-D quality; the "A" and the "T" in the drawing we might call the "Rodeo" drawing are also angular, and drawn as serifed characters. Like the lettering on the clubs, Flannigan's characters seem to be without sound or semantic meaning; but in the top drawing there are also words: "Song Fellow" and "WAVE STATAY" ("Wave Station"). The spread out letters in the "Rodeo" drawing could also be read as spelling out the word "ACT," though there also appears to be a letter "I" above and between the "A" and the "C" (it could also be an upside-down "T"). The tree resembles a letter "Y" with a mop of leaves that almost completely overlaps the body of the ridden emu in the section above.

Through the use of the "bar" in these two drawings, Flannigan works with the concept of framing within the pictures, using it differently in these two examples reproduced by van Toorn (the originals are held by the Museum of South Australia, further examples are reproduced in Sayers 64–66). In the first, the text is separated, in the upper section, from the buildings and so on, that represent the station. The words "WAVE STATAY" resemble a sign and are larger than the buildings. In Flannigan's spelling, "Station" comes to contain the word "Stay," which could refer to where he wanted to stay, that is, in his country, or on the station, or might be read as referring to his stay in prison. The words have a greater prominence than the station or settlement in this drawing. Yet above these words is the smaller text "Song Fellow," as if representing Flannigan himself, commenting on what is below. Here Flannigan frames words outside and separate to settlement. In the "Rodeo" drawing, the scene is very different. It could depict a rodeo or a carnival. There are no buildings, but there is land depicted in the bottom half. There is not the same separation either, as the tree and the figure riding the bucking horse overlap the upper and lower sections. The letters are separate, but they break out of their own outlines or frames; they link to each other and appear to have branches or vines extending from them. They also break from the abstraction of language in their providing apparent support for a number of acrobatic human figures.

In the drover texts and in Flannigan's drawings we arguably have the opposite to Livon-Grosman's definition of the baroque as "nature...extend[ing] or multiply[ing] itself in cultural products": rather, the cultural product of the word extends itself in literal nature, in the drover case, and in representations of nature, in Flannigan's. Flannigan appears to present two alternatives in these drawings. The first shows language as material that is static, and as equivalent (or possibly superior) to buildings; the second shows language as a living equivalent that is part of a dynamic world of people, animals and trees. Octavio Paz's more banal formulation of the baroque is closer here: "In almost all the baroque poets may be observed a conscious use of the natural world" (25), yet Flannigan's joyful representation is a more literal use than the presumably semantic one that Paz refers to.

In concluding with Flannigan there is a return to the violence and wounding of settlement: and to the "un-homed." Like Kelly, Flannigan was also hanged, following a guilty verdict at a murder trial. He could be said to be depicting two versions of home in his drawings, of station life and country, while living his last months in jail. While Williams and Davenport offer examples of the deferred desire of being "homed," and the drovers were literally "outsiders" by profession, the Wiradjuri clubs are "unhomed" texts in that they are designed for use outside the home (whether in hunting, or in defence or attack), as well as being sites of letters isolated from the alphabet. Flannigan's drawings speak of the typical ambiguity of the displaced person: of his preimprisonment home of Wave Hill Station, as well as the bush that the station displaced.

Conclusion

In an essay on "the creolization of the psychoanalytic concept of trauma," Pheng Cheah writes, "For at least two decades, it has been the task of postcolonial theory, loosely termed, to remind critical theory of its Eurocentric limits and to point to different forms of theorization that may arise in colonial and postcolonial space" (83–84). Australian literature cannot avoid the European inheritance that comes with the English language (and the Roman alphabet), but it is already a mixed one. Writing in the context of the literary colonization of Peru, José Carlos Mariategui cites nineteenth-century Italian critic Francesco de Sanctis, who states:

> The idea of a national literature is an illusion... The imagination and style now known as orientalism are not particularly of the Orient but of all the East and of all barbaric, primitive literatures. Greek poetry has Asiatic elements, Latin poetry has Greek, and Italian poetry has both Greek and Latin. (188)

Sanctis rejects the notion of literature as a settled phenomenon: it is one that would require isolation. Australian literature, therefore, is not and never was, settled. From its beginning it was being made and remade by writers of different cultures, whether Indigenous, Chinese, convict Irish, or working or middle-class English settlers. These writers invented new material practices of lettering style, syntax, and punctuation usage, as well as new and networked affects, tones and ironies. The results—in writing—were bound to be interesting. Yet even the most open literary anthologies and histories tend, if only by lack of explicit framing, to present such texts as of historical rather than poetic interest: reifying the work as an effect of colonization, rather than an effect of (a potentially effective) writing practice. This is perhaps a problem with the word "literature," in that it emphasizes writing as a noun, rather than as a verb. The words "literature" (and by extension "letters"), "poetics," and "writing" are so taken for granted as part of the assemblage of literary studies that they are used interchangeably, yet all have the power to frame in distinct ways. A word like "poetics" emphasizes making (from the Greek *poieo*), and appears to be a more active term than that of literature, as it refers to the writing/making practice of the poet; as well as, in the broader sense of making, which has currency in a wide range of other disciplines. Yet, as Stephen Owen notes, "poetics," as distinct from the Chinese *tso* (which refers to literary composition more broadly) refers specifically to the making of "plots" and is therefore, in its Aristotelian origin, associated more with narration and fiction (or history or journalism) than with poetic form (77). The etymology of "literature" is later: Latin, rather than Greek, it derives from the "letter" (Concise 588). In etymological terms, then, "literature," which might sound broader, is a more specific term than "poetics." It can also be thought of as an active term, if we remember its etymology, and think of it as a lettering practice. The term "writing" is therefore actively related. Deriving is from the Old English "*wrītan*," meaning "scratch, score, write," from the Germanic "*wrītan*": "orig. of symbols inscribed with sharp tools on stone or wood" (1246). This relation of the terms "writing" and "lettering" suggests marking, rather than the making of the Greek-derived term of "poetics." Marking is a visual term, and in the sense of making boundaries, it is also a spatial one. There are etymological roots for both these meanings: the Old Norse *marka*, meaning "observe," and the Germanic *marko*, meaning "boundary" (619). I am not suggesting that we might escape the Greek aspect of English, such as, in particular, the connotations of composition, the poem and the book that the word "making" suggests. But there are other historical components: origins that suggest that poetics, being also writing and lettering, must account for the visual marks on the page, the bodily act of marking the page, and, in terms of boundaries, the limits of the page. Even an oral poetics, which is also a form of writing (mentally and verbally) and lettering (in that letters form words), potentially has questions to ask regarding marking (for example, what is seen by, and of, the performer) and boundaries (of performance space, for example). Literacy can also be defined as a practice of the letter (perhaps a rethinking regarding the "letter" as epistolary genre is possible here too). Lettering includes the use (or avoidance) of punctuation, as well as the use of space, on the page, including the conceptual page of boab, water tank, or club: and screen. All writing becomes conceptual with word processing: making, marking, lettering. Technological developments, not least the internet, also put pressures on the concept of national literatures.

To produce—or invent—a space for what I call unsettled Australian writing, a space that is not merely an extension of the space of English literature, may require further thinking in terms of comparative as well as conceptual models of writing. As we open up this space, I expect that connections will be made between this unsettled literature and that of the transnational, worldly, contemporary: as well as between the unsettled and (what has appeared to be) the settled. To be able to do so enriches both, enabling us to read Australian writing with a greater sense of a networked poetic history, rather than of its novelty or its canonical aspiration. The unsettled does not seek to displace the settled, but to unsettle it. This means seeing a richer relation between the works in the anthologies and those that are not; between those that appear to be creative works and those that appear to be historical documents; it also suggests there may be new—punctuation-attentive, spatially accented—approaches to reading these settled texts: that may not be so settled after all.

Bibliography

Ackland, Michael. "Poetry from the 1890s to 1970." *The Cambridge Companion to Australian Literature*. Ed. Elizabeth Webby. Cambridge: Cambridge UP, 2000. 74–104. Print.

———. *That Shining Band: A Study of Australian Colonial Verse Tradition*. St Lucia: U of Queensland P, 1994. Print.

Adamowicz, Elza. *The Surrealist Collage in Text and Image: Dissecting the Exquisite Corpse*. Cambridge: Cambridge UP, 1998. Print.

Adorno, T. W. *Notes to Literature: Vol. 1*. Trans. Sherry Weber Nicholsen, New York: Columbia UP, 1991. Print.

Agamben, Giorgio. *The End of the Poem: Studies in Poetics*. Trans. Daniel Heller-Roazen, Stanford: Stanford UP, 1999. Print.

Ahmed, Sara. "Happy Objects." *The Affect Theory Reader*. Eds. Melissa Gregg and Gregory J. Seigworth. Durham: Duke UP, 2010. 29–51. Print.

Anderson, Benedict. *Imagined Communities: Reflections on the Origin and Spread of Nationalism*. London: Verso, 2006. Print.

Andrews, Bruce, and Charles Bernstein, eds. *The L=A=N=G=U=A=G=E Book*, Carbondale: Southern Illinois UP, 1984. Print.

Ashcroft, Bill. "Reading Post-Colonial Australia." *Postcolonial Issues in Australian Literature*. Ed. Nathanael O'Reilly. Amherst: Cambria P, 2010, 15–40. Print.

Ashcroft, Bill, Gareth Griffiths, and Helen Tiffin, eds. *The Post-Colonial Studies Reader*. Abingdon: Routledge, 1995. Print.

Assmann, Jan. *Religion and Cultural Memory*. Trans. Rodney Livingstone, Stanford: Stanford UP, 2006. Print.

Attali, Jacques. *Noise: The Political Economy of Music*. Trans. Brian Massumi, Minneapolis: U of Minnesota P, 1992. Print.

Attwood, Bain, and Andrew Markus, eds. *The Struggle for Aboriginal Rights: A Documentary History*. St Leonards: Allen & Unwin, 1999. Print.

Auden, W. H. "The Orators." *The English Auden: Poems, Essays and Dramatic Writings 1927–1939*. Ed. Edward Mendelson. London: Faber, 1977. 59–110. Print.

Bacon, Jono. *The Art of Community: Building the New Age of Participation*, Sebastopol: O'Reilly, 2009.

Barnes, Katherine, "'With a smile barely wrinkling the surface': Christopher Brennan's Large Musicopoematographoscope and Mallarmé's Un Coup de dés." *XIX: Dix-Neuf,* Number 9, October 2007. 44–56. Web.

Barthes, Roland. *Camera Lucida: Reflections on Photography.* Trans. Richard Howard, London: Vintage, 2000. Print.

———. *Criticism and Truth.* Trans. Katrine Pilcher Keuneman, London: Athlone, 1987. Print.

———. *The Pleasure of the Text.* Trans. Richard Miller, New York: Noonday P, 1975. Print.

Bataille, Georges. *Visions of Excess: Selected Writings 1927–1939.* Trans, ed. Allan Stoeckl, with Carl Lovitt and Donald M. Leslie, Jr. Minneapolis: U of Minnesota P, 1985. Print.

Batchen, Geoffrey. "*Camera Lucida*: Another Little History of Photography." *The Meaning of Photography.* Eds. Robin Kelsey and Blake Stimson, Williamstown: Sterling and Francine Clark Art Institute, 2008. 76–91. Print.

Bate, Jonathan. *The Song of the Earth.* London: Picador, 2000. Print.

Baudelaire, Charles. *Intimate Journals.* Trans. Christopher Isherwood, London: Methuen, 1949. Print.

Bennelong. "Letter to Mr Philips, Lord Sydney's Steward." Heiss and Minter. 9.

Bennett, Bruce. "Literary Culture Since Vietnam: A New Dynamic." Bennett and Strauss. 239–264.

Bennett, Bruce, and Jennifer Strauss, eds. *The Oxford Literary History of Australia.* Melbourne: Oxford UP, 1998. Print.

Benterrak, Krim with Stephen Muecke, and Paddy Roe. *Reading the Country: Introduction to Nomadology.* Fremantle: Fremantle Arts Centre P, 1996. Print.

Berger, John. *About Looking.* London: Writers and Readers, 1980. Print.

Bernstein, Charles. *A Poetics.* Cambridge: Harvard UP, 1992. Print.

———. "Introduction to Ezra Pound." *Poetry Speaks.* Eds. Elise Paschen and Rebekah Presson Mosby (Sourcebooks, 2001). Web.

———. "The Task of Poetics, The Fate of Innovation, and the Aesthetics of Criticism." *The Consequence of Innovation: 21st Century Poetics.* Ed. Craig Dworkin. New York: Roof, 2008. 37–57. Print.

Birns, Nicholas. *Theory after Theory: An Intellectual History of Literary Theory from 1950 to the Early 21st Century.* Peterborough: Broadview P, 2010. Print.

Bird, Delys. "The 'Settling' of English." Bennett and Strauss. 1998. 21–43.

Bohn, Willard. *Reading Visual Poetry.* Madison: Fairleigh Dickinson UP, 2011. Print.

———. *The Aesthetics of Visual Poetry 1914–1928.* Cambridge: Cambridge UP, 1986. Print.

Bollobas, Eniko. *Charles Olson.* New York: Twayne, 1992. Print.

Bonwick, Richard. "The History of Yarra Bend Lunatic Asylum, Melbourne." MA Thesis. University of Melbourne, 1996. Web.

Brandenstein, C. G. von, and A. P. Thomas. *Taruru: Aboriginal Song Poetry from the Pilbara,* Honolulu: UP of Hawaii, 1975. Print.

Brennan, Christopher. *Musicopoematographoscope & Pocket Musicopoematographoscope*. Ed. Axel Clark. Sydney: Hale & Ironmonger, 1981. Print.

———. *The Prose of Christopher Brennan*. Sydney: Angus & Robertson. 1962. Print.

Breton, Andre. *Earthlight*. Trans. Bill Zavatsky and Zack Rogow. Los Angeles: Sun and Moon, 1993. Print.

Brodsky, Isadore. *Bennelong Profile: Dreamtime Reveries of a Native of Sydney Cove*. Sydney: University Co-Operative Bookshop, 1973. Print.

Brody, Jennifer DeVere. *Punctuation: Art, Politics, and Play*. Durham: Duke UP, 2008. Print.

Brophy, Kevin. "Aboriginal Voices Resist Colonial History." *Eureka Street*. 18. 13. June 27, 2008. Web.

Brown, Alexander, and Brian Geytenbeek. *Ngarla Songs*. Fremantle: Fremantle Arts Centre P, 2003. Print.

Brown, Susan. "Determined Heroines: George Eliot, Augusta Webster, and Closet Drama by Victorian Women." *Victorian Poetry*. Vol. 33, No. 1, Women Poets, Spring, 1995. 89–109. Print.

Browning, Robert. *The Poems Vol. II*. Ed. John Pettigrew. Harmondsworth: Penguin, 1981. Print.

Bru, Sascha. *Democracy, Law and the Modernist Avant-Gardes: Writing in the State of Exception*. Edinburgh: Edinburgh UP, 2009. Print.

Buckley, Vincent, ed., *The Faber Book of Modern Australian Verse*. London: Faber, 1991. Print.

Bush, Ronald. "'Quiet, Not Scornful'? The Composition of *The Pisan Cantos*." Rainey. 169–211.

Cameron, Sharon. *Lyric Time: Dickinson and the Limits of Genre*. Baltimore: John Hopkins UP, 1979. Print.

Campbell, David A. *Greek Lyric In Four Volumes: I Sappho Alcaeus*, trans. Campbell, Cambridge: Harvard UP, 1982. Print.

Campos, Augusto de. "Yale *Symphosymposium* on Contemporary Poetics and Concretism: A World View from the 1990s." Jackson, Vos and Drucker. 375–380.

Campos, Haroldo de. *Novas: Selected Writings*. Evanston: Northwestern UP, 2007. Print.

Carey, Peter. *True History of the Kelly Gang*. St Lucia: U of Queensland P, 2000. Print.

Carter, Paul. "The Forest in the Clearing: The Environmental Poetics of John Shaw Neilson." Rutherford and Holloway. 2010. 133–157.

———. *The Lie of the Land*. London: Faber, 1996. Print.

———. *The Road to Botany Bay: An Essay in Spatial History*. London: Faber, 1987. Print.

———. "Turning the Tables—or, Grounding Post-colonialism." *Text, Theory, Space: Land, Literature and History in South Africa and Australia*. Eds. Kate Darian-Smith, Liz Gunner, and Sarah Nuttall. London: Routledge, 2006. 23–34. Print.

Certeau, Michel de. *The Practice of Everyday Life*. Trans. Steven Rendall. Berkeley: U of California P, 1988. Print.

Clark, Axel. *Christopher Brennan: A Critical Biography*. Carlton: Melbourne UP, 1980. Print.

———. "Introduction." *Musicopoematographoscope*. By Christopher Brennan. Sydney: Hale & Ironmonger, 1981. Print.

Cluver, Claus. "Concrete Poetry: Critical Perspectives from the 90s." Jackson, Vos and Drucker. 265–286.

Collis, Stephen. *Phyllis Webb and the Common Good: Poetry / Anarchy / Abstraction*. Vancouver: Talonbooks, 2007. Print.

Conley, Thomas. *Toward a Rhetoric of Insult*. Chicago: U of Chicago P, 2010. Print.

Cooke, Stuart. *Speaking the Earth's Languages: A Theory for Australian-Chilean Postcolonial Poetics*. Amsterdam: Rodopi, 2013. Print.

Craven, Peter. "Black Canons: Craven Writes Back." *Crikey*. Sep. 14 2009. Web.

———. "Obscuring the Heritage: The Macquarie Anthology." *Australian Book Review*. Sep. 2009, No. 314. 7–8. Print.

Culler, Jonathan. *Structuralist Poetics: Structuralism, Linguistics and the Study of Literature*, Ithaca, NY: Cornell UP, 1976. Print.

Cunningham, Sophie. "The Black and White of the Australian Literary Canon." *Crikey*. Sep. 4 2009. Web.

Cutts, Simon. "The Aesthetic of Ian Hamilton Finlay." *Wood Notes Wild: Essays on the Poetry of Ian Hamilton Finlay*. Ed. Alec Finlay. Edinburgh: Polygon, 1995. 32–35. Print.

Davidson, Ian. *Ideas of Space in Contemporary Poetry*. Houndmills: Palgrave, 2007. Print.

Dawes, William. *William Dawes's Notebooks on the Aboriginal Language of Sydney 1790–91*. London: Hans Rausing Endangered Language Project and SOAS Library Special Collections, School of Oriental and African Studies, in conjunction with the Darug Tribal Aboriginal Corporation, Blacktown, 2009. http://www.dnathan.com/eprints/dnathan_etal_2009_dawes.pdf. Web.

Delbridge, Arthur, Editor-in-chief. *Macquarie Concise Dictionary*. Macquarie University: Macquarie Library, 2002. Print.

Deleuze, Gilles, and Claire Parnet. *Dialogues II*. Trans. Hugh Tomlinson and Barbara Habberjam. New York: Columbia UP, 2002. Print.

Deleuze, Gilles, and Felix Guattari. *Kafka: Toward a Minor Literature*. Trans. Dana Polan. Minneapolis: U of Minnesota P, 1986. Print.

Dewey, Anne Day. *Beyond Maximus: The Construction of Public Voice in Black Mountain Poetry*. Stanford: Stanford UP, 2007. Print.

Diepeveen, Leonard. *Changing Voices: The Modern Quoting Poem*. Ann Arbor: U of Michigan P, 1993. Print.

Dixon, Robert. "Literature and Melodrama." Bennett and Strauss. 66–86.

Drucker, Johanna. "A Note on Historical Context and Basic Concepts." Jackson, Vos and Drucker. 39–64.

DuPlessis, Rachel Blau. *Pound, Eliot, Zukofsky, Olson, Creeley, and the Ends of Patriarchal Poetry*. Iowa City: U of Iowa P, 2012. Print.

Dutton, Geoffrey, ed. *Australian Verse from 1805: A Continuum*. Adelaide: Rigby, 1976. Print.
Dworkin, Craig. *Reading the Illegible*. Evanston: Northwestern UP, 2003. Print.
Edwards, Chris. *People of Earth*. Sydney: Vagabond, 2011. Print.
Elliott, Brian. *Adam Lindsay Gordon*. Melbourne: Sun, 1973. Print.
———. *The Landscape of Australian Poetry*. Melbourne: F.W. Cheshire, 1967. Print.
Espinosa, César. *Corrosive Signs: Essays on Experimental Poetry (Visual, Concrete, Alternative*. Trans. Harry Polkinhorn, Washington: Maisonneuve, 1990. Print.
Fagan, Kate. "'A Fluke? [N]ever!': Reading Chris Edwards." *Journal for the Association for the Study of Australian Literature* 12 (2012): 1–12. Web.
Farrell, Michael. "The Black or Unfair Image: The Babington Letter as a Sonnet." *Journal for the Association for the Study of Australian Literature*. 8 (2008). 7–16. Web.
Felski, Rita. *Doing Time: Feminist Theory and Postmodern Culture*. New York: New York UP, 2000. Print.
———. *Uses of Literature*. Malden: Blackwell, 2008. Print.
Finlay, Alec, ed. *Wood Notes Wild: Essays on the Poetry of Ian Hamilton Finlay*. Edinburgh: Polygon, 1995.
Fitzgerald, John. *Big White Lie: Chinese Australians in White Australia*. Sydney: U of New South Wales P, 2007. Print.
Forrest-Thomson, Veronica. *Poetic Artifice: A Theory of Twentieth-Century Poetry*. Manchester: Manchester UP, 1978. Print.
Foucault, Michel. *Language, Counter-memory, Practice: Selected Essays and Interviews*. Ithaca, NY: Cornell UP, 1993. Print.
Fredman, Stephen. *Poet's Prose: The Crisis in American Verse*. Cambridge: Cambridge UP, 1990. Print.
Freeland, Cynthia. "Photographs and Icons." *Photography and Philosophy: Essays on the Pencil of Nature*. Ed. Scott Walden. Malden: Blackwell, 2008. 50–69. Print.
Freud, Sigmund. "The Uncanny." *Art and Literature: Jensen's* Gradiva, *Leonardo da Vinci and Other Works*. Trans. James Strachey. Ed. Albert Dickson. London: Penguin, 1988. 339–376. Print.
Friedlander, Jennifer. *Feminine Look: Sexuation, Spectatorship, Subversion*. Albany: State U of New York P, 2008. Print.
Frost, Lucy. *No Place for a Nervous Lady: Voices from the Australian Bush*. Fitzroy: McPhee Gribble, 1984. Print.
Frye, Northrop. *T.S. Eliot*. Edinburgh: Oliver and Boyd, 1965. Print.
Gaile, Andreas, ed. *Fabulating Beauty: Perspectives on the Fiction of Peter Carey*. Amsterdam: Rodopi, 2005. Print.
Garton, Stephen. "The Dimensions of Dementia." *Constructing a Culture*. Eds. Verity Burgmann and Jenny Lee. Fitzroy: McPhee Gribble, 1988. Print.
Gibson, Ross. *Seven Versions of an Australian Badland*. St Lucia: U of Queensland P, 2002. Print.

Giddens, Anthony. *The Constitution of Society: Outline of the Theory of Structuration.* Cambridge: Polity, 1984. Print.
Gilmore, Mary. *The Collected Verse of Mary Gilmore: Vol. 1, 1887–1929.* Ed. Jennifer Strauss. St Lucia: U of Queensland P, 2004. Print.
Godwin, Luke. "The Fluid Frontier: Central Queensland 1845–63." Russell. 101–118.
Goffman, Erving. *Frame Analysis: An Essay on the Organization of Human Experience,* Cambridge, MA: Harvard UP, 1975. Print.
Goldsmith, Kenneth. "Being Boring." *American Poets in the 21st Century: The New Poetics.* Claudia Rankine and Lisa Sewell, eds. Middletown: Wesleyan UP, 2007. 361–367. Print.
———. *Uncreative Writing.* New York: Columbia UP, 2011. Print.
———. "Why Conceptual Writing? Why Now?" *Against Expression: An Anthology of Conceptual Writing.* Dworkin, Craig and Kenneth Goldsmith, eds. Evanston: Northwestern UP, 2011. xviii–xxii. Print.
Goodstein, Elizabeth. *Experience Without Qualities: Boredom and Modernity.* Stanford: Stanford UP, 2005. Print.
Goodwin, James. *Autobiography: The Self Made Text.* New York: Twayne, 1993. Print.
Grossman, Michele. "Bad Aboriginal Writing: Editing, Aboriginality, Textuality." *Meanjin.* 60.3 (2001). 152–165. Print.
———. "When they write what we read: Unsettling Indigenous Australian Life-writing." *Australian Humanities Review.* 39–40, Sep. 2006. Web.
———. "Xen(ography) and the Art of Representing Otherwise: Australian Indigenous Life-Writing and the Vernacular Text," *Postcolonial Studies.* 8.3 (2005). 277–301. Web.
Halden-Sullivan, Judith. "The Game of Self-Forgetting: Reading Innovative Poetry Reading Gadamer." *Reading the Difficulties: Dialogues with Contemporary American Innovative Poetry.* Eds. Thomas Fink and Halden-Sullivan. Tuscaloosa: U of Alabama Press, 2014. 127–145. Print.
Harpur, Charles. *The Poetical Works of Charles Harpur.* Ed. Elizabeth Perkins. Sydney: Angus & Robertson, 1984. Print.
Harris, Norman. "Letter to Jim Bassett." Heiss and Minter. 25–28.
Harrison, Martin. *Who Wants to Create Australia?* Sydney: Halstead, 2004. Print.
Harrison, Robert Pogue. *Forests: The Shadow of Civilization.* Chicago: U of Chicago P, 1992. Print.
Harrison, Rodney. "Historical Archaeology in the Land of the Black Stump." Mayne. 85–112. Print.
Hartman, Charles O. *Free Verse: An Essay on Prosody.* Evanston: Northwestern UP, 1980. Print.
Heiss, Anita, and Melodie-Jane Gibson. *Barani: Sydney's Aboriginal History.* http://www.sydneybarani.com.au/sites/aboriginal-people-and-place/ Web.
Heiss, Anita, and Peter Minter. Eds. *Macquarie PEN Anthology of Aboriginal Literature.* Crows Nest: Allen & Unwin, 2008. Print.

Heyward, Michael. *The Ern Malley Affair*. St Lucia: U of Queensland P, 1993. Print.

Hobbs, Andrew. "Ngarla People Win 11,000sqkm Pilbara Land Claim." *WA Business News*. 30 May 2007. Web.

Hodge, Bob, and Vijay Mishra. *Dark Side of the Dream: Australian Literature and the Postcolonial Mind*. North Sydney: Allen & Unwin, 1990. Print.

Howe, Susan. *Singularities*. Hanover: Wesleyan UP, 1990. Print.

Huang, Guiyou. "Chinese Literature" and "Chinese Translation." Tryphonopoulos and Adams. 58–61.

Hunt, Jane E. "Finding a Place For Women in Australian Cultural History: Female Cultural Activism in Sydney, 1900–1940." *Australian Historical Studies*. Oct 2004, Vol. 36 Issue 124, 221–237. Print.

Indyk, Ivor. "There's Life in the Corpus Yet," *The Australian*. 5 August 2009. Web.

Innes, Lyn. "Resurrecting Ned Kelly." *Sydney Studies in English*. Vol. 29, 2003. 83–94. http://openjournals.library.usyd.edu.au/index.php/SSE/article/view/574. Web.

Iser, Wolfgang. *Acts of Reading: A Theory of Aesthetic Response*. London: Routledge & Kegan Paul. 1978. Print.

Jackson, K. David, Eric Vos, and Johanna Drucker, eds. *Experimental–Visual–Concrete: Avant-Garde Poetry Since the 1960s*. Amsterdam: Rodopi, 1996. Print.

Jackson, Noel. *Science and Sensation in Romantic Poetry*. Cambridge: Cambridge UP, 2008. Print.

Jennings, Kate. *Mother I'm Rooted: An Australian Women Poets Anthology*. Fitzroy: Outback, 1975. Print.

Jones, Ian. *Ned Kelly: A Short Life*. Port Melbourne: Lothian, 1995. Print.

Jones, Jennifer. *Black Writers White Editors: Episodes of Collaboration and Compromise in Australian Publishing History*. North Melbourne: Australian Scholarly, 2009. Print.

Jong, Ah Sing. *Diary* [Manuscript]. 1866–1872. Melbourne, State Library of Victoria.

———. *A Difficult Case: An Autobiography of a Chinese Miner on the Central Victorian Goldfields*. Eds. Ruth Moore and Jim Tully. Daylesford: Jim Crow 2000. Print.

Joris, Pierre. *A Nomad Poetics*. Middletown: Wesleyan UP, 2003. Print.

Jose, Nicholas, Gen. ed. *Macquarie PEN Anthology of Australian Literature*. Crows Nest: Allen & Unwin, 2009. Print.

Jullien, Francois. *Detour and Access: Strategies of Meaning in China and Greece*. Trans. Sophie Hawkes. New York: Zone, 2000. Print.

Kane, Paul. *Australian Poetry: Romanticism and Negativity*. Cambridge: Cambridge UP, 1996. Print.

———. "Preface." Gaile. xi–xiv.

Keats, John. *Complete Poetry and Selected Prose of Keats*. Ed. Harold Edgar Briggs. New York: Random House, 1967. Print.

Kelly, Ned. *The Jerilderie Letter*. Ed. Alex McDermott. Melbourne: Text, 2001. Print.

———. "The Jerilderie Letter." Online Version, State Library of Victoria. Web.

Kenner, Hugh. *The Pound Era*. London: Faber, 1972. Print.

Kenny, Robert. *The Lamb Enters the Dreaming: Nathanael Pepper and the Ruptured World*. Melbourne: Scribe, 2007. Print.

Kinsella, John. *Contrary Rhetoric: Lectures on Landscape and Language*. Eds. Glen Phillips and Andrew Taylor. Fremantle: Fremantle P, 2008. Print.

———. *Spatial Relations Volume Two: Essays, Reviews, Commentaries, Chorography*. Amsterdam: Rodopi, 2013. Print.

———, ed. *The Penguin Anthology of Australian Poetry*. Camberwell: Penguin, 2009. Print.

Kirkpatrick, Peter. "New Words Come Tripping Slowly." *Cambridge History of Australian Literature*. Ed. Peter Pierce. Cambridge: Cambridge UP, 2009. Print. 199–222.

Kotz, Liz. *Words To Be Looked At: Language in 1960s Art*. Cambridge: MIT Press, 2007. Print.

Kristeva, Julia. *Desire in Language: A Semiotic Approach to Literature and Art*. New York: Columbia UP, 1980. Print.

Kwasny, Melissa. ed. *Toward the Open Field: Poets on the Art of Poetry 1800–1950*. Middletown: Wesleyan UP, 2004. Print.

Lambert, Gregg. *The Return of the Baroque in Modern Culture*. London: Continuum, 2006. Print.

Lawson, Henry. *Collected Verse: Volume One 1885–1900*. Sydney: Angus & Robertson, 1967. Print.

Lefevbre, Henri. *The Production of Space*. Trans. Donald Nicholson-Smith. Malden: Blackwell, 1991. Print.

Lehman, David, ed. *Great American Prose Poems: from Poe to the Present*. New York: Scribner, 2003. Print.

Lewis, Darrell. "The Bush Has Friends to Meet Him." Mayne. 277–303.

———. *The Murranji Track: Ghost Road of the Drovers*. Rockhampton: Central Queensland UP, 2007. Print.

Lionnet, Francoise, and Shu-mei Shih, eds. "Introduction." Lionnet and Shih. 1–33.

Lionnet, Francoise, and Shu-mei Shih, eds. *The Creolization of Theory*. Durham: Duke UP, 2011. Print.

Livon-Grosman, Ernesto. "Transcending National Poetics: A New Reading of Lezama Lima." *Selections* by José Lezama Lima. Berkeley: U of California P, 2005. Print.

Mackellar, Dorothea. *I Love A Sunburnt Country: The Diaries of Dorothea Mackellar*. Ed. Jyoti Brunsdon. North Ryde: Angus & Robertson, 1990. Print.

———. Official Dorothea Mackellar Website. dorotheamackellar.com.au. Web.

Macneil, Rod. "Time After Time: Temporal Frontiers and Boundaries in Colonial Images of the Australian Landscape." Russell. 47–67. Print.

Madsen, Deborah L. "Writing Chinese Diaspora: After the 'White Australia Policy.'" *Australia Made: A Multicultural Reader.* Eds. Sonia Mycak and Amit Sarwal. Sydney: Sydney UP, 2010. 158–172. Print.
Mallarmé, Stéphane. *Collected Poems.* Trans. Henry Weinfield. Berkeley: U of California P, 1994. Print.
Mariategui, José Carlos. *Seven Interpretive Essays on Peruvian Reality.* Austin: U of Texas P, 1971. Print.
Martin, Susan K. "Dead White Male Heroes." Gaile. 301–317.
Martin, Sylvia. *Passionate Friends: Mary Fullerton, Mabel Singleton and Miles Franklin.* London: Onlywomen, 2001. Print.
Matthews, Steven. *Les Murray.* Manchester: Manchester UP, 2001. Print.
Maushart, Susan. *Sort of a Place Like Home: Remembering the Moore River Native Settlement.* Fremantle: Fremantle Arts Centre P. 1993. Print.
―――. *Sort of a Place Like Home: Remembering the Moore River Native Settlement.* 2nd ed. Fremantle: Fremantle Arts Centre P. 2003. Print.
Mayne, Alan, ed. *Beyond the Black Stump: Histories of Outback Australia.* Kent Town: Wakefield, 2008. Print.
McBride, Patrizia C. "The Game of Meaning: Collage, Montage, and Parody in Kurt Schwitters' Merz." Modernism/modernity. Vol. 14, No. 2, April 2007, 249–272. Print.
McCaffery, Steve. *The Darkness of the Present: Poetics, Anachronism and the Anomaly.* Tuscaloosa: U of Alabama P, 2012. Print.
McCann, Andrew. "Writing and Commodity Capitalism." *Authority and Influence: Australian Literary Criticism 1950–2000.* Eds. Delys Bird, Robert Dixon and Christopher Lee. St Lucia: U of Queensland P, 2001. 329–340. Print.
McCooey, David. "Fiction and Poetry from 1950." Jose. 41–48.
McDermott, Alex. "Introduction." *The Jerilderie Letter.* By Ned Kelly. Melbourne: Text, 2001. Print.
McGann, Jerome. *A Critique of Modern Textual Criticism.* Chicago: U of Chicago P, 1983. Print.
―――. *The Textual Condition.* Princeton: Princeton UP, 1991. Print.
McLaren, John. "Unsettling the Southland: Myths of Possibility and Origin." *Bernard Hickey: A Roving Ambassador: Essays in his Memory.* Eds. Maria Renata Dolce and Antonella Riem Natale. Udine: Forum, 2009. 195–205. Print.
McQuillan, Martin. "Foreword." Jacques Derrida. *Geneses, Genealogies, Genres and Genius: The Secrets of the Archive.* New York: Columbia UP, 2006. Print.
Mead, Philip. *Networked Language: Culture & History in Australian Poetry.* North Melbourne: Australian Scholarly, 2008. Print.
Menzies, Robert. "The Forgotten People." Jose. 407–410.
Michaels, Eric. *The Aboriginal Invention of Television in Central Australia, 1982–1985.* Canberra: Australian Institute of Aboriginal Studies, Institute Report, 1986. Print.
Middleton, Peter. *Distant Reading: Performance, Readership, and Consumption in Contemporary Poetry.* Tuscaloosa: U of Alabama P, 2005. Print.

Mignolo, Walter. "I Am Where I Think: Remapping the Order of Knowing." Lionnet and Shih. 159–192.

———. "Literacy and Colonization: The New World Experience." *1492–1992 Rediscovering Colonial Writing.* Eds. René Jara and Nicholas Spadaccini. Minneapolis: Prisma Institute, 1989. 51–96. Print.

Miller, D. A. *Jane Austen or the Secret of Style.* Princeton: Princeton UP, 2003. Print.

———. *The Novel and the Police.* Berkeley: U of California P, 1988. Print.

Milne, Esther. *Letters, Postcards, Emails: Technologies of Presence.* New York: Routledge, 2010. Print.

Mitchell, Adrian. *Charles Harpur.* South Melbourne: Sun, 1973. Print.

Monroe, Jonathan. *A Poverty of Objects: The Prose Poem and the Politics of Genre.* Ithaca: Cornell UP, 1987. Print.

Morgan, George. *Unsettled Places: Aboriginal People and Urbanisation in New South Wales.* Kent Town: Wakefield, 2006. Print.

Muecke, Stephen. "Can You Argue With the Honeysuckle?" Rutherford and Holloway. 48–52.

———. *No Road (Bitumen All the Way).* Fremantle: Fremantle Arts Centre P, 1999. Print.

———. "Preface." George Dyuŋgayan's *The Bulu Line: A West Kimberley Song Cycle.* Ed Stuart Cooke. Glebe: Puncher and Wattmann, 2014. Print.

———. "'Something Wrong? Oh Must Be Ghost': Writing Different Existences." *Hidden Agendas: Unreported Poetics.* Ed. Louis Armand. Prague: Literaria Pragensia, 2010. 175–178. Print.

———. *Textual Spaces: Aboriginality and Cultural Studies.* Sydney: U of New South Wales P, 1992. Print.

Nadel, Ira B. "Visualizing History: Pound and the Chinese Cantos." Rainey. 151–166.

Nancy, Jean-Luc. *The Inoperative Community.* Ed. Peter Connor. Trans. Peter Connor, Lisa Garbus, Michael Holland and Simona Sawhney. Minneapolis: U of Minnesota P, 1991. Print.

Ngai, Sianne. *Ugly Feelings.* Cambridge: Harvard UP, 2005. Print.

Nicholls, Peter. "*The Chinese Written Character as a Medium for Poetry: A Critical Edition* (Review)." *Modernism/Modernity.* 17.3. Sep. 2010. 694–696. Print.

Nietzsche, Friedrich. *The Gay Science.* Ed. Bernard Williams. Trans. Josefine Nauckhoff. Cambridge: Cambridge UP, 2001. Print.

Noland, Carrie, and Barrett Watten, eds. *Diasporic Avant-Gardes: Experimental Poetics and Cultural Displacement.* New York: Palgrave, 2009. Print.

Noonuccal, Oodgeroo—see Kath Walker.

Normington-Rawling, J. *Charles Harpur, An Australian.* Sydney: Angus & Robertson, 1962. Print.

Noyes, John K. "Nomadic Landscapes and the Colonial Frontier: the Problem of Nomadism in German South West Africa." Russell. 198–215.

Ong, Walter. *Orality and Literacy: The Technologizing of the Word.* London: Routledge, 2002. Print.

Owen, Stephen. *Readings in Chinese Literary Thought*. Cambridge: Council on East Asian Studies Harvard U, 1992. Print.
Paterson, A. B. *Selected Poems*. Sydney: Angus and Robertson, 1996. Print.
Payne, Mark. *The Animal Part: Humans and Other Animals in the Human Imagination*. Chicago: U of Chicago P, 2010. Print.
Paz, Octavio. ed. *Mexican Poetry: An Anthology*. London: Thames and Hudson. Print.
Pepper, Thomas. *Singularities: Extremes of Theory in the Twentieth Century*. Cambridge: Cambridge UP, 1997. Print.
Perkins, Elizabeth. "Introduction." *The Poetical Works of Charles Harpur*. By Charles Harpur. Sydney: Angus & Robertson, 1984. xi–xliii. Print.
———. "Literary Culture 1851–1914: Founding a Canon." Bennett and Strauss. 47–65.
Perloff, Marjorie. *The Dance of the Intellect: Studies in the Poetry of the Pound Tradition*. Cambridge: Cambridge UP, 1985. Print.
———. *Unoriginal Genius: Poetry by Other Means in the New Century*. Chicago: U of Chicago P, 2010. Print.
———. *Wittgenstein's Ladder: Poetic Language and the Strangeness of the Ordinary*. Chicago: U of Chicago P, 1996. Print.
Pheng, Cheah. "Crises of Money." Lionnet and Shih. 83–111.
Picchione, John. *The New Avant-Garde in Italy: Theoretical Debate and Poetic Practices*. U of Toronto P, 2004. Print.
Pilger, John. *A Secret Country*. Vintage: London, 1992. Print.
Plug, Leendert. "On Tempo in Dispreferred Turns: A Recurrent Pattern in a Dutch Corpus." *Where Prosody Meets Pragmatics*. Eds. Dagmar Barth-Weingarten, Nicole Dehé and Anne Wichmann. Bingley: Emerald, 2009. 225–256. Web.
Plumwood, Val. "Decolonizing Relationships with Nature." Ashcroft, Griffiths and Tiffin. 503–506.
Pound, Ezra. "A Few Don'ts By an Imagiste." *Poetry*. Vol. 1, No. 6 (Mar., 1913). 200 206. Web.
———. *The Pisan Cantos*. London: Faber, 1973. Print.
———. *Selected Poems*. New York: New Directions, 1957. Print.
Price, Mary. *The Photograph: A Strange Confined Space*. Stanford: Stanford UP, 1994. Print.
Prichard, Katherine Susannah. "Marlene." Jose. 379–385.
Quartermain, Peter. *Disjunctive Poetics: From Gertrude Stein and Louis Zukofsky to Susan Howe*. Cambridge: Cambridge UP, 1992. Print.
———. "Sound Reading." *Close Listening: Poetry and the Performed Word*. Ed. Charles Bernstein. New York: Oxford UP, 1998. 217–230. Print.
Rainey, Lawrence, ed. *A Poem Containing History: Textual Studies in the* Cantos. Ann Arbor: U of Michigan P, 1987. Print.
Ramraj, Victor. "Diasporas and Muticulturalism." *New National and Post-Colonial Literatures*. Ed. Bruce King. Oxford: Clarendon Press, 1996. 214–229. Print.

Rasula, Jed. *This Compost: Ecological Imperatives in American Poetry*. Athens: U of Georgia P, 2002. Print.

———. "Understanding the Sound of Not Understanding." *Close Listening: Poetry and the Performed Word*. Ed. Charles Bernstein. New York: Oxford UP, 1998. 233–261. Print.

Ravenscroft, Alison. *The Postcolonial Eye: White Australian Desire and the Visual Field of Race*. Farnham: Ashgate, 2012. Print.

Reid, Anthony, ed. *The Chinese Diaspora in the Pacific*. Aldershot: Ashgate, 2008. Print.

Reiman, Donald H. *The Study of Modern Manuscripts: Public, Confidential, and Private*. Baltimore: Johns Hopkins UP, 1993. Print.

Reynolds, Henry. *With the White People*. Ringwood: Penguin, 1990. Print.

———. *Why Weren't We Told: A Personal Search for the Truth of Our History*. Ringwood: Penguin, 2000. Print.

Rose, Deborah Bird. *Dingo Makes Us Human: Life and Land in an Aboriginal Australian Culture*. Cambridge: Cambridge UP, 1992. Print.

Rothenberg, Jerome, and Jeffrey C. Robinson. *Poems for the Millennium Vol. 3: Romantic and Postromantic Poetry*. Berkeley: U of California P, 2009. 655. Print.

Russell, Lynette, ed. *Colonial Frontiers: Indigenous-European Encounters in Settler Societies*. Manchester: Manchester UP, 2001. Print.

Russo, Katherine E. *Practices of Proximity: The Appropriation of English in Australian Indigenous Literature*. Newcastle upon Tyne: Cambridge Scholars, 2010. Print.

Rutherford, Jennifer. "*Kairos* for a Wounded Country." Rutherford and Holloway. 1–11.

———. "Undwelling; or Reading Bachelard in Australia." Rutherford and Holloway. 111–125.

Rutherford, Jennifer, and Barbara Holloway, eds. *Halfway House: The Poetics of Australian Spaces*. Crawley: UWAP, 2010. Print.

Ryan, Jan. "Chinese Australian History." *Creating Australia: Changing Australian History*. Eds. Wayne Hudson and Geoffrey Bolton. St Leonards: Allen and Unwin, 1997, 71–78. Print.

Sacerdoti, Giorgio. *Irony Through Psychoanalysis*. London: Karnac, 1992. Web.

Saper, Craig. "Under Cancellation: The Future Tone of Visual Poetry." Jackson, Vos and Drucker. 309–316.

Sarduy, Severo. "The Baroque and the Neobaroque." Zamora and Kaup. 270–291.

Sayers, Andrew. *Aboriginal Artists of the Nineteenth Century*. Melbourne: Oxford UP, 1994. Print.

Schlunke, Katrina. "Unsettling Whiteness." *Unmasking Whiteness: Race Relations and Reconciliation*. Ed. Belinda McKay. Nathan: Centre for Public Culture and Ideas, Griffith U, 2004. 173–179. Print.

Schmidgall, Gary, ed. "Introduction." *Selected Poems 1855–1892: A New Edition*. By Walt Whitman. New York: St Martin's, 1999. Print.

Sedgwick, Eve Kosofsky, ed. *Novel Gazing: Queer Readings in Fiction.* Durham: Duke UP, 1997. Print.
Serres, Michel. *The Parasite.* Trans. Lawrence R. Schehr. Baltimore: Johns Hopkins UP, 1982. Print.
Shakespeare, William. *The Tempest. The Complete Works of William Shakespeare: Comprising His Plays and Poems.* London: Spring, 1967. 1–20. Print.
Shaviro, Steven. *Passion and Excess: Blanchot, Bataille and Literary Theory.* Tallahassee: Florida State UP, 1990. Print.
Shen, Yuanfang. *Dragon Seed in the Antipodes.* Carlton Sth: Melbourne UP, 2001. Print.
———. "Sojourners or Settlers? Early Chinese Immigrants in Australia." ANU, 27 Feb. 1999. Web.
Shoemaker, Adam. *Black Words, White Page: Aboriginal Literature 1929–1988.* St Lucia: U of Queensland P, 1989. Print.
Silliman, Ron. *The New Sentence.* New York: Roof, 1989. Print.
Skinner, Jonathan. "Editor's Statement." *ecopoetics.* no.1, winter 2001. 5–7. Print.
Siegel, Jeff. "Chinese Pidgin English in Southeastern Australia: The notebook of Jong Ah Siug." *Journal of Pidgin and Creole Languages.* Vol. 24, No. 2, 2009. 306–337. Web.
Slemon, Stephen. "Unsettling the Empire: Resistance Theory for the Second World." Ashcroft, Griffiths and Tiffin. 102–106. Print.
Smith, Keith Vincent. *Mari Nawi: Aboriginal Odysseys.* Dural: Rosenberg, 2010. Print.
Sontag, Susan. *On Photography.* London: Penguin, 2002. Print.
———. *Regarding the Pain of Others.* New York: Farrar, Strauss and Giroux, 2003. Print.
Soper, Kate. *What Is Nature?: Culture, Politics and the non-Human.* Oxford: Blackwell, 1995. Print.
Spacks, Patricia Meyer. *Boredom: The Literary History of a State of Mind.* Chicago: U of Chicago P, 1995. Print.
Spender, Dale. *Writing a New World: Two Centuries of Australian Women Writers.* London: Pandora, 1988. Print.
Spicer, Jack. *My Vocabulary Did This To Me: The Collected Poetry of Jack Spicer.* Eds. Peter Gizzi and Kevin Killian. Middletown: Wesleyan UP, 2008. Print.
Spivak, Gayatri Chakravorty. "Preface." *Of Grammatology.* By Jacques Derrida. Baltimore: Johns Hopkins UP, 1997. Print.
Stallybrass, Peter, and Allon White. *The Politics and Poetics of Transgression.* Ithaca: Cornell UP, 1986. Print.
Stefans, Brian Kim. "A Quick Graph: On Martin Johnston/Paragraphs from an Unwritten Letter to John Tranter." *Jacket* 11 (Apr. 2000). Web.
Stein, Gertrude. *Look at Me At Me Now and Here I Am: Writings and Lectures 1909 45.* London: Penguin, 1990. Print.
Steiner, Peter. *Russian Formalism: A Metapoetics.* Ithaca: Cornell UP, 1984. Print.
Stevens, Wallace. *The Collected Poems.* New York: Vintage, 1954. Print.

Stewart, Susan. *Poetry and the Fate of the Senses*. Chicago: U of Chicago P, 2002. Print.

Stewart, Kathleen. *A Space on the Side of the Road: Cultural Poetics in an "Other" America*. Princeton: Princeton UP, 1996. Print.

Strehlow, T. G. H. *Songs of Central Australia*. Sydney: Angus & Robertson, 1971. Print.

Svendsen, Lars. *A Philosophy of Boredom*. Trans John Irons. London: Reaktion, 2005. Print.

Switzer, Renee. *The Age*. "Castlemaine Pigs out on Pork Revival." *The Age*. 16 March 2006. Web

Sykes J. B. ed. *The Concise Oxford Dictionary: of Current English*. Oxford: Oxford UP, 1982. Print.

Taggart, John. *Songs of Degrees: Essays on Contemporary Poetry and Poetics*. Tuscaloosa: U of Alabama P, 1994. Print.

Tarlo, Harriet. "Women and Ecopoetics: An Introduction in Context." *How2* 3:2. http://www.asu.edu/pipercwcenter/how2journal/vol_3_no_2/ecopoetics/index.html. Web.

Taylor, Andrew. *Reading Australian Poetry*. St Lucia: U of Queenland P, 1986. Print.

Troy, Jakelin. *The Sydney Language*. Canberra: Australian Dictionaries Projects, AIATSIS, 1994. Print.

Tryphonopoulos, Demetres P., and Stephen J. Adams, eds. *The Ezra Pound Encyclopedia*. Westport, CT: Greenwood, 2005. Print.

Van Toorn, Penny. *Writing Never Arrives Naked: Early Aboriginal Cultures of Writing in Australia*. Canberra: Aboriginal Studies, 2006. Print.

Vickery, Ann. *Stressing the Modern: Cultural Politics in Australian Women's Poetry*. Cambridge: Salt, 2007. Print.

Von Hallberg, Robert. *Charles Olson: The Scholar's Art*. Cambridge: Harvard UP, 1978. Print.

Vos, Eric. "Critical Perspectives on Experimental, Visual and Concrete Poetry: an Introduction to this Volume (with an Appendix on Carlfriedrich Claus)." Jackson, Vos and Drucker. 23–38.

Walker, Kath. *My People: A Kath Walker Collection*. Milton: Jacaranda, 1970. Print.

Wallace-Crabbe, Chris. "Poetry and Modernism." Bruce Bennett and Jennifer Strauss. 217–238.

Walsh, Michael, and Colin Yallop, eds. *Language and Culture in Aboriginal Australia*. Canberra: Aboriginal Studies Press, 2007. Print.

Ward, Russel. *The Australian Legend*. Melbourne: Oxford UP, 1960. Print.

———. "*Felons and Folk-songs*." On native grounds: Australian writing from Meanjin quarterly. Ed. Clement Christesen. Sydney: Angus & Robertson, 1968. Print.

Waterhouse, Richard. *The Vision Splendid: A Social and Cultural History of Rural Australia*. Fremantle: Curtin U, 2005. Print.

Webby, Elizabeth, ed. *Colonial Voices: Letters, Diaries, Journalism and Other Accounts of Nineteenth-Century Australia.* St Lucia: U of Queensland P, 1989. Print.
Weil, Simone. *Gravity and Grace.* Abingdon: Routledge, 2007. Print.
Wentworth, W. C. "Australasia." Australian Poetry Library. Web.
Werner, Marta. *Emily Dickinson's Open Folios: Scenes of Reading, Surfaces of Writing.* Ann Arbor: U of Michigan P, 1996. Print.
White, Hayden. *Tropics of Discourse: Essays in Cultural Criticism.* Baltimore: Johns Hopkins UP, 1985. Print.
White, Richard. *Inventing Australia: Images and Identity 1688–1980.* Sydney: Allen and Unwin, 1981. Print.
Whitman, Walt. *Selected Poems 1855–1892: A New Edition.* Ed. Gary Schmidgall. New York: St Martin's, 1999. Print.
Wilde, William. *Australian Poets and their Works: A Reader's Guide.* Oxford: Oxford UP, 1996. Print.
Wolfe, Carey. "Introduction." *Zoontologies: The Question of the Animal.* ed Wolfe. Minneapolis: U of Minnesota P, 2003. ix-xxiii. Print.
Wolfreys, Julian. *Readings: Acts of Close Reading in Literary Theory.* Edinburgh: Edinburgh UP, 2000. Print.
Woodcock, Bruce. "Unsettling Illusions: Carey and Capital in *Jack Maggs.*" Gaile. 263–273.
Woodward, Dennis. *Australia Unsettled: The Legacy of Neo-liberalism.* Sydney: Pearson Education, 2005. Print.
Yépez, Heriberto. *The Empire of Neomemory.* Trans. Jen Hofer, Chistian Nagler, and Brian Whitener. Oakland: Chainlinks, 2013. Print.
Zamora, Lois Parkinson, and Monika Kaup, eds. *Baroque New Worlds: Representation, Transculturation, Counterconquest.* Durham: Duke UP, 2010. Print.

Index

Ackland, Michael, 4–5, 15, 39, 86
Adorno, T. W., 83, 89
Agamben, Giorgio, 21, 51, 113
Alcaeus, 114
alphabet, 73, 77, 94, 96, 97, 186, 192, 183, 194, 195
analphabetical, 186
anthologies, 7, 8, 10, 17, 19, 26, 31, 32, 47, 48, 65, 118, 131, 150, 178, 189, 195, 197
  see also Macquarie PEN anthologies
anthologists, 11, 66
anthologizing, 14, 27, 65, 66, 83, 86, 138, 141
antisettlement, 7, 52
  see also unsettlement
Apollinaire, Guillaume, 81
appropriation, 5, 40, 65, 77, 78–9, 82, 83, 100, 124, 133, 141, 144, 148, 165, 170, 171, 192
Ashcroft, Bill, 134–5
assemblage, 6–7, 10, 15, 29, 31, 32, 41, 52, 62, 64, 67, 72, 73, 74, 75, 91, 92, 97, 99, 104, 108, 117, 120, 123, 124, 127, 129–30, 131, 132, 134, 135, 137, 138, 139, 140, 142, 144, 146, 149, 150, 152, 153, 161, 164–5, 171, 178, 183, 186, 189, 192, 193, 196
Assmann, Jan, 159–61, 165
Auden, WH, 100

"Babington Letter, The," 14, 46
ballads, 4, 22, 27, 40–4, 50, 54, 150
Barnes, Katherine, 83, 138–9, 140, 142, 149, 150
baroque. *See* neobaroque
Barthes, Roland, 56, 85, 92–3, 111, 115, 119, 123, 125, 126, 155, 156, 167, 170, 172
Bataille, Georges, 167, 171
Batchen, Geoffrey, 166
Bate, Jonathan, 47, 144–5, 146, 148, 150–2
Baudelaire, Charles, 19, 112, 113, 114, 115, 116
Bennelong, 3, 13–18, 26–38, 64, 82, 86, 100, 103, 170, 176
Berger, John, 166, 171–2
Bernstein, Charles, 31, 65, 79, 82, 95, 97
biodiversity, 141, 144–5, 148–51
Bird, Delys, 7–8, 32
Birns, Nicholas, 136
Boake, Barcroft, 5
Bohn, Willard, 83, 140, 142, 170
Bollobas, Eniko, 146
Bonwick, Richard, 64
boredom, 10, 12, 22, 107–27
Bradman, Don, 139
Brennan, Christopher, 11, 12, 76, 83, 109, 119, 120, 129, 138–50, 152
Brodsky, Isadore, 16, 26–7, 30, 36, 37
Brody, Jennifer DeVere, 80, 113, 170

"Bromide." *See* Fullerton
Brophy, Kevin, 99, 104
Brown, Alexander, 129, 130, 131, 134, 136–8, 187
Brown, Susan, 93–4
Browning, Robert, 121, 122
Brunsdon, Joy, 85, 87, 88–9, 90–1, 92, 94–5, 96, 97
bullocks. *See* cattle
Byrne, Joseph, 14, 18, 19, 27, 45, 48, 49, 51, 52, 54, 56, 58

Cage, John, 123
Cambridge, Ada, 21
Cambridge History of Australian Literature, 67
canons, 7, 10–11, 64, 66, 82, 91, 108, 119, 123, 125, 126, 127, 138, 140, 150, 152, 197
capitalization, 27, 45, 58, 69, 75, 144, 181
Carey, Peter, 16, 17, 19, 20, 59
Carter, Paul, 1, 5, 13, 23, 28–9, 30, 56, 57, 61, 150, 163, 178, 180
Case, The. *See* Jong, Ah Sing
cattle, 15, 21, 24, 40, 51, 53, 56, 57, 58, 96, 131, 132, 135, 179–80, 182, 183, 184, 185, 188
Certeau, Michel de, 41, 78–9, 89, 100, 190
Chinese Australians, 63–7, 69, 71, 72, 74, 77, 100, 151, 153, 184, 195
see also Jong, Ah Sing
Chinese language, 67–8, 71–4, 76, 77, 78, 80, 82
Chinese poetics. *See* tso
Christian, 22, 115, 141, 171
Clark, Axel, 129, 138, 139, 140–1, 142, 145, 149
Clarke, Marcus, 107, 117
clearing, 23, 40, 45, 61–2, 148–9
closet drama, 93–4, 100
Cluver, Claus, 30, 81, 83, 97
code, 11, 26, 33, 72, 74, 80, 85–97, 102, 120, 157, 186–7

collaboration, 18, 27, 34, 125, 129, 130, 131, 135, 148, 154, 168
collage, 18, 82, 108, 119–27, 140–4, 147, 164
Collis, Stephen, 103–4
conceptual poetics, 3, 65, 78, 79, 82, 127, 144, 148, 187, 196–7
concrete poetry, 72, 74, 75, 79–84, 96, 97, 106, 140, 170, 192
Conley, Thomas, 59
Cooke, Stuart, 68, 163
country, 2, 4, 7, 13, 21, 27, 30, 32, 36, 37, 54, 68, 69, 85, 86–7, 94, 95–6, 98, 105, 131, 133, 135, 139, 165, 168, 172, 175, 179, 180, 182, 194
see also earth, land, landscape
Craven, Peter, 31
Creeley, Robert, 148
creole, 24, 25, 68
Culler, Jonathan, 123
Cunningham, Sophie, 31

Dada, 140, 164
Danayarri, Hobbles, 102
Daniehy, Daniel, 4
Dante, 21
Davenport, Sarah, 12, 175, 178, 181–3, 194
Davidson, Ian, 75, 76, 84, 91, 190
Dawes, William, 28
decorum, 189
Deleuze, Gilles and Claire Parnet, 6, 116–17, 142, 164–5
see also assemblage
Deleuze, Gilles and Felix Guattari, 6, 51–3, 64, 73, 76, 142
Dewey, Anne Day, 148
diaspora, 66, 67–9, 73, 83
Dickinson, Emily, 22, 23, 25, 52, 81, 82–3
dictation, 14, 18, 27, 113
see also scribes
Diepeveen, Leonard, 119, 124, 125, 142–4

dogs, 15, 19, 20, 24, 37, 41, 51, 53, 57, 60, 157, 170, 192
drawings, 12, 13, 64, 67, 74, 75, 76, 164, 175, 192–4
see also illustration, maps, visual poetry
driving, 93, 133, 134, 135
drought, 44, 133
drover messages, 11, 12, 175, 183–92, 194
Drucker, Johanna, 81–2, 141, 142
ducks, 46, 47, 55
Duncan, Robert, 146, 148
DuPlessis, Rachel Blau, 148
Dutton, Geoffrey, 139
Dworkin, Craig, 31, 82, 87, 95, 163

earth, 40, 42, 55, 57, 61, 62, 90, 96, 151
see also country, land, landscape
ecopoetics, 12, 47, 144, 150, 151
ecosystem, 141, 144, 145
editing, 48, 83, 94, 97, 99, 124, 138, 154, 155, 161–5, 167, 169, 170, 171, 173, 193
editors, 6, 11, 17, 18, 22, 26, 41, 42, 46, 59, 77, 79, 87, 88, 99, 103, 106, 108, 117, 129, 130, 135, 140, 151, 157, 161, 162–4, 165, 167, 169, 170, 172, 173, 192
Edwards, Chris, 139, 148
Eisenstein, Sergei, 144
Eliot, George, 93–4
Eliot, TS, 82, 123, 143, 144
Elliott, Brian, 15, 134, 140
empathy, 133, 138
Emu Plains, 43, 49
emus, 193
England, 14, 27, 29, 30, 33, 34, 35, 37, 40, 41, 44, 54, 90, 98, 107, 120, 123, 127, 181
Eora, 14, 27, 28, 30, 32, 35, 36, 37
see also Wangal
ethics, 23, 102, 146, 148–9, 169, 171, 172
etymology, 30, 40, 55, 93, 103, 137, 154, 159, 166, 176, 186, 189, 196

everyday, 41–2, 76, 87, 88–9, 91–100, 106, 109, 123, 131, 132, 133, 138, 157, 163, 166
exophonic, 78, 83, 192

Federation, 77, 86, 91, 98, 103, 138
Felski, Rita, 72, 88, 89, 91, 93, 96, 98, 100, 103
feminism, 89, 132
fences, 55, 74, 75, 133, 134–5, 138, 161, 184, 186, 189, 190
Fenollosa, Ernest, 73, 82
Finlay, Ian Hamilton, 83
fish, 14, 26, 157
Fitzgerald, John, 65
Fitzpatrick, Constable Alexander, 21, 23, 24, 26
Flannigan, Charlie, 12, 76, 175, 193–4
Fogarty, Lionel, 8, 9, 189
Forrest-Thomson, Veronica, 84, 87, 97
Foucault, Michel, 3, 10, 101, 136
Frank the Poet, 43
Fredman, Stephen, 112, 113, 118, 141
free verse, 42, 79, 147
freedom, 21, 22, 63, 67, 69, 71, 82, 83, 84, 112, 115, 120, 133, 184, 190
Friedlander, Jennifer, 156, 172
Frost, Lucy, 175, 178–82
Fullerton, Mary, 11, 12, 107–10, 118–27, 141, 176
futurism, 140, 146

game, 14, 15, 20–1, 26, 83
games, 12, 85, 108, 110, 118–27, 131
Geytenbeek, Brian, 129, 130–2, 133, 136–8, 187
Gibson, Ross, 7, 27, 29, 40, 98, 101
Giddens, Anthony, 6
Gilligan, Gladys, 12, 153–74, 176
Gilmore, Mary, 83, 119
Goffman, Erving, 30
Goldsmith, Kenneth, 3, 123, 124, 144
Goodstein, Elizabeth, 111, 116
Gordon, Adam Lindsay, 5, 15

218 • Index

grammar, 6, 7, 16, 21, 22, 27, 37, 45, 47, 48, 50–1, 66, 72, 77, 79, 99, 117, 126, 158, 171, 175, 177, 180, 188
  see also literacy, punctuation, spelling
Grossman, Michelle, 154, 156–7, 161–6, 169, 170, 173
guns, 15, 44, 58, 100
  see also shooting

Hall, Stuart, 24
handwriting, 14, 18, 40, 48, 62, 71, 73, 81, 82, 84, 125, 139, 140, 143, 148, 149, 170, 187, 193
  see also drawings, drover messages
Harpur, Charles, 4, 11, 12, 15, 40, 56, 64, 96, 107–19, 123, 126, 127, 143, 177
Harris, Max, 189
Harris, Norman, 11, 85, 86, 91, 98–106, 150, 153, 188
Harrison, Martin, 1, 6
Harrison, Robert Pogue, 186
Harrison, Rodney, 2, 151
Hartman, Charles O, 106
Hartman, Geoffrey, 82
Heiss, Anita and Melodie-Jane Gibson, 29
Heiss, Anita and Peter Minter, 13, 26, 27, 32–3, 35, 36, 37, 85, 99, 101–2
hens, 64, 70, 137
Heyward, Michael, 120
Hodge, Bob and Vijay Mishra, 105, 139
horse riding, 23, 42, 131, 134, 193, 194
horses, 15, 23, 39, 40, 41, 42, 46, 47, 50–1, 52, 53, 55, 56, 58, 62, 110, 111, 115, 118, 131, 134, 177, 179, 180, 183, 193, 194
  see also Ruita Cruta and Wombat
Howe, Susan, 25, 70, 163
Huggins, Jackie, 154
Huggins, Rita, 154
humor, 24, 58, 60, 105, 132, 133, 177, 189

hunting, 11, 12, 13, 14–16, 19, 20–30, 34, 38, 44, 56, 57, 58, 60, 84, 135, 147, 157, 159, 172, 178, 191, 192, 194
hyperbole, 26, 55, 58
hypotaxis, 141–2

ideology, 3, 5, 22, 86, 87, 137
illustrations, 60, 64, 76, 77–8, 80, 81, 88–9, 131, 162, 165–6
  see also drawings, maps, photography, visual poetry
Indyk, Ivor, 17, 21, 44
insults, 57, 59, 70, 143
intertextuality, 36, 78
invention, 15, 41–2, 44, 65, 66, 67, 71–2, 73, 74, 76–7, 78, 80, 81, 83, 84, 86, 87, 92–3, 96, 100, 101, 109, 120, 127, 145, 173, 176, 177, 191, 195, 197
Ireland, 21
Irish, 13, 16, 21, 26, 42–3, 49–50, 59, 66, 85, 195
irony, 22, 25, 32, 33, 37, 51, 56, 58, 61, 83, 94, 103, 104, 105, 110, 113, 120, 122, 127, 138, 141, 150, 153, 167, 173, 174, 177

Jerilderie Letter, The, 7, 13–27, 31, 38, 39–62
Jingkiri, Miriny-Mirinymarra, 131–4, 176
Jingkiri, Wirrkaru, 134
Jones, Ian, 14, 16, 18, 19–20, 27, 40, 42, 43, 52, 60
Jones, Jennifer, 103, 162, 164, 165, 166, 173
Jong, Ah Sing, 11, 63–84, 96, 176, 192
Joris, Pierre, 10, 183
Jose, Nicholas, 5–6, 13, 85, 118

Kaalyamarra, Yintilypirna, 134
Kafka, Franz, 51, 52
Kane, Paul, 6, 20, 108, 115
kangaroos, 15, 134, 140, 157

Keats, John, 5, 113, 144–5, 148, 149
Kelly, Dan, 21, 23, 56, 58–9
Kelly, Ned, 7, 13–27, 31, 38, 39–62, 64, 67, 82, 86, 107, 146, 147, 176, 180, 181, 194
Kimberley, The, 130, 136, 163
Kinsella, John, 2, 44, 138
Kristeva, Julia, 22
Kwasny, Melissa, 77, 147

Lambert, Gregg, 191
land, 2, 3, 5, 8, 9, 15, 23, 24, 36, 40, 41, 43, 44, 45, 52, 53, 61, 62, 68, 85, 100, 102, 105–6, 130–1, 133, 135, 149, 156, 168, 169, 191, 194
landscape, 1, 5, 9, 20, 142, 148, 168
see also clearing, country, earth
language poetry, 79, 125
Lawson, Henry, 7, 100, 119
Lefebvre, Henri, 76, 89, 100, 131, 158, 178
Lehman, David, 113, 115
Lewis, Darrell, 11, 175, 183, 184–5, 188, 190
Lima, Jose Lezama, 190
literacy, 4, 5, 16, 17, 18, 27, 29, 32, 34, 39, 50, 51, 52, 78, 84, 99, 104–5, 165, 173, 177, 181, 188, 196
literated, 154
literature, 2, 5–6, 7–8, 9–10, 17, 18, 19, 32–3, 41, 45, 64, 67, 72, 73, 84, 90, 91, 93, 99, 102, 104, 108–9, 110, 113, 115, 118, 119, 121, 123, 127, 131, 134, 139, 146, 151, 152, 189, 191, 193, 195–7
Livon-Grosman, Ernesto, 190, 194
lowercase, 47, 48
lyric, 4, 87, 92, 112, 114, 115, 119, 149, 150, 167, 169

Mabo, 2
Mackellar, Dorothea, 11, 85–100, 106, 119
Macneil, Rod, 62

Macquarie PEN Anthology of Aboriginal Literature, 7, 26, 99, 119
see also Heiss and Minter
Macquarie PEN Anthology of Australian Literature, 6, 7, 8, 16, 26, 31, 32, 47, 65, 99, 118, 119
see also Jose, Nicholas
Madsen, Deborah L, 65–6, 72
magpies, 21, 51, 59
Mallarmé, Stéphane, 74, 76, 80, 81, 82, 119, 139–41, 142, 145–50
Malley, Ern, 4, 9, 22, 50, 119–20, 125, 139, 189
manuscript, 17, 45, 48, 63, 69, 82, 162, 166, 187–8
maps, 66, 67, 74–6, 81, 162
Mariategui, José Carlos, 195
Martin, Susan K, 19, 20
Martin, Sylvia, 122, 124, 125, 127
Maushart, Susan, 153–74
McCaffery, Steve, 190
McCann, Andrew, 9–10, 107, 117
McCooey, David, 17
McDermott, Alex, 13, 16, 18, 19, 21, 26, 40, 42, 46, 47–8, 49–50, 52, 58, 60
McGann, Jerome, 18, 77, 78, 84, 148
McLaren, John, 8–9
Mead, Philip, 1, 6, 8, 9–10, 16, 22, 26, 28, 66, 67, 84, 91, 92, 102, 103, 109, 110, 120, 171, 175
Menzies, Robert, 89–90, 98
metamorphosis, 51–2, 57, 59
metaphor, 14, 19, 23, 24, 25, 27, 32, 39, 40, 41, 42, 44–5, 47, 50, 51, 52, 53, 57, 59, 70, 94, 95, 98, 129, 135, 140, 142, 145–6, 164, 182, 184, 190
Michaels, Eric, 168
Middleton, Peter, 98
Mignolo, Walter, 27, 32
Miller, D. A., 30, 85, 86, 94, 101, 102, 104
Milne, Esther, 19, 26, 30, 31, 34, 37, 43, 58

Minter, Peter
  see Heiss, Anita and Peter Minter
Mitchell, Adrian, 11, 110, 127
Monroe, Jonathan, 73, 113, 114, 115, 116, 117
Moore, Marianne, 123, 143
Moore, Ruth and Jim Tully, 63, 64, 66, 67, 76, 79, 81, 83
Moore River Native Settlement, 153–74
mosquitoes, 50–1, 52, 60–1, 95, 120, 181
Muecke, Stephen, 1, 15, 21, 32, 33, 35, 135, 163, 168–9
Murray, Jilalga, 131
Murray, Les, 24, 151
"My Country," 86, 94, 95–6, 98
  see also Mackellar, Dorothea

Nancy, Jean-Luc, 103–4, 170–1
national culture, 5, 7, 9, 10, 11, 16, 17, 20, 33, 39, 40, 43, 44, 48, 49, 62, 65, 66, 67, 73, 74, 77, 84, 86, 90, 96, 97, 98, 102, 106, 108, 110, 115, 127, 140, 175, 176, 177, 195, 196
Neilson, John Shaw, 23, 119
neobaroque, 12, 175, 189–91, 192, 194
Neville, A. O., 12, 105–6, 132, 153, 154–5, 159, 162, 167, 169, 170
Ngai, Sianne, 19, 111
Ngarla Songs, 12, 129–38, 151, 152, 187
Nietzsche, Friedrich, 44–5, 93, 96, 101, 109, 118
nomadic, 10, 135, 160, 168, 176, 178, 180, 182, 183–4, 190
non-semantic, 84, 97
Noongar, 11
Noonuccal, Oodgeroo, 15, 162, 165, 166
Norfolk Island, 26, 43, 49
Normington-Rawling, James, 4

Olson, Charles, 12, 23, 129, 145, 146–9, 189
Ong, Walter, 18, 52, 53–4, 73, 80, 82, 99, 124, 126

oral culture, 18, 39, 52, 53–4, 77, 79, 80, 82, 126, 129, 153, 156–7, 165, 173, 187, 196
Owen, Stephen, 196

page poetics, 3, 11, 19, 39, 45, 47–8, 56, 71, 81, 82, 84, 135–6, 138, 140–1, 143, 145–50, 163, 164, 166, 169, 171, 173, 184, 186, 187, 190, 192, 196
parataxis, 53, 69, 70, 73, 83, 141–2
parody, 12, 22, 28, 35, 121, 122, 134, 137, 138, 140, 146, 149, 171, 173, 176
pastoral, 1, 9, 38, 39, 44, 50, 52, 57, 60, 61, 138, 176, 184
Paterson, Banjo, 22, 50, 119
Perkins, Elizabeth, 108, 110–11, 112, 114, 115, 118, 139
Perloff, Marjorie, 1, 35, 65, 66, 73, 78, 82, 83, 84, 140, 142, 146, 148–9, 163, 164, 167, 171
Phar Lap, 139
Phillip, Governor Arthur, 26, 32
photography, 48, 50, 56, 59, 60, 131, 135, 140, 153, 154–6, 159, 164, 165–73
Pilbara, 130, 131
Pilger, John, 101
ΠO, 8, 9, 17, 189
plough, 11, 12, 22, 23, 39–62, 106, 181
police, 7, 14, 16, 19, 20–6, 40, 42, 46, 47, 48, 52, 54, 56–61, 101, 102, 110, 111, 113, 114, 118, 159, 181
politeness, 26, 28, 29, 31, 34, 37, 135
politics, 4, 9, 10, 11, 19, 30, 32, 33, 102–3, 104, 106, 108, 114, 131, 148–9, 154, 176–7
Porter, Peter, 39
Pound, Ezra, 51, 65, 73–4, 77–8, 80, 81–2, 116, 122, 123, 143, 151
print culture, 18, 82, 171
prose, 3, 45, 47, 48, 50, 88, 94, 103, 108, 114, 116, 117, 142, 145, 149, 164, 179, 191

prose poetry, 3, 5, 20, 24, 74, 92, 103, 106, 108, 111, 112, 114–17, 126, 145, 147, 149, 164, 191
punctuation, 3, 8, 11, 25, 27, 28, 29, 30, 34, 45, 52, 54, 66, 67, 68, 71–2, 73, 76, 80, 83, 84, 87, 96, 97, 104, 106, 107, 108, 111, 113, 125, 131, 135–7, 143, 144, 147, 149, 167, 170, 171, 172–3, 177, 179, 182–3, 185–6, 189, 192, 195, 196, 197
  colons, 27–8, 30, 31, 34, 35, 170
  commas, 27, 35, 45, 48, 52, 66, 71, 81, 135, 180, 188
  dashes, 83, 96, 115, 121, 193
  ellipses, 112, 113, 115, 116, 143
  exclamation marks, 96, 136, 143, 146
  full stops, 45, 48, 52, 96, 105, 185–6, 188
  hyphens, 66, 79, 80, 121, 136–7, 143, 149
  question marks, 106
  quotation marks, 7, 8, 83, 143
  semicolons, 27, 83
  underlining, 61, 83, 107, 121, 122, 123, 125, 126, 127
punctum, 170, 172, 186
punning, 7, 34, 47, 59, 105, 113, 149–50, 181, 186

Quartermain, Peter, 3, 51, 70, 77, 124–5, 142

race, 67, 68, 100, 183, 184
racism, 32, 59, 100, 151, 162
rain, 56, 57, 106
Ramraj, Victor, 67–8
Rasula, Jed, 3, 52, 92, 146, 148
Ravenscroft, Alison, 37, 100–1, 163
Reiman, Donald H, 187–8
religion, 12, 50, 105, 127, 159–60, 165, 171
  see also sacred, spirituality
repetition, 21, 28, 31–2, 36–7, 46, 47, 49, 54, 56, 58, 66, 67, 68, 71, 81, 88, 131, 137, 155, 166, 167

Reynolds, Henry, 101, 177, 178
rhyme, 28, 47, 50, 52, 56, 61, 104, 105, 115, 121, 122, 185, 188
rhythm, 21, 22–3, 28, 32, 47, 50, 54, 68, 71, 79, 81, 104, 105, 116, 126, 136, 147, 150, 163, 169, 185
Rimbaud, Arthur, 114, 115
Roberts, Tom, 88, 91
Roe, Paddy, 133, 135, 168, 169
Rose, Deborah Bird, 102
Ruita Cruta, 50, 51, 52
  see also Wombat
Russo, Katherine, 33, 87, 95, 99
Rutherford, Jennifer, 34, 90, 176–7, 178

sacred, 15, 39–40, 159, 167
  see also religion, spirituality
Schlegel, Friedrich, 113
scribes, 27, 28, 41, 45, 166, 169
secrets, 11, 72, 85–8, 92–3, 95–6, 98, 100–2, 104, 132, 186
Sedgwick, Eve Kosofsky, 2
semantics, 6, 22, 30, 33, 35, 47, 52, 73, 77–8, 79–80, 87, 89, 91, 92, 94, 95, 102, 103, 108, 113, 116, 122, 123, 124, 135, 136, 137, 145, 146, 149, 169, 170, 177, 193, 194
  see also non-semantic
sentences, 21, 24, 27, 28, 30, 34–5, 36, 45, 50, 51, 53, 60, 66, 71, 74, 81, 104, 113, 115, 117, 126, 141, 155, 156, 157, 158, 164, 167, 169, 179, 180
Serres, Michel, 15, 23, 30, 31, 40, 51, 56, 61, 100, 148
Shakespeare, William, 119, 120, 121–2, 125
shared history, 2, 7, 8
Shen, Yuanfang, 63, 64, 66–7, 68–72, 79, 83
shit, 21, 53, 55, 56, 57, 61, 188
Shoemaker, Adam, 8, 32, 33, 36, 37, 102, 103
shooting, 19, 23, 24, 51, 56, 57, 58, 134, 159

silence, 22, 61, 80, 81, 86, 102, 106, 150, 163, 169, 170, 190
Silliman, Ron, 31, 83, 94, 95
Sim, Lorraine, 96, 99
Simmel, Georg, 93, 100
Slessor, Kenneth, 4, 9
Sontag, Susan, 92, 171, 172
sound, 24, 26, 45, 46–7, 49–50, 51, 52, 60, 72, 78, 79, 80, 81, 87, 104–5, 116, 122, 135, 136, 138, 144, 146, 179, 181, 185, 188, 193
  see also silence
Sousa Andrade, Joaquim de, 142
Spacks, Patricia Meyer, 109–10, 111, 115, 120
spears, 14, 15, 26–7, 28, 30, 34–5, 37
speed, 23, 110, 111, 115, 116, 125, 126, 134, 136, 147
spelling, 17, 18–19, 27, 47, 50, 83, 98, 99, 104–5, 179, 180–1, 188, 193–4
Spicer, Jack, 116
spirituality, 4, 162, 168
  see also religion, sacred
Stein, Gertrude, 83, 190
Steiner, Peter, 24, 80
Stevens, Wallace, 65
Stewart, Kathleen, 72, 73, 84
Stringybark Creek, 16, 21, 23–5, 58–9
style, 15, 24, 28, 29, 30, 91, 103, 115, 133
  writing style, 20, 27, 30, 31, 44, 53, 54, 56, 57, 59, 67, 68, 69, 72, 77, 79, 98, 105, 130, 139, 140, 141, 143, 145, 149, 158, 170, 180, 188, 189, 190, 195
surrealism, 120, 140, 146
Swift, Jonathan, 70, 99
swimming, 104
syntax, 27, 36, 54, 66, 68, 71, 77, 79, 111, 147, 195

Taggart, John, 22, 23, 25
Tasmania, 41, 42–3, 44, 40, 50, 54

Taylor, Andrew, 5–6
terra nullius, 2, 4, 45, 172
textual criticism, 18, 84
  see also McGann, Jerome
Tranter, John, 9
tso, 196
Tucker, Margaret, 162, 165, 166
Tynjanov, Jurij, 24, 50, 80
typography, 71, 82, 83, 84, 91, 139, 140, 141, 145, 148, 149, 165, 170, 192, 193

unicorns, 56
unsettlement, 1, 2, 4, 6, 7, 9–10, 22, 68, 85, 138, 171, 174, 175, 191

Van Diemen's Land. *See* Tasmania
Van Toorn, Penny, 13, 17, 26, 27, 28, 29, 30, 32, 36, 99, 175, 186, 192–3
vernacular, 16, 21, 30, 55, 60, 62
vernacular text, 154, 163
Vickery, Ann, 119, 124
Vico, Giambattista, 51
visual poetics, 5, 10, 11, 48, 66, 67, 68, 69, 71, 72, 74, 77, 78–9, 80, 81–2, 83, 84, 87, 88–9, 92, 94, 96, 97, 124, 135, 137, 142, 143, 145, 146, 155, 161–2, 163–4, 165, 166, 168, 169, 170, 172, 173, 190–1, 192, 193, 196
visual prosody, 66, 80, 83, 92, 94, 164, 170, 172
voice, 3, 17–19, 52, 54, 58, 65, 96, 103, 107, 143, 144, 146, 149, 150, 165, 169, 173

walking, 20, 162, 168
Wangal, 26, 27, 35, 36
  see also Eora
Ward, Russel, 15, 37, 40, 41, 43, 59, 64, 107, 127, 184
Webby, Elizabeth, 17, 18, 21, 65
Weil, Simone, 56

Wentworth, William, 44, 45
Werner, Marta, 82–3, 84
White, Patrick, 134
White, Richard, 40, 44, 191
White Australia Policy, 10, 66, 98
Whitman, Walt, 51, 83, 142
Williams, Ann, 119
Wiradjuri, 12, 175, 192, 194
Wittgenstein, Ludwig, 35, 120
Wombat, 50, 52
  see also Ruita Cruta
Wombat Ranges, 16

wombats, 21, 45, 51, 52, 59
Woolf, Virginia, 96, 99
Wright, Judith, 9, 175

Yarra Bend Asylum, 63, 64, 66
Yarralin, 102
Yepez, Heriberto, 147
yirraru, 130–8, 151
  see also *Ngarla Songs*
Yirrkala Bark Petition, 101–2

Zizek, Slavoj, 22, 156